Developing Applications with Enterprise SOA

SAP PRESS

SAP PRESS is a joint initiative of SAP and Galileo Press. The know-how offered by SAP specialists combined with the expertise of the publishing house Galileo Press offers the reader expert books in the field. SAP PRESS features first-hand information and expert advice, and provides useful skills for professional decision-making.

SAP PRESS offers a variety of books on technical and business related topics for the SAP user. For further information, please visit our website: *www.sap-press.com*.

Stefan Hack, Markus A. Lindemann
Enterprise SOA Roadmap
2008, 411 pp.
978-1-59229-162-5

Carsten Bönnen, Mario Herger
SAP NetWeaver Visual Composer
2007, 517 pp.
978-1-59229-099-4

Horst Keller, Sascha Krüger
ABAP Objects: ABAP Programming in SAP NetWeaver
2007, 1062 pp.
978-1-59229-079-6

Jan Rauscher, Volker Stiehl
The Developer's Guide to the SAP NetWeaver Composition Environment
2008, approx. 300 pp.
978-1-59229-171-7

Martin Huvar, Timm Falter,
Thomas Fiedler, Alexander Zubev

Developing Applications
with Enterprise SOA

Galileo Press

Bonn • Boston

ISBN 978-1-59229-178-6

© 2009 by Galileo Press Inc., Boston (MA)
1st Edition 2009

German Edition first published 2008 by Galileo Press, Bonn, Germany.

Galileo Press is named after the Italian physicist, mathematician and philosopher Galileo Galilei (1564–1642). He is known as one of the founders of modern science and an advocate of our contemporary, heliocentric worldview. His words *Eppur si muove* (And yet it moves) have become legendary. The Galileo Press logo depicts Jupiter orbited by the four Galilean moons, which were discovered by Galileo in 1610.

Editor   Florian Zimniak
English Edition Editor   Jon Franke
Translation   Paul Read
Copy Editor   Ruth Saavedra
Cover Design   Tyler Creative
Layout Design   Vera Brauner
Production   Irus Warkus
Typesetting   Publishers' Design and Production Services, Inc.
Printed and bound in Canada

Contents at a Glance

Contents

4   Components of SOA Middleware 67

5   Interaction Models for SOA Middleware 103

6 Developing an Enterprise Service 143

7 Developing an Enterprise Service – Based Consumer Application 175

IT departments today have to adapt to business changes at least at the same pace as the company as a whole and even be able to predict these changes. Implementing enterprise service-oriented architecture (enterprise SOA) allows you to be more flexible while more effectively keeping costs under control. The concept of enterprise SOA goes beyond that of Web services in that it provides a company-wide infrastructure for the business use of Web services.

1 Introduction to Enterprise Service-Oriented Architecture

Enterprise SOA allows you to develop new applications based on existing business solutions, thus enhancing the value of your existing systems and automating new processes. Enterprise SOA makes the following possible:

Benefits of enterprise SOA

▶ **Rapidly adapt business processes**
Enterprise SOA makes application functionalities available in the form of enterprise services and allows them to be combined flexibly. This makes implementation faster and upgrades more efficient, as they can be made when needed and without impacting system availability.

▶ **Win new customers**
Enterprise SOA lets you use Web services to open up new customer segments.

▶ **Out-task**
Enterprise SOA lets you connect to external partners and make use of services, reducing costs and capital commitments, allowing you to focus fully on your core competencies – and all this with no impact on transparency and control for critical processes.

▶ **Extend and automate your value chain**
Enterprise SOA lets you determine and automate the conditions of a

business relationship and thus extend business models and value chains with optimal speed and transparency.

▶ **Innovate**
The primary benefit of enterprise SOA is that SAP's® partners and customers can use enterprise SOA to implement innovative solutions that build on existing systems.

1.1   About this Book

As you would expect, a lot can be written about enterprise SOA and its use in business processes and system landscapes. To cover all areas would go far beyond the scope of this book. We have focused here primarily on SAP NetWeaver's® technical features and tools. This is the first book to offer application developers and software architects an introduction to software development using the tools and the infrastructure provided by SAP enterprise SOA. It describes the components, such as the Enterprise Services Repository and services registry, service runtime, and configuration framework and explains methodologies and metamodels for developing your own enterprise services and combining them in scenarios to build applications. The book looks at both the service provider side and the service consumer side. Other books from SAP PRESS cover broader themes such as implementing an enterprise SOA landscape (Stefan Hack, Markus A. Lindemann: *Implementing Enterprise SOA*, SAP PRESS 2007), a detailed study of the generic concepts behind enterprise SOA (Dan Woods: *Enterprise Services Architecture: SAPs Building Plan for Next Generation Business Applications*, SAP PRESS 2004), and specific concepts and tools in an enterprise SOA landscape, such as the using Visual Composer for model-driven application development (Carsten Bönnen, Mario Herger: *SAP NetWeaver Visual Composer*, SAP PRESS 2007).

Following on from this introductory section, we look at what enterprise SOA actually is and what benefits it offers users from both a business and a technical perspective.

SOA middleware   Chapter 2, The Building Blocks of SOA Middleware, is devoted to the subject of SOA middleware. The SOA middleware concepts described form the overall basis for managing service-based landscapes. Chapter 2 outlines the requirements and benefits of a central repository, a central registry, and a universal service bus and its technology components. We investigate different perspectives of a system landscape with enterprise SOA and the different types of applications needed in an SOA landscape. Finally, we round off the overview by looking at the management of heterogeneous SOA landscapes.

Starting with Chapter 3, Model-Driven Business Process Development, the information presented in the previous sections is applied to the actual SOA middleware tools. In Chapter 3, we describe the different development phases needed for model-driven service development. The procedure is illustrated with a business example. This chapter thus provides an overview of the approach to modeling processes and services with specific configurations.

Development phases

In Chapter 4, Components of SOA Middleware, you learn about the components that SOA middleware provides to support the model-driven software development process described in the previous chapter. The individual phases from Chapter 3 are used to illustrate what objects can be modeled, what tools are needed, and what entities are generated. Chapter 4 describes additional tools used during the service creation process to help improve development efficiency.

Components of SOA middleware and service development

Now that we are familiar with how services are developed, Chapter 5, Interaction Models for SOA Middleware, discusses models for interaction between components. Explanations are offered of terms such as *reliable communication* and *message exchange pattern,* and interaction models such as asynchronous or synchronous communication.

Interaction models

Based on this information, Chapter 6, Developing an Enterprise Service, looks at the specific steps required to model and implement a service on the provider side. Building on the description of the modeling approach on the application platform described in Chapter 1, Chapter 6 describes in detail the design and implementation phase. Here, ABAP is our target provider platform. We also cover publishing a service for use in consumer applications.

Modeling and implementation on the provider side

In Chapter 7, Developing an Enterprise Service-Based Consumer Application, we switch perspectives to look at how a consumer application can use the SOA system landscape. First, we explain what an application

Consumer side

developer must do to ensure that an application can be configured and subsequently executed correctly. Then we describe the main steps of the process of developing a consumer application. The development process is illustrated using specific examples.

Configuring the
overall scenario

Once the provider and consumer side have been implemented, the overall scenario can be configured. Chapter 8, Configuring an Enterprise Service-Based Scenario, describes the procedure. Chapter 8 shows what technical settings can be made to the service runtime to configure communication between consumer and provider. This includes specific security settings, parameters for reliable communication, and the actual call addresses (URLs).

The appendix also includes a section with a brief description of the main standards relevant for Enterprise SOA. This information may be helpful in understanding the previous chapter.

Software
availability

Some of the procedures described in this book are not generally available at press time, in the spring of 2008. SAP NetWeaver functionality will, however, be available soon. Each chapter notes the SAP release with which each part will be available. If there is no note, the functionality is already in the currently available releases. You can find details of releases and service packs in the SAP Developer Network (SDN)[1] in the release notes for SAP NetWeaver and SAP NetWeaver Process Integration.

As has been common practice for some time, test versions of SAP NetWeaver are available for download from the SDN. These test versions are an ideal way of testing the functionality described in this book.

As already mentioned, some of the tools and functions described here are fresh from the development departments at SAP. The screens and descriptions are as up-to-date as can be. Nonetheless, there may be discrepancies resulting from continued maintenance and development work. In addition to the book updates available on the Internet (*www.sap-press. de/1101* and *www.sdn.sap.com* - SOA Middleware, SAP NetWeaver Process Integration), you can find information about changes in the online documentation (*www.help.sap.com*) and on SDN in the sections: Enter-

---

1 The SAP Developer Network: *http://sdn.sap.com*

prise SOA, SAP NetWeaver Process Integration (SOA Middleware), and
SAP NetWeaver in general.

1.2   Definition of Enterprise SOA

Let's begin by taking a look at a generic definition of an SOA that was
circulated by Gartner in the mid-1990s and subsequently quoted or
reworded by various sources.

SOA concerns a paradigm that describes the use of services in distributed
systems. The main assumption here is that the responsibility for operating the services can be in different locations.

Using services in distributed systems

The central concept is that of the *service*. Services used in an SOA have
the following characteristics:

► Services are offered in a system landscape and made available to
potential consumers through a search mechanism. Typically, we think
of this as being a central registration in a directory.

► The directory makes available the descriptions and, more importantly,
the interface of the service. The interface and its metadata form a
complete description of the service. No information about the implementation needs to be known.

► Use of services is platform independent. To describe a service, there
are no restrictions concerning programming languages or platforms.

► A service is self-contained. It can be executed independently without
constraints.

These characteristics describe the technical view of a service. If a system
landscape is implemented technically as described above, new scenarios
can be built more easily than before. The implementation of services is
a necessary precondition for an SOA.

Technical view of services

Functionalities and services can be easily combined to make new processes based on the services, a network of systems, and the service
administration.

A large part of this book deals with how to implement services and use
them in new business scenarios. However, this definition does not go far

enough for that. If we look at serious scenarios in the business world, the purely technical view of an SOA is not sufficient. This view only defines what exchange formats are used; it does not define what business content is exchanged. Technical integration is nevertheless important (and for SOA essential), but it is only a small part of the solution. The part that is not considered in the technical SOA view is *semantic integration*.

Enterprise services It only makes sense to use a service if the purpose, that is the semantics, is known in addition to the technical definition, for example, the interface signature. An enterprise service is therefore a Web service that conforms to particular criteria:

▶ The service is designed in accordance with the methodology prescribed by SAP.

▶ The service is embedded in the business processes within the overall context of an SAP solution.

▶ The service metadata is stored in a central directory.

Enterprise services are thus digital containers for innovative processes. The enterprise services can be recombined as needed into new business processes that can even reach beyond company boundaries. Enterprise services are composed of all the important information about the business context in which they are being used, for example, what industry-specific solutions the service is implementing. They are also largely standardized to allow their use in as many scenarios as possible. All this additional business information is administered centrally in a directory. This allows the business context as well as the technical context to be understood by service consumers.

This information is essential for the success of SOA, particularly in a world in which many thousands of services exist.

Extending SOA SAP has a wealth of experience in building business applications. It was always of vital importance that the processes implemented by SAP applications meet customer requirements to optimally describe their business scenarios. Enterprise SOA is the logical step toward transforming the definition of a technical SOA into the real business world. Compared with technical services, the model is enhanced to include a concrete view on meaningful business scenarios. This approach differentiates SAP from all other providers. The two sections that follow shed more light on these two areas.

To sum up, here is the definition of enterprise SOA:

> *Enterprise SOA is the model of an architecture that enables innovation and standardization in the same environment, thus allowing IT departments to meet their companies' demands for speed and efficiency.*

Definition of
enterprise SOA

1.3 Enterprise SOA from the Perspective of Business Processes

As the definition of enterprise SOA states, implementing a new architecture always involves new goals and challenges. In the sections that follow, we look into issues companies have to resolve in the course of their business activities and how enterprise SOA can help. Section 1.3.1, The Challenges of Today's Business World, briefly presents the challenges that typically arise from the conventional architecture of software solutions. Section 1.3.2, New Challenges in Attaining Company Goals, looks at how this affects decisions made by companies, and in section 1.3.3, Enterprise SOA: A New Architecture for New Business Models, we describe the role of enterprise SOA in resolving these issues.

1.3.1 The Challenges of Today's Business World

If we look at current company architectures, we see that they are marked by a high degree of heterogeneity. They are composed of a mix of different systems and applications. As well as company-wide applications, best-of-breed solutions and enterprise resource planning (ERP) systems, there are typically also legacy systems. A central role—particularly from the perspective of mission-critical applications—is played by the company-wide applications. These applications are often developed to facilitate the integration of different information systems. This is what makes their role central.

Limiting factors for flexibility

Ongoing and rapid change in the business world has led to a need for greater business agility and flexibility, which can no longer be supported by conventional application architectures for two reasons:

▶ **Low flexibility**
Applications in use today are typically characterized by a very large amount of code that is difficult to modify. Such applications can often be configured in the broader sense, but the processes implicitly embedded in the code place great restrictions on flexibility for changes. Each change, be it due to the required integration of a partner or the introduction of new products and services, generates high costs and delays in implementation. In many cases, the IT architecture presents an obstacle for short-term innovation in business initiatives.

▶ **Heterogeneity**
Even when using comprehensive company-wide application packages, the IT landscape of large companies consists mostly of isolated implementations that are dedicated to specific functions or business units. To make matters worse, most large companies, as a result of takeovers and spinoffs, end up with an IT infrastructure that consists of a network of various systems that are difficult to integrate.

This means that to execute a typical business process, it is necessary to integrate a variety of subprocesses from different organizational units, diverse systems, and frequently even external resources and services. As this integration requires great effort, it is sometimes only done half-heartedly. Thus, there is a great potential for improvement in this area.

Enterprise application integration

In the 1990s, one important approach to resolving these problems was the concept of *enterprise application integration* (EAI). At the heart of EAI was the ability of business processes and scenarios to be connected through application-specific interfaces. This made for reliable processes that performed well. Nevertheless, the EAI paradigm is of no help in resolving the issues described above. EAI scenarios focus on the integration of individual applications. This is no way to resolve the integration of many applications arising from the high level of heterogeneity. This way, only a small portion of the necessary processes is optimized.

If we also consider the available tools, it quickly becomes clear that they are not suited to EAI-to-EAI integration. For this reason, only a small number of the issues can be resolved through EAI in the long term.

A further weak point of EAI was the limited benefit of integrating processes. The focus was on integrating data and exchange formats. Only a few tools support the cross-system integration or processes, as is necessary for complex scenarios such as synchronizing stocks.

Yet another critical aspect of EAI is its cost. Limited options and high expenditures mean that from today's perspective, EAI is no longer an ideal response to the issues described above.

1.3.2 New Challenges in Attaining Company Goals

To attain both personal goals and company goals, a CEO today has to implement a business strategy faster than the competition. The goals are to tap into new sources of income, reduce costs, and increase efficiency. To achieve all that, it is often necessary to adapt existing business processes or to introduce new business processes.

Traditionally, the typical business model of a company considers only internal business processes. Typical scenarios emerge from the areas of human resources management, finance, or logistics and make up the backbone of the company's processes. Based on established business processes, these stable, effective, and efficient processes perform the core tasks of a company.

Internal business processes

Internal processes are often not sufficient to meet the demands of new globalized markets. Additionally, there are the challenges that arise as a result of mergers and acquisitions of companies. The situation is exacerbated by new competitors in the global markets as well as the rapid growth of companies and markets. Traditional processes are often overstrained, the pace of innovation is slow, and it becomes difficult to attain the envisioned goals. Figure 1.1 illustrates the way these factors interconnect.

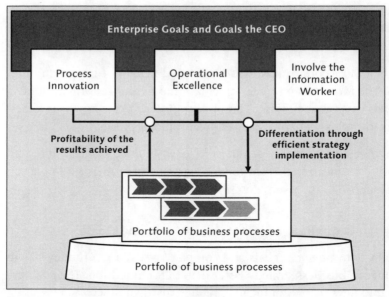

Figure 1.1 Influences on the Portfolio of Business Processes

An IT landscape must under no circumstances be allowed to become a bottleneck in the implementation of new business ideas. It is necessary to build a flexible and innovation-friendly system landscape.

1.3.3 Enterprise SOA: A New Architecture for New Business Models

SOA by evolution

Enterprise SOA is a new architecture driven by business processes. This allows the disadvantages of a traditional system architecture detailed above to be circumvented. The goal of implementing new and innovative processes is thus greatly accelerated. Nonetheless, existing processes are still supported without changes. The introduction of enterprise SOA can therefore be referred to as *SOA by evolution—not by revolution*.

If a company implements enterprise SOA, it can:

▶ Merge existing standalone processes into new and innovative end-to-end processes.

▶ Adapt specific processes as needed.

▶ Seamlessly and simply implement the execution and design of processes that extend beyond company boundaries. In this way, processes, resources and competencies can be better exploited within a company and by partners.

Enterprise SOA thus contributes greatly to exploiting the untapped potential of business processes inside and outside a company. It also offers new tools that a company can use to exploit the process design to obtain the maximum benefit from the business model. In this way, enterprise SOA prepares the way to easily implement changes to a business model and constitutes the link between the goals of a company and the view of a business model, as shown in Figure 1.2.

Simple changes to the business model

Figure 1.2 Enterprise SOA Seen as the Link Between Company Goals and Business Processes

Merging existing standalone processes into new and innovative end-to-end processes is one of the most important tasks of the new architecture. For example, in the world of commerce, it is common practice to undercut competitors' prices. To do this, the process must often be supported

Linking processes innovatively

by people at individual subsidiaries. They need to perform some tasks manually:

▸ Find out which products and which competitors to check out.

▸ Visit the competitors and collect data.

▸ Calculate the new lower price for the individual items.

▸ Refer data to the category manager for approval (by email, fax, or phone).

▸ Wait for the confirmation, which again is sent manually.

▸ Change the price in the system.

These manual steps require a great deal of effort, and the collected data is not directly synchronized with the data in the core processes. With enterprise SOA, this process can be automated and integrated into existing processes. Figure 1.3 shows this example again in its new and more efficient form.

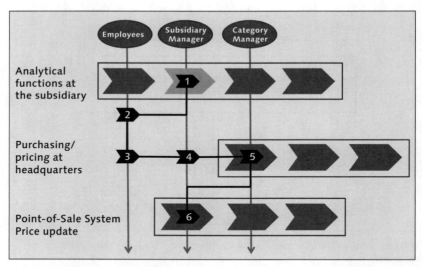

Figure 1.3 The End-to-End Process Including Existing Subprocesses with Enterprise SOA

The individual steps are as follows:

1. The subsidiary manager determines the products and the competitors to be checked.
2. Employees check the competitor's prices.
3. Employees report back the data.
4. The subsidiary manager calculates proposed prices.
5. The category manager verifies and approves the proposed prices.
6. The data is transferred electronically, and the point of sale (POS) system at the subsidiary is changed.

The number of steps remains the same, but they are triggered by the employees, and parts of the processes are described by existing subprocesses in existing systems. On the one hand, this allows many manual steps to be replaced with automated steps. On the other hand, the linking of the subprocesses on different systems makes for faster and more efficient scenario processing, as the data can be transferred with much greater speed and with less effort. The error tendency is greatly reduced. This streamlining frees up additional resources. This allows the subsidiary manager to use the time saved for other useful activities. An additional benefit is the fact that the data collected is not only available in the one subsidiary, but can also be used at higher levels. This increases the flexibility and reduces the risk in the decision process.

The second important aspect of enterprise SOA is the *selective need-based reorganization of processes*. Enterprise SOA allows you to adapt existing processes to new business requirements with much greater efficiency. In turn, the necessary changes can be delivered to the appropriate department very quickly and at low cost.

Redesigning processes

Let's look at the example of the telecommunication industry. New technologies, adapting existing technologies, and innovations require a steady stream of new products and services, yet many of the necessary process steps remain the same, for example, the order process, packaging and shipping, and invoicing. The essential difference is in the provisioning of the different products. In the traditional perspective, the end-to-end process had to be redefined for each new product—only to map the differences in the provisioning process for the products.

With enterprise SOA, the overall process can be divided into separate substeps that can be interchanged as required. The parts that are shared remain stable and can be reused again and again. Any changes needed are only made selectively to individual subprocesses. Figure 1.4 illustrates this. One overall process is enough to represent the new products and services. Subprocesses 1 and 2 as well as 4 and 5 remain stable. Depending on the product or service, only step 3 is changed and executed. In this way, the costs of running the process can be minimized. At the same time, processes can be more flexibly used and adapted to changes in market requirements.

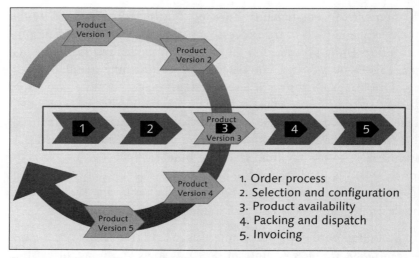

Figure 1.4 Selective Change to Individual Subprocesses with Enterprise SOA

Simplicity of process design and execution

Finally, let's look at the last aspect of enterprise SOA: the seamless and simple execution and design of processes beyond company boundaries. This means processes, resources, and competencies can be better exploited in a company and by partners.

As an example, let's look at the calculation of taxes by the tax authority, as is common in many countries. The tax authority can use enterprise SOA to integrate multiple partners into the process in order to accelerate the overall procedure. These partners include the taxpayer, the subsidiaries involved and, for example, banks. Figure 1.5 shows the scenario with the subprocesses and the partner network beyond company boundaries:

1. Enter the tax data in an electronic form.
2. Identify the tax process.
3. Check the tax data.
4. Synchronize the data with the external subsidiaries.
5. Compare the data with external data.

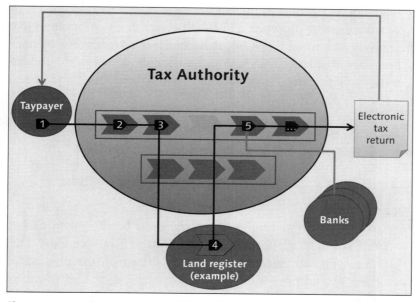

Figure 1.5 Including Taxpayers and External Partners in the Tax Calculation Process with Enterprise SOA

Compared with the manual process, there are multiple benefits:

▸ The taxpayer provides the tax data electronically.

▸ The tax authority can process the data directly, without re-entering it.

▸ The external subsidiaries are automatically integrated into the process to verify the data.

- ▶ External information (such as messages from banks) are automatically included in the calculation.

- ▶ The result is automatically sent to the taxpayer.

- ▶ Run-of-the-mill tax cases can be largely processed automatically. This allows the tax authority to concentrate on exception processing and complex individual cases.

Enterprise SOA links business models

Enterprise SOA is used to link the different drivers of a new and flexible business model. It puts companies in a position to merge isolated data containers into one unified view on the company. Additionally, it exploits the existing processes and subprocesses in a significantly more efficient way and makes it possible to minimize the overall costs by reusing processes. The enterprise SOA technology described in the following sections helps extend processes and operate them in an end-to-end perspective.

1.4   Enterprise SOA: A Technical Perspective

Characteristics of modern IT landscapes

Modern IT landscapes must have three essential characteristics:

- ▶ **Open technology**
  A company's custom-developed software can be integrated just as easily as standard applications from various software vendors. Furthermore, you can describe value chains based on the division of work that extend beyond the organizational, system, and company boundaries.

- ▶ **Modular functionality**
  Functionalities are implemented as Web services that communicate with each other through standardized interfaces. Their coordination is handled by a technological platform. This yields completely new ways to combine and network functions. At the same time, the implementation effort is dramatically reduced.

- ▶ **Powerful development tools**
  User-friendly development tools allow new solutions to be quickly developed and integrated into the existing environment.

The sections that follow take a more detailed look at these areas from different perspectives. Beginning with Chapter 2, The Building Blocks of SOA Middleware, these themes are covered in greater depth.

1.4.1   Web Services: The Base of Enterprise SOA

Even today, communication between applications is based largely on manually defined, proprietary interfaces and message formats. To continue to meet the above-described requirements for business processes, communication must be based on a standardized technology.

Here, Web services can help simplify processes. They work with web-based interfaces that can be integrated into a company's business scenarios and that are based on widely accepted, open standards. In this way, communication beyond system boundaries and even company boundaries is made significantly easier.

Section 1.2, Definition of Enterprise SOA, already described the fundamental characteristics of a service. From this, we can derive the following definition:

Definition

> *A Web service is a modularized, executable entity that can be called in heterogeneous system landscapes beyond computer boundaries. Communication is based on open and generally accepted Internet standards.*

Put simply, Web services are a set of Internet technologies and standards for interoperability between distributed software systems.

SAP NetWeaver—the technological base for all SAP applications—implements the standards needed to use Web services. SAP NetWeaver also provides the tools to develop services, the runtime environment, and the management tools.

Web services form the foundation of the Enterprise SOA *open technology* and are the reason it is so flexible. Enterprise SOA prevents dependency on proprietary technologies.

1.4.2 System Landscape and System Architecture in Enterprise SOA

One of the most important factors when using enterprise SOA is problems that occur with the existing system landscape. Particularly in large companies, the system landscape is marked by heterogeneous systems and the use of diverse technologies. This gives rise to a variety of problems if a company tries to operate cross-company scenarios in this landscape. In practice, it takes a lot of work to interconnect the individual systems. Also, each time process-dependent components, logical elements, or interfaces are changed in one of the systems, extensive modifications are needed. For example, if a company decides to switch to a different customer relationship management (CRM) system, the new system must be modified for each interface.

Divide a landscape into functional units

If you are running a system landscape with enterprise SOA, many of these problems can be resolved. Enterprise SOA aims to divide an existing landscape into functional units. Each of these units is represented to the outside world by processes and services. The services encapsulate the business function. These services are based on the above-described technical concept for Web services and are available in the system landscape to all consumers. This means the implementation of a service can be easily changed, without interrupting the business process.

Converting a system landscape and its applications to enterprise SOA has even more benefits. The main benefit is that the conversion can be done successively.

SAP ships many services as part of enterprise SOA. These services are available for various applications, such as SAP ERP or SAP CRM, as well as in industry-specific solutions. This is an ideal basis for getting the greatest benefit from enterprise SOA with the least effort.

SAP NetWeaver also offers the tools and mechanisms needed to integrate all kinds of applications into service-oriented scenarios. In addition to the SAP systems, it is crucial to be able to integrate legacy systems, custom developed software, or partner systems.

Data exchange in an enterprise SOA landscape is based, by definition, on communication through services. For new systems and scenarios, communication takes place—as described in the service definition—by means of Web protocols such as SOAP. Nevertheless, not all systems in an SOA landscape are in a position to support these protocols directly. This is often the case with legacy systems. With enterprise SOA, these systems can still be integrated. For connectivity, at runtime the SOA middleware uses the protocols available in the legacy systems. In addition, proprietary services are assigned the necessary descriptions from the Web service world and are available to the enterprise SOA landscape as fully fledged services. SOA middleware forms a level of abstraction for proprietary services to integrate them seamlessly into the enterprise SOA landscape.

This combination of complete services and powerful development tools makes it very easy to get started in the enterprise SOA world. Enterprise SOA allows for old and new scenarios to be run in parallel. Depending on a particular customer situation, this makes for practical planning of projects, resources, and costs. With each further step toward SOA, almost as a matter of course, new scenarios present themselves, as well as new ways to put the available services to practical use.

The architecture and the system landscape will change during the course of projects. Enterprise SOA helps you consolidate a system landscape, dismantle dependencies between systems and technologies, and go further toward attaining the goal of flexibility. A system landscape with many point-to-point connections and proprietary interfaces can thus be made into an adaptable and efficient architecture. The *modularity* of the system landscape on different levels is crucial for enterprise SOA.

1.4.3 SAP NetWeaver: Integration and Development Platform

SAP NetWeaver forms the technological base of enterprise SOA. It is a universal platform that allows companies to build user-defined applications or to integrate their existing applications and infrastructures. This simplifies the development, installation, and administration of services.

With SAP NetWeaver, SAP offers both a technology platform that abstracts the underlying hardware and system software (operating systems, database systems, networks) and tools, frameworks, and services to develop business applications. As all SAP applications were implemented on SAP NetWeaver, SAP NetWeaver forms the foundation for all SAP applications. However, SAP NetWeaver can also be used independently of the SAP applications as a standalone integration and composition platform.

SAP NetWeaver is an open technology platform based on established standards, which makes integration significantly less complex. It is composed of components for system integration, enables access to information, and offers an efficient development platform for applications and services.

SAP NetWeaver allows you to unleash the potential capacity of your existing technologies—paving the way for new systems—both SAP systems and non-SAP systems.

Faced with intensifying competition, it is all the more important for companies to react quickly to new market requirements. This is why SAP developed its enterprise service-oriented architecture (Enterprise SOA). SAP NetWeaver forms the technology basis, and SAP applications are the functional core. This gives companies a concrete plan for a service-oriented IT strategy that allows innovations to be implemented considerably faster than before.

2 The Building Blocks of SOA Middleware

Today, companies are forced to constantly change and adapt their business processes. There are many reasons for this, such as the need to differentiate oneself from competitors, reduce costs by standardizing and consolidating, and make changes required by legal provisions. The most important benefit of enterprise SOA is that it allows existing processes to be adapted flexibly while allowing new processes to be created easily. It further aims to reduce IT costs for implementation, integration, and maintenance.

In the future, business processes will be modeled using enterprise services, which can be combined in almost any way. Enterprise services describe business processes using open standards. This allows applications, processes, or data to be combined independently of the operating system and to be used by partners, vendors, or customers alike, through the Internet or a portal—flexibly, quickly, and simply. In this way, company strategy and IT strategy mesh tightly. This partnership between IT and business experts yields process-oriented solutions that establish new competitive advantages.

To attain this goal, it is necessary to have a powerful infrastructure that lets you easily provide services, consume services, and enable integration based on services.

2.1 SOA Middleware for all Types of Applications

If we consider enterprise SOA as a basis for applications and IT solutions, we can distinguish between three main types of service-based applications (see Figure 2.1):

- *Platform applications* provide many predefined processes for standard and mission-critical applications. Their flexibility is achieved by simplicity of configuration and simplicity of extensibility. SAP offers two different platforms: The SAP Business Suite with SAP ERP for large companies, and Business ByDesign for small and medium-sized businesses.
- *Extension applications* extend the platform applications, for example, in order to provide industry-specific processes.
- *Composite applications* address individual requirements, ranging from simple platform extensions to completely new business processes.

Platform applications

The *platform applications* are developed by SAP and shipped to customers. They offer a wide variety of configuration options and allow customers to run the core processes of their business model, and to easily modify it if needed. The platform applications make up the backbone of the SAP Business Suite and the solutions for mid-sized companies. With its Business Suite, SAP offers a wide range of processes and applications. These processes account for the success of SAP, but also for that of the many companies throughout the world that use these processes.

Extension applications

Extensions are not made available by modifying the stable platform, but instead by implementing *extension applications*. Some of these extensions are offered by SAP to extend the platform applications. These include, for example, the industry solutions, but also additional solutions in the SAP Business Suite. Partners and independent software vendors (ISVs) also offer their own extension applications. These solution extensions are applications that are developed by independent partners and that provide cross-solution and -industry functionality. These applications can be integrated seamlessly into your SAP environment, adding new functionalities to your SAP solutions. To ensure a high standard of quality, SAP tests and evaluates the partner solutions are tested. Their compatibility with SAP solutions is then certified.

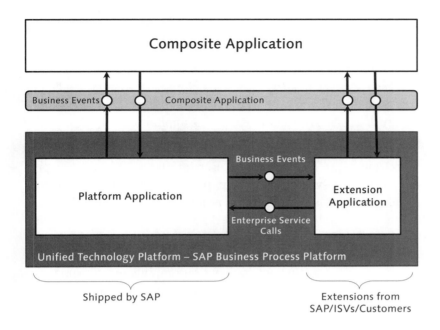

Figure 2.1 The Three Types of Applications

Composite applications are notable for the fact that they typically use services and messages from the platform and extension applications. The large number of core processes and functions allows you to build user-friendly applications that meet the specific requirements of business processes in any customer situation. SAP offers a wide range of composite applications. Partners and customers too use SAP NetWeaver to build composite applications quickly and economically. The *SAP NetWeaver Composition Environment* (SAP NetWeaver CE) provides the development environment as well as the stable runtime environment. This allows applications from existing systems to be integrated into user-centric applications. SAP NetWeaver CE supports application development based on Java EE 5, currently the most stable Java technology.

Composite applications

All three types of applications communicate with each other by calling enterprise services or by exchanging messages (events) at the business level. This allows the applications to be decoupled and facilitates the adaptation of parts of the system landscape. This requires that the infra-

Role and function of SOA middleware

35

structure used supports secure communication that can be effectively monitored.

The SOA infrastructure must be in a position to enable end-to-end business processes, integrating legacy systems, third-party systems, and older SAP releases. It must also support the seamless integration of new applications, such as SAP xApps (SAP composite applications).

Typically, these projects are customer-specific and involve creating services and messages and integrating user interfaces and business processes. Thus, these systems become an integral part of platform, extension, and composite applications. It is also essential for SOA middleware to be able to decouple the different technologies and to create a unified abstraction level. Services and applications shipped by SAP also have a comprehensive set of metadata, which describes the semantics of the interfaces and the functions of the application. This greatly simplifies integration, as this information that is essential for integration no longer needs to be supplied with costly manual effort.

2.2   Different Entry Points, One Integration Platform

In the previous section, we looked at the requirements for SOA middleware from the perspective of the different application types. Additional requirements also arise due to the system landscape architecture in a specific customer situation. Depending on the size and constellation of the system landscape, the infrastructure must support a variety of approaches. There are three ways to use SOA middleware:

▶ The integrated shipment with the SAP applications is known as *Packaged Integration*.

▶ The SOA middleware can support the simplified creation of *composite applications*.

▶ The SOA middleware can be used as an *SOA backbone*. It then forms the backbone of your global SOA strategy.

When we discuss packaged integration, we are looking at end-to-end scenarios in application-to-application (A2A) and business-to-business (B2B), such as *order-to-cash*. In these scenarios, the application logic is connected from different systems using the integration logic of the service infrastructure. Here, the scenario definition, the services used, the mappings between the interfaces, the connectivity options, and the corresponding processes are included in the SAP shipment. The sceanrio operator is given all the necessary objects and metadata and is thus able to easily integrate business partners into the process. The SOA middleware is an integral part of the application systems. This type of scenario has a long tradition at SAP, with these scenarios being shipped with SAP NetWeaver Exchange Infrastructure. The SOA middleware takes over this procedure, thus securing your company's inventments in existing scenarios or enabling new scenarios to be easily implemented.

Packaged integration

Composition scenarios typically use a wide range of services and messages from other applications. The SOA middleware provides easy and standardized access to these objects. The many connectivity options are also often used to consume services. One typical example is querying the inventory in an external system from a composite application. The SOA middleware offers a wide range of options for doing this, including, for example, calling a Web service as a remote function call (RFC) or as an IDoc (intermediate document). Other options include an HTTP call or a SOAP message. In this way, a composite application can easily access services—regardless of in which language or technology the service was implemented.

Simplified creation of composite applications

SOA middleware can also be used as the central backbone for global and company-wide communication and integration. The SOA middleware instances are distributed across the whole system landscape. Despite the varied uses and the sometimes highly heterogeneous distribution, the SOA middleware ensures that the landscape can be configured and managed centrally. One important aspect of this is that even legacy systems can be encapsulated using the SOA middleware and their services made available for all processes.

SOA backbone

Table 2.1 presents an overview of the different ways SOA middleware can be used.

	Packaged Integration	Simplified Creation of Composite Applications	SOA Backbone
Example	Order-to-cash, form-based access to enterprise services for business partners	Query the inventory in an external system	Build an SOA landscape in a global company
Benefits	Easy access to B2B networks, simple configuration, integrated monitoring and error handling	High user productivity on a stable platform	Consolidated system landscape with unified connectivity, integrated policy for SOA development and runtime, high performance, scalability
Focus	Service bus for B2B connectivity	ES Repository for the composition of services, service bus is a technology component, efficient use of services	(Distributed) Service bus, ES Repository is the central repository, SOA management
SOA benefits	Services for B2B scenarios	Easy to call services, services and messages enhanced by semantic information	Standards for integration, encapsulation of legacy systems, common and re-usable SOA objects, integrated policy

Table 2.1 Different Uses of SOA Middleware

The three uses for SOA middleware described previously usually exist in a hybrid form in a real system landscape. The concept of SOA middleware aims to gradually bring all scenarios over to the SOA paradigm. You can do this step by step and in accordance with customer-specific requirements. This means that any investments already made are protected, allowing a target-oriented evolution into the world of SOA.

2.3 Building Blocks of SAP SOA Middleware

SOA middleware is composed of three basic blocks that are needed for a secure and efficient infrastructure. These building blocks support the scenarios and their requirements described in the previous sections:

▸ Enterprise Services Repository including the development tools for SOA objects

▸ Service bus

▸ SOA management

2.3.1 The Enterprise Services Repository

The *Enterprise Services Repository* (ES Repository) makes up the modeling and design-time environment for SOA middleware. All three above-described types of applications are supported. The ES Repository plays a special role in SOA middleware. Based on predefined rules, SOA-specific objects are defined and stored in the ES Repository. These objects can be, for example, enterprise services.

Modeling and design-time environment

All SOA-specific objects shipped by SAP adhere to a unified methodology with regard to their definition within a business context, their interface design, and their implementation. The main cornerstones of this methodology are a common metamodel for all services, based on the SAP concept of global data types and service interfaces, embedding each service in a business context, the graphical modeling of all related entities, including the business processes, and the central storage of all of the above-mentioned design objects in the ES Repository. Accordingly, the ES Repository offers the following functionality for service enabling:

▸ *Defining service interfaces* that represent the foundation of enterprise services

▸ Creating *modeling objects* that reflect the SAP concept of business-oriented process modeling

▶ *Global data types*, defined throughout the SAP system and based on the *Core Component Technical Specification* (CCTS) that ensures that the data types are aligned with each other and can be reused

Services Registry In addition to the generic, universal definitions in the ES Repository, the concrete characteristics of a service must be described in the system landscape. For this reason, the ES Repository has the Services Registry. Whereas the ES Repository contains the design information, it is the task of the Services Registry to manage the information needed to call a service.

For example, if the service to call the inventory is defined in the ES Repository, then this service can exist more than once in the actual system landscape. Each subsidiary can manage its own inventory. If SAP systems are used in each case, and an enterprise service is implemented accordingly, then the definition of that enterprise service will exist only once in the ES Repository. The interface and the semantics are always the same for all implementations. So, how does the consumer of this service know which services can be called and where? This information is administered in the Services Registry. The Services Registry would contain a reference to the generic definition in the ES Repository and the necessary data such as the call URL or the port for each active implementation. Simply put, the ES Repository contains the generic data, and the Services Registry contains the implementation-specific data.

A further important aspect is shown in Figure 2.2. So-called *outside-in development* is the basis for unified service implementation in a distributed landscape. Here, the development process begins in the ES Repository, not in the target system. As we said, in the ES Repository, the metadata for the objects are based on consistent rules and a consistent methodology. To implement a service from this metadata, a proxy is generated using this data. This ensures reuse and conformance to rules in the system landscape. Chapter 3, Model-Driven Business Process Development, and Chapter 4, Components of SOA Middleware, describe these approaches in detail.

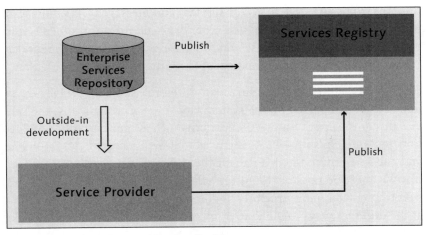

Figure 2.2 ES Repository and Services Registry

The main advantage for ES Repository users is complete transparency regarding which enterprise services are used to provide which business logic. The openness of the ES Repository also allows you to use it to administer non-SAP services, not just SAP services. This means that all the services in a landscape are visible, and the ES Repository is the central infrastructure component for administering an SOA landscape. The introduction of the Services Registry imposes a clear separation between generic definition and the runtime-specific parameters. This supports transparency in a heterogeneous and complex system landscape. Enhancing the definitions in the ES Repository with semantics and the application context make it that much easier to subsequently integrate services into different scenarios.

Benefits of ES Repository and Services Registry

2.3.2 The Service Bus

A *service bus* is a communication infrastructure that is responsible for the seamless integration of different systems into a system landscape. This technology component connects the providers and consumers of services. The service bus has the important task of abstracting from the underlying technical communication and technology protocols, such as HTTP or Java Message Service. This gives the communication partners

Communication infrastructure

the easiest possible way to access services and messages. This must also be possible for legacy systems and older communications protocols. It is vitally important that all transactions that are processed using the service bus are secure, transparent, and scalable.

Interaction pattern   As described above, it is essential that different — including legacy — systems can be connected in one system landscape. Consequently, the service bus must support interaction patterns such as request/reply, notification, and publish/subscribe. It is crucial to have a powerful development and runtime environment to adapt the different data and message formats. It must be possible to ensure efficient conversion of formats and data through mapping structures and implementing protocols. If we look at the different ways to build an IT infrastructure, a service bus must do justice to the most diverse scenarios. The service bus must support all of these scenarios, regardless of whether it is a part of the application server, the central hub, or a distributed system landscape with different hubs and servers.

In addition to the central definitions of the SOA objects in the ES Repository, the local object characteristics in the application systems also play a part. The local objects contain the actual implementation of the business application. The service bus allows these local objects to be easily integrated and make this functionality available centrally to the processes. Based on the definitions in the ES Repository and on the configuration in the Services Registry, proxies are generated in different programming languages. It is through these proxies that the application functionality is encapsulated and called at runtime.

Mechanisms to support communication   The service bus offers a set of mechanisms, as described in Chapter 5, Interaction Models for SOA Middleware, to support communication beyond system boundaries. These include primarily *reliable communication*, for example, *exactly once* or *exactly once in order*. Also of critical importance is locking processed objects, or transactionality.

However, it is not only the technical implementation of protocols and scenarios that is used in daily operation. The service level agreements are also essential for the success of an SOA landscape. As described above for SOA management, these rules can be defined for the service bus and in turn for the different applications. This ensures that the rules are adhered to during operation and that appropriate responses are made if errors occur.

All the previously mentioned properties of a service bus must be based on recognized standards. Only in this way is it possible to ensure that a uniform SOA-based infrastructure is built from the heterogeneous and proprietary technologies. These standards are of particular importance in the area of communication and connectivity. Some of these standards will be covered in more detail later in this book.

If we look at the capabilities of the service bus, we can see that it brings together the functionalities of a service runtime, which enables service-based communication, and the integration runtime, which offers mapping, routing, and business process management.

The properties of a service bus enable systems to be seamlessly integrated in a system landscape, connecting platform applications and their core processes with business partners' systems and composite applications. The many options for interoperability on a technical level allow you to integrate components from third-party vendors, SAP systems, and other integration solutions. This is made more efficient through support for numerous universally recognized standards for Web services, Java, communication, and the Internet. The abstraction and the underlying technology in the *service abstraction layer* helps implement the integration with the least effort and at low cost. Different approaches for distributing the functions offered through the service bus in central or distributed systems ensure that you have the flexibility to meet the requirements of different customer landscapes. Figure 2.3 summarizes these benefits.

Benefits of the service bus

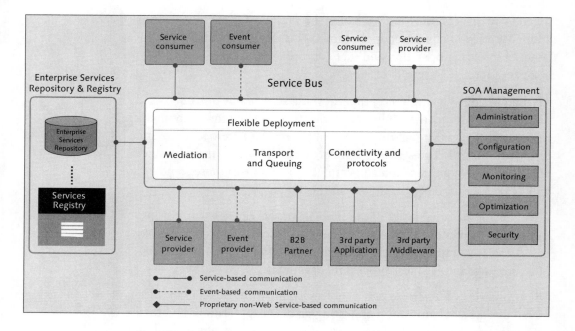

Figure 2.3 Overview of SOA Middleware

2.3.3 SOA Management

Managing an SOA landscape, especially in typical heterogeneous constellations, is the third main building block of SOA middleware. SOA management focuses on the following areas:

▶ Configuration

▶ Monitoring

▶ Security

▶ Change services in the system landscape

A toolset ensures that the applications in the system landscape can be monitored at any point in the lifecycle. SOA management supports all operational phases, starting with building the landscape through the initial configuration and operation to the change management for system components and applications. This is also the central location for managing users and their roles and authorizations and for auditing applications.

44

To take the previously described steps, SOA management supports compliance with an integrated policy, enabling the configuration and execution of applications to conform as closely as possible to the SOA paradigms. This makes configuration easier and reduces the frequency of errors during daily operation. Having a policy common to all applications also allows existing applications to be changed or new applications to be integrated in a highly efficient way. A variety of active and passive monitoring tools are available to analyze the system landscape and the applications. When considering the many ways to use the service bus, SOA management is of vital importance. Only if the system landscape is managed centrally is it possible to keep the administration costs and effort in check. In the world of central, monolithic applications, this was comparatively easy. Distributed systems that include partners and customers have completely new requirements for managing the connected entities.

Integrated policy

If we look at an SOA landscape from the perspective of a security expert, it quickly becomes clear that SOA management also needs to devote serious attention to security in a system landscape. If we were to attempt to decentrally implement all the rules for system accesses, user and role administration, authorizations, and auditing, we would — apart from the rapid increase in costs — greatly increase the risk of security vulnerabilities. Consequently, SOA management must also focus on these issues, which are already familiar from traditional system landscapes run by SAP customers. The SOA management part of SOA middleware builds on experience gained here and supports implementation in complex SOA landscapes.

Security

The last important task for SOA management is change management in a system landscape. Changes that are needed in widely distributed landscapes sometimes have a significant effect on other applications and components. Managing services is a good example of this. Chapter 8, Configuring an Enterprise Service-Based Scenario, shows what steps and options SAP SOA middleware can offer here.

Change management

Based on the model-driven approach of the SAP *application platform*, SOA management allows plug-and-play configuration of composite applications. This minimizes the effort required to integrate the applications into a system landscape. SOA management also supports the entire lifecycle of applications and landscapes. This makes it very efficient to monitor and manage security, communication, and integration in multiple large

Benefits of SOA management

installations. Taken together, these issues form the essential requirements for running an SOA landscape successfully and cost-effectively. With SOA management, users can set up rules and service-level agreements, which are then checked in their actual landscape at runtime and form the basis for successful collaboration between all technologies and applications.

Table 2.2 summarizes the importance and the benefits of the SOA middleware components.

SOA Middleware Component	Description	Benefits
ES Repository	▸ Model process components for designing services ▸ Repository for reusable SOA objects ▸ Comprehensive modeling and development tools ▸ Development of services for all application types	▸ Store SOA objects with their semantics ▸ Services are easy to find and use (for SAP and non-SAP systems) ▸ Built-in rules for designing services
Service bus	▸ Access to business logic through services and events ▸ Central or distributed run-time systems ▸ Integral part of PI and SAP Composition Environment ▸ Message routing and mapping ▸ Adapt different interface types	▸ Seamless integration of all application types ▸ Based on Web service standards ▸ Interoperable ▸ Simplicity through a unified abstraction layer
SOA management	▸ Service contracts (policies) for services ▸ Security ▸ Lifecycle management ▸ SOA landscape monitoring and analysis	▸ Scalable from very few up to many thousand services ▸ Plug and play for composite applications ▸ Monitored execution of services based on rules

Table 2.2 Building Blocks of SOA Middleware and Their Meaning

2.4   Summary

SOA middleware is an important part of SAP NetWeaver. It adds SOA-specific functions to established SAP NetWeaver Exchange Infrastructure mechanisms that have been validated by many customers. This enables support for many types of applications, as shown in Figure 2.1. These exist as various types in real-life system landscapes.

SOA middleware supports a wide variety of scenarios, irrespective of whether the installation is small with only a few systems or a large customer with several hundred systems. In Section 2.2 Different Entry Points, One Integration Platform, we therefore described the different approaches to running SOA middleware. On the one hand, SAP SOA middleware model is highly scalable; on the other hand, it ensures that you can switch from one model to another without any difficulty. One thing all models have in common is that SAP solutions can be installed, configured, and run seamlessly and with minimum effort. This is due to the preconfigured integration of SAP solutions. The shipped packages also include a complete set of metadata, which allows the available services and functions to be understood and integrated automatically.

Considering the wide range of possible composite applications, the ES Repository tools and the model-driven approach, the outside-in approach for implementation, and the SAP NetWeaver tools make the process of creating composites very efficient.

Composite applications

All the functions of SOA middleware are based on accepted standards — mainly from the fields of communication, Web services, and, building on that, security and management. This allows any standards-based non-SAP systems to be integrated smoothly.

Finally, SOA management allows you to efficiently install, configure, and run a heterogeneous, SOA-based system landscape. Monitoring and error handling are done centrally, independently of the architecture of system landscape.

Figure 2.4 summarizes this once more.

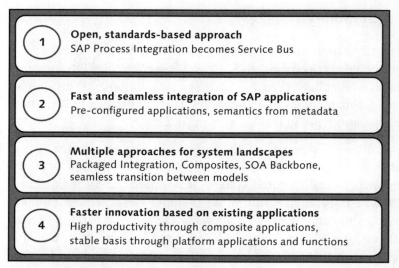

Figure 2.4 Summary of the Benefits of SOA Middleware

SAP ships the application platform in a number of different versions, so as to best accommodate the requirements of large enterprises, mid-sized companies, and small companies. This chapter offers you an overview of the approach used to model processes and services in each of the platform variants.

3 Model-Driven Business Process Development

A model-based development process is used to describe business processes on the business process platform. Modeling, naturally, has a central role in model-driven software development. Modeling makes the software development process more effective and more efficient and creates components that are suited for reuse. This chapter offers a brief introduction to the SOA development process, focusing on the role of process modeling and the different process model types.

The development of business applications can be divided into three phases: *specification*, *design* and *implementation*. This modeling process allows the complexities of a business process to be made transparent on different abstraction layers for different developer groups. Each of these phases has its own models and entities, which are closely interrelated, as shown in Figure 3.1.

Development phases

In the *specification phase*, application requirements are mapped to business process models. The business process models contain process models and process integration models to define a static view of process components, their internal structure, and the relationships between them. The main focus is on integration and service orchestration among process components, and less on specific business process functionality.

Specification

In the *design phase*, the details of the service interfaces are defined. The models from the specification phase form the basis for the design-time

Design

entities. Here, the service models are created, which determine the service definitions, that is, the operations, parameters, and data types.

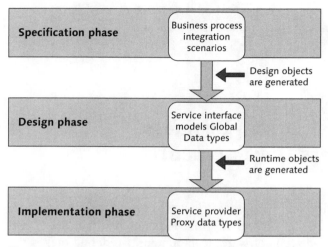

Figure 3.1 Relationships between Models and Entities in Each Development Phase

Implementation

In the *implementation phase*, the executable code is created. The services modeled in the design phase are turned into a platform-dependent representation. This step, known as *proxy generation*, creates the interfaces and implementation classes for the services. These generated entities are then enhanced with business and integration logic, which is normally programmed manually. The sections that follow explain the individual modeling phases in greater detail.

3.1 Specification

Mapping requirements

The development cycle begins with the specification phase, in which requirements for the business applications are mapped to suitable models. The specification phase starts with portfolio planning. Here, you identify the application requirements and functionalities that the software application will provide. Portfolio planning produces a list of application scenarios and a description of the functions to be implemented.

Technical process models

The results of portfolio planning are passed on to the technical process models. The following steps are performed:

- Define the business processes on a non-technical level.
  Result: Process model

- Identify the function components needed by the integration scenario. These are business objects, process components, and deployment units.
  Result: Business object overview

- Define the interaction between the process components in the integration scenario.
  Result: Integration scenario model

- Specify the communication details between the process components, identify the enterprise services needed, and model the sequence of service calls.
  Result: Process component model and process component interaction model

Figure 3.2 shows the relations between these steps.

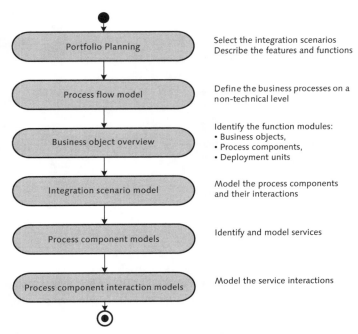

Figure 3.2 Overview of the Specification Phase

Top-down Process modeling in the specification phase is done via a top-down approach. The modeling begins with the rough modeling, which is described by the integration scenario model. From this model, two more detailed models are derived: the process component model and the process component interaction model.

However, before the integration scenario model is built, a software architect defines the process model and the business object overview based on that. In the following sections, you will learn more about the individual steps in the specification phase.

3.1.1   Process Model

After the portfolio has been planned, the first step is to build the process model. The aim of this model is to represent the process flow on the application level, that is, to abstract it from technical implementation details. The modeler defines the flow using standardized models, such as the *Business Process Modeling Notation*. Typically, the process flow is modeled using activities, control flows, and operators that determine the control flows (decisions, divisions, connections).

The example in Figure 3.3 shows the process flow for material order processing.

3.1.2   Business Object Overview

Basic building blocks Next, you define the business object overview. Here, you identify the basic building blocks that make up the business processes in the following order:

▶ Business objects

▶ Process components

▶ Deployment units

When the business object overview is complete, the next step is to define the interaction between the process components using the integration scenario model.

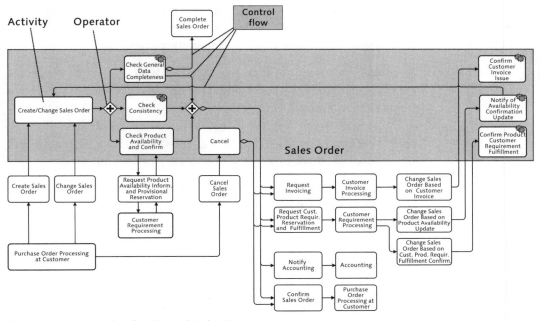

Figure 3.3 Process Flow for Material Order Processing

3.1.3 Integration Scenario Model

Process components group semantically related steps together. To flexibly group the business process platform entities, the semantically related process components are grouped into *deployment units*. This grouping is set up so that each deployment unit can be installed on a separate system. Thus, interaction between process components from different deployment units always takes place through the A2A enterprise service interaction. On the other hand, interactions within a process component are normally done by direct communication through method calls or function module calls.

Process components

Process components are self-contained and make up the reusable units in the business process architecture that are used in multiple integration scenarios. The entities in a process component and the services it provides are represented graphically by a process component model. A process component is composed of one or more business objects and typically represents a self-contained functional area within a company,

Reusable units

such as order requirements processing. Within process modeling, these process components are self-describing, reusable components that can be combined to describe different integration scenarios.

Interaction of components

The interaction of all the process components in a business process is known as an *integration scenario* and is represented graphically by an integration scenario model. Integration scenarios describe end-to-end business processes, which are composed of subprocesses defined through process components. The integration scenario model represents the highest level of abstraction in the design and implementation.

An integration scenario, as represented in Figure 3.4, describes a business scenario using the following three entities:

▶ Deployment units

▶ Process components

▶ Interactions between process components

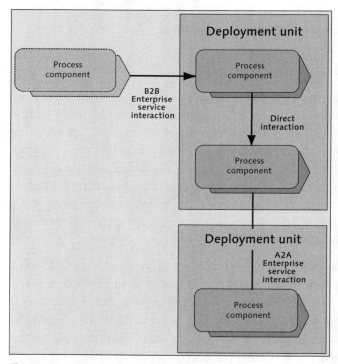

Figure 3.4   Example of an Integration Scenario

The interaction between two process components is represented in the integration scenario model as an arrow indicating the direction of the process flow. For communication beyond deployment unit and B2B, this interaction is refined through a dedicated model: the process component interaction model.

The integration scenario model is the entry point for a series of other more detailed models. On one hand, there is the process component model, which described the details of a process component. On the other hand is the process component interaction model that refines the cross-deployment unit and B2B communication.

3.1.4 Process Component Model

A process component model provides details of the internal structure of a process component. It describes the business objects and the service interface operations of the consumer and the provider.

Process components can contain one or more business objects, but each business object belongs to exactly one process component. A business object represents a class of uniquely identifiable entities in business life, for example, *sales order* or *business partner*. An operation is the abstract description of a functionality or process provided through a service. Each operation is part of a service interface, which represents the grouping of semantically related operations.

Business objects

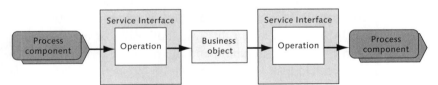

Figure 3.5 Process Component Model

3.1.5 Process Component Interaction Model

The precise interaction of two process components is graphically represented by a process component interaction model. Here, the modeling is restricted to the interactions that are implemented by services. Direct interactions between process components in the same deployment unit

Connecting process components

55

are not specified in detail within the model. The process component interaction model defines how the outbound interfaces of one process component are connected with the inbound interfaces of another component. Figure 3.6 illustrates this situation.

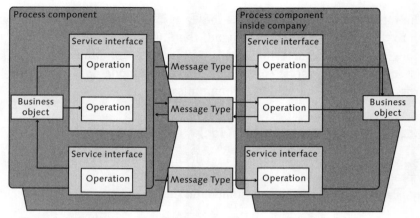

Figure 3.6 Process Component Interaction Model

Typically, the interaction between two process components contains several steps. For this reason, request-confirmation interaction models are often more complex than those described in Figure 3.6. In the figure, a request call is sent from one process component to another, followed by a confirmation call, which is sent in the opposite direction. It is important to note that this interaction model is not a request-response message exchange pattern in the sense of SOAP (see Chapter 5, Interaction Models for SOA Middleware). In this case, both calls, or messages, are defined as part of a single operation, and the response to the request is sent synchronously. In the request-confirmation interaction model, both calls are defined as separate, asynchronous operations belonging to two service interfaces, whose only relationship with each other is through the process component interaction model.

In this way, the process component interaction model is used to define relationships between service interfaces or operations that cannot be formulated on the SOAP or WSDL level but are nevertheless needed to fully describe process relationships.

The process component model and the process component interaction model essentially contain the same types of objects. To be more precise, the two models present two different views of the same data model:

▶ The process component interaction model represents the *connection-oriented view*. It contains only parts of two related process components which are relevant for a specific interaction. It also contains the definition of the SOAP messages to be exchanged and the sequence of the service calls.

▶ The process component model represents the *structure-oriented* view of the data. It contains all the business objects and all the service interfaces and operations that are called or provided within the process component.

As such, the process component model and the process component interaction model are the connective links on the path from modeling to design. All the entities specified in these models have an equivalent in the design-time level. Both models are used to generate the corresponding design-time entities.

3.2 Design

After the specification phase comes the design phase, where you define in detail how the individual business process components will look. This step is still on a very abstract model level.

In the design phase, the data structures are created from the business object models, and the service interfaces are defined. The data types and service operations are modeled independently of any particular programming language. These service operations handle the exchange of the business documents (described by their data types) that are processed within the process steps. Service operations are used primarily for A2A and B2B communication and are therefore based on open E-business standards. The underlying metamodel for service interfaces and data types is based on the World Wide Web Consortium (W3C) standards *Web Services Description Language* (WSDL) and *XML Schema* (XSD).

Global data types The quality of a service is determined to a significant extent by the data types used in it, as the data types have the greatest influence on how easily a service can be implemented on the provider side and used by a consumer. The service interfaces are defined using *global data types* (GDTs). A GDT is a business world data type that is defined and consolidated throughout the SAP landscape and complies with established Internet and business standards or their extensions.

Governance process for data types Data types are defined under strict guidelines in accordance with a unified SAP modeling process (a governance process) that ensures that existing types are reused and that new types are subject to certain rules. Naming rules for data types comply with ISO11179, ensuring that the names of the data types and their elements correspond exactly to the semantic meaning. To increase reuse, SAP has defined GDTs that uniquely specify frequently reoccurring entities (such as currency and date). A mainstay of data modeling is ensuring the integrity of the data types among each other, which can be done by deriving them from a common object model. The individual data types needed for a particular scenario can then be obtained by aggregating the types from the business object model. A complex data type is created by using the object hierarchy to combine the fine-grained business object types into this course-grained type.

Standardized interfaces based on GDTs Semantic integration of components is an important unique selling point in competition with other software vendors. In addition to the tools and frameworks for this, SAP also ships the business content (process integration content) that is needed for communication between systems and their components. This content is designed in accordance with international standards. This outside-in approach ensures that SAP (inside) speaks the language of the business world (outside). The basis for this is formed by an integrated business object model that describes the business-relevant concepts and relationships and is harmonized across industry and business sectors. The implementation of semantic integration across industry and business sectors is due, to a large extent, to the SAP normed data types.

Principles of typing Data types determine the types of unified elements in business objects or operations, which generally have a hierarchical structure. The types of their leaf elements are determined by GDTs, in accordance with the following principles:

▶ If the same semantic state occurs, then the type is always determined by the same GDT.

▶ The types of all leaf elements are determined by GDTs.

GDTs are based on a set of fundamental types, known as *core component types* (CCTs):

Core component type

▶ **Amount**
Amount with a currency unit

▶ **BinaryObject**
Data stream consisting of any binary characters

▶ **Code**
Abbreviated representation of a value, a method, or a property

▶ **DateTime**
Timestamp of a calendar

▶ **URI**
Unique digital address in the form of a uniform resource identifier

▶ **Identifier**
Unique identifier of an object

▶ **Indicator**
Binary code specifying a state (0/1 or true/false)

▶ **Measure**
Physical measure with the unit

▶ **Numeric**
Decimal value

▶ **Quantity**
Quantity with the unit

The CCTs were specified by the UN/CEFACT in the ebXML Framework and are based on the W3C XML Schema definition. The CCTs do not possess any business semantics; they merely describe a structure. Only GDTs have business semantics.

In summary, GDTs have the following properties and benefits:

Properties and benefits of GDTs

▶ They represent reusable data types that are used to define enterprise services. Identical attributes in different service interfaces are always described by the same global data type or a derivative of it.

▶ They are defined throughout all application areas and adhere to high standards. This is guaranteed by the Governance Process for Business Content, which was developed by the SAP Process Integration Council and is monitored by them.

▶ Their content is based on open business and industry standards, such as RosettaNet.

▶ They were developed in accordance with the modeling methodology described in the international standards ISO 15000-5 and UN/CEFACT Core Component Types Specification (CCTS). This methodology, with its well-defined, controlled, semantics-oriented vocabulary and pre-defined XML Schema fragments, is specifically designed for building a consistent business data model.

▶ Technically, GDTs are defined using the XML Schema.

This is the foundation for a consistent, non-technology-driven data type world, based on business-oriented semantics, throughout all SAP applications and especially for service interfaces.

Figure 3.7 shows a metamodel summarizing the entities described in the sections on the specification and design phases.

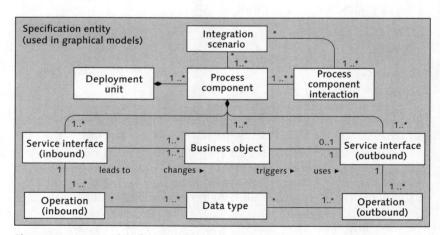

Figure 3.7 Metamodel of the Specification and Design Entities

3.3   Implementation Phase

Up until this phase, we are still working on a very abstract modeling level. The actual mapping onto a runtime system and a programming language is done in the final phase, the *implementation phase*, in which the individual components are implemented.

Mapping at runtime

In this phase, it is important that the transition from an abstraction phase to the next phase is done through an automatic generation process. Only in this way can consistency between the individual abstraction phases be achieved. After the services are modeled in the design phase, proxy generation occurs. In proxy generation, the metadata descriptions of the services and data types are used to create a representation, known as a *proxy*, in the ABAP development system or in the SAP NetWeaver Developer Studio for Java (support for .NET proxies is planned for the future). In this phase, the metadata and programming language constructs for ABAP or Java, such as DDIC types, ABAP, or Java classes or interfaces, are created.

Proxy generation

ABAP and Java developers only work with the corresponding proxies in their familiar development environment; they do not need to be concerned with the technical side of communication and of conversion to an XML document. A service is implemented by defining a method for each service operation defined in the ES Repository in the corresponding ABAP or Java class. A service is called using generated typed consumer proxies or generic interfaces in the infrastructure. In both cases, methods are made available to execute the service operations defined in the ES Repository.

The infrastructure offers additional framework functionality in addition to proxy generation, such as transaction control, which can be used both to implement and to consume services. This functionality is a part of the SOA middleware programming model and is not described in the ES Repository. You can find a detailed description of service implementation in Chapter 6, Developing an Enterprise Service.

3.4   Example of a Modeling Process

We will now use a simple example to illustrate the entities and model types introduced in the previous sections. Figure 3.8 shows the inter-action of process components in a simple sales process integration scenario.

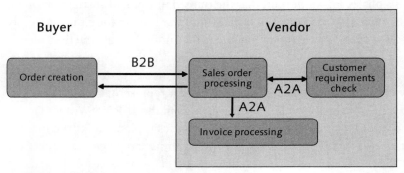

Figure 3.8   Interaction of Process Components

This simplified integration scenario illustrates the process from ordering a product through processing the sales order, and invoicing. It involves the following steps:

Process steps

1. A customer submits an order in his system. This involves business objects such as the sales order, the product, and the business partner.

2. When the order is completed, an electronic message is sent to the vendor so the order can be processed. In the vendor's system, a process component is started that creates a quote from the order. This takes place in the CRM deployment unit.

3. In this procedure, an availability check is first made to verify whether the products are available in the quantity ordered.

4. If the check is positive, an order confirmation is sent to the buyer, and invoicing is triggered.

The sections that follow will step through the modeling process for the vendor side of this process. We will not consider the buyer side, as we are working on the assumption that the purchase order is sent by an order application of another company. Consequently, this step is neither modeled nor implemented.

For this scenario, we identify four business objects: *SalesOrder*, *Customer-Requirement*, *CustomerInvoiceRequest,* and *CustomerInvoice*. These business objects are located in three process components, as shown in Figure 3.9.

Business objects

It should also be possible for each process component to run in a separate system. For that reason, the process components are distributed over three deployment units.

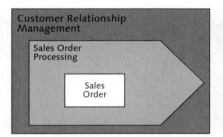
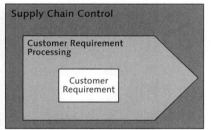
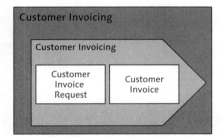

Figure 3.9 Components for the Vendor Side

3.4.1 Integration Scenario Model

When the business object overview has been completed, the next step is to use the integration scenario model to define the interaction between the process components. The scenario *Sell from Stock* is shown in Figure 3.10.

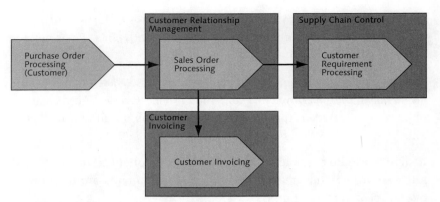

Figure 3.10 Interaction between the Process Components

In this example, the interactions needed in the vendor's system are implemented through asynchronous services between the process components. It is assumed here that the individual process components are defined in different deployment units and may potentially be installed in different systems.

3.4.2 Process Components

Figure 3.11 shows the process component model for the *SalesOrderProcessing* process component.

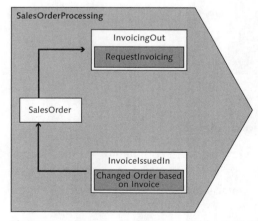

Figure 3.11 Process Component Model for the SalesOrderProcessing Process Component

The graphic shows an example of the entities in a process component model. In the center of the diagram, the *SalesOrder* business object is shown. This is the central object in the sales process. From this object, the process of generating the invoice is triggered. This process kicks in after the sales order has been correctly saved in the system. This process step is implemented through the service interface *InvoicingOut* with the *RequestInvoicing* operation, which is shown at the top-right of the diagram. Another interface in the *SalesOrderProcessing* process component is the inbound interface for invoice creation. This interface can be used to notify the invoicing part of sales processing that the invoice has been created for the sales order. The interface is also described as a service interface with an operation.

3.4.3 Process Component Interaction Model

Following on from that example, Figure 3.12 shows the process component interaction model for the *SalesOrderProcessing* and *InvoiceProcessing* process components.

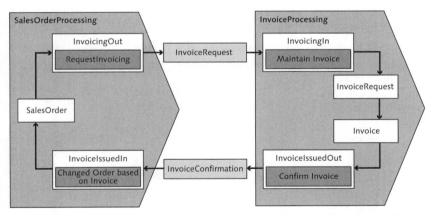

Figure 3.12 Process Component Interaction Model for SalesOrderProcessing and InvoiceProcessing

On the left of the diagram is the *SalesOrderProcessing* process component with the *SalesOrder* business object and the two service interfaces *InvoicingOut* and *InvoiceIssuedIn*. Also, in this graphic the interactions are modeled with the *InvoiceProcessing* process component. There are two process steps: the asynchronous interaction *InvoiceRequest*, which is located between the *SalesOrderProcessing* and *InvoiceProcessing* process components. The graphic also shows some internal details about the process components, particularly the *SalesOrder* business object within the *SalesOrderProcessing* component, which initiates communication to invoicing, and the consumer service interface *InvoicingIssuedOut*, which contains the consumer operation *RequestInvoicingIn*, used for communication. The same types of entities are used on the provider side, that is, the process component *InvoiceProcessing*. The service interface *InvoicingIn* with the operation MAINTAIN INVOICE makes up the inbound interface of the process component. When it is called, this interface generates an invoice request (the business object *InvoiceRequest*) by calling operations in the business logic. The next internal process step is to create an invoice from the invoice request. When the invoice has been created, communication changes direction. The confirmation process for the *SalesOrder* process component is called through the service operation CONFIRM INVOICE in the service interface *InvoicingIssuedOut*.

This causes the business document *InvoiceConfirmation* to be sent to the process component *SalesOrderProcessing*, where is it processed within the service operation *Change Order based on Invoice* in the service interface InvoiceIssuedIn. At the same time, the business object *SalesOrder* is modified by adding the invoice information. This last step in the process chain completes the process of order creation.

In this chapter, you will learn which components SOA middleware provides to support the model-driven software development process explained in the previous chapter. This chapter also introduces the modeling environment of the ES Repository, the implementation platforms, and the Services Registry.

4 Components of SOA Middleware

In the last chapter, we explained the model-driven development approach on the SAP application platform. For the specification phase, you need suitable modeling tools that allow you to build the integration scenarios with the process components and their interactions. Working with these models, you need tools to allow modelers to define the interfaces for the services and their data types. To support this process, SOA middleware offers a central development repository to manage the models. The *ES Repository* stores the data and process models, and, through the *Enterprise Services Builder,* provides a practical development environment to optimally support developers in building the models. The ES Repository and the dedicated Enterprise Services Builder evolved out of the Integration Repository and the Integration Builder in SAP NetWeaver Process Integration (PI). Section 1.1 ES Repository explains this environment in greater detail.

Overview

To make it possible to implement services, SOA middleware lets you generate proxies for the consumer and provider side, based on the definitions in the ES Repository. To accomplish this, a programming-language-specific representation of the abstract model is generated in the provider system, based on the metadata in the service model. This entity is known as a *service definition*. It contains the generated programming language constructs (normally an object-oriented interface with methods and parameters), as well as other metadata, which we will be looking at in greater detail in the following chapters. An application developer subsequently implements this service definition, and in doing so, abstracts

Service definition

it from all its technical communication details, allowing the proxy user to focus fully on the implementation of the business processes. The tools for implementing and using service interfaces are embedded in the standard SAP NetWeaver development environment. Specifically, this refers to the ABAP Workbench, the SAP NetWeaver Developer Studio, and the Visual Composer. As these service proxies are a central part of implementation, proxies and proxy generation are covered in greater detail in Section 4.2 Development Environment and Tools.

Implementing consumer applications

In addition to the modeling capabilities of enterprise services, SOA middleware offers tools for implementing consumer applications. In this scenario, the Services Registry plays a pivotal role. After the implementation phase, services are published in the Services Registry. While the consumer application is being modeled, it is determined which services will be consumed by the application. To do this, the modeler searches the Services Registry for published service models and services that could potentially be called and that can be used in the consumer application. When modeling the consumer application and browsing the Services Registry, modelers use their specific development environment. Depending on the actual scenario, this environment can be:

▶ The Java development environment and the SAP NetWeaver Developer Studio for modeling Composite Applications

▶ The Visual Composer for modeling UI applications

▶ The ABAP Workbench

Service consumer

Before the consumer application is implemented, an application developer generates the service consumers, based on the metadata of the service model or the service. A service consumer includes the proxy definitions, which are the programming language–specific representations of the service call—the counterpart of the service definition on the provider side. Then, the consumer application is implemented, and the generated proxy call definition is integrated into the program logic.

Configuration scenario

The second task of the Services Registry comes to bear in the configuration scenrio, as it tells the configuration framework which services need to be configured to allow the consumer to call them. To enable a consumer to call a service, the technical settings of the Web service runtime must be specified, for example, the security settings and the call address.

These settings are made when the service is being configured. The entities created in this step are known as *service endpoints*.

Service endpoints are the entities that can be called by a service consumer. The service is configured through a configuration framework, which is able to centrally configure all the services and service consumers in a system landscape. For this reason, the configuration framework also accesses the Services Registry to check for all the entities that are potentially relevant for configuration. When the service endpoints have been generated, they are published to the Services Registry, as they are the main points of reference for the configuration of the service consumers.

Service endpoints

Similar to the provider side, the consumer application uses the configuration framework that enables the entire system landscape to be configured from one central entry point. When the service consumers are configured, the configuration framework automatically checks the Services Registry for all relevant service endpoints. The information about whether endpoints can be called by a particular consumer application is made available to the infrastructure when the service consumer is published to the Services Registry. The proxy definition is configured with the technical settings that will be used by the runtime for the service call. This makes up the service consumer configurations. You can find more details about the configuration scenario with the Services Registry in Chapter 8, Configuring an ES-Based Scenario.

Configuring service consumers

In addition to the design and configuration tools, SOA middleware offers another component for enterprise SOA in the form of the SOA runtime. SOA runtime is composed of the service runtime, which handles communication between the service consumer and the service provider using Web service standards. This service runtime has the following enhancements to the SAP NetWeaver Process Integration (PI) Integration Server:

Service runtime

▶ Adaptors for processing additional communication protocols

▶ Integration logic processing, for example, mapping, routing, or process logic

These extended functionalities of SOA middleware enable the implementation of integration scenarios; that is, they provide support for scenarios in which consumer and provider have different requirements or are not known to each other directly.

Figure 4.1 shows an overview of the main components of SOA middleware and how they interact.

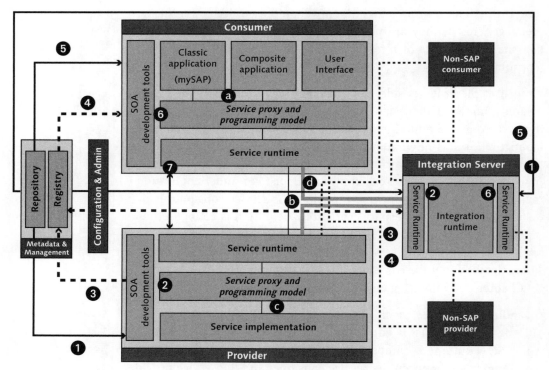

Figure 4.1 Components of SOA Middleware and How They Interact

Connectors ❶–❼ show the processes that take place at design and configuration time, and ⓐ–ⓓ show the processes at application runtime:

❶ Read the ES Repository metadata in the provider system

❷ Generate the provider proxy objects

❸ Publish the services to the Services Registry

❹ Browse the Services Registry

❺ Read the ES Repository metadata in the consumer system

❻ Generate the consumer proxies

❼ Configure and monitor the consumer and provider

ⓐ The consumer application calls the consumer proxy

ⓑ The service runtime calls the service in the provider system

ⓒ The service provider is called in the provider system

ⓓ Alternatively, the service call is routed through the Integration Server to an external system

4.1   ES Repository

The ES Repository is the central SOA middleware component for managing the metadata that is created when business processes are modeled. The ES Repository stores both the models from the design phase and the objects from the specification phase. This means the entire modeling process can be implemented using one repository with one development environment.

Working with a central repository in a development landscape offers modelers several benefits. A central storage location for all enterprise service objects in a development landscape is needed to resolve two core issues in development. One is that a semantically unique design object should be defined only once within a platform. Avoiding redundancies and supporting reuse of design objects are thus essential features of the ES Repository. The other benefit is being able to find out which users are affected when a design object is changed. These two requirements are best met by a central repository that stores all the objects in a service landscape. Additionally, the ES Repository development environment contains a number of functions that exploit the central modeling paradigm to offer functions that support modelers in their work.

Benefits of a central repository

One of the core ideas behind the ES Repository is to allow design objects to be defined both independently from the platform (for example, SAP Business Suite or SAP Business ByDesign) and the programming language (for example, Java or ABAP). This allows modelers on the one hand to

Platform independence

focus on the business context without having to concern themselves with implementation issues and on the other hand also allows components to be reused in the different platforms. This is particularly important if you need to run B2B processes between different platforms.

Tools The development environment needs to provide suitable tools for each step in the development process. For the specification phase, in which the integration scenarios are modeled, the ES Repository offers an integrated version of the IDS Scheer ARIS Toolset. You can use this toolset to graphically model diagrams for process components and their interactions. For the design phase, in which the service interfaces are defined, the development environment offers user-friendly editors that provide a high level of abstraction from WSDL and XSD, allowing developers to again focus on the semantic structure of the data. The conversion of the models to specification-compliant source code is done by the development tools.

Figure 4.2 shows an overview of the functions of the ES Repository.

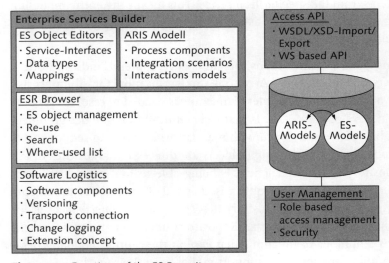

Figure 4.2 Functions of the ES Repository

4.1.1 Enterprise Services Builder

The Enterprise Services (ES) Builder is used to define and manage objects in the ES Repository. The development environment offers practical editors for the service entities such as data types and service interfaces, as well as tools needed for managing the lifecycle of an object. These tools primarily include transport tools and the version management capabilities of the ES Repository. Figure 4.3 shows the ES Builder user interface. To the left is the navigation bar, which you use to select objects in the ES Repository for processing in an object editor (on the right).

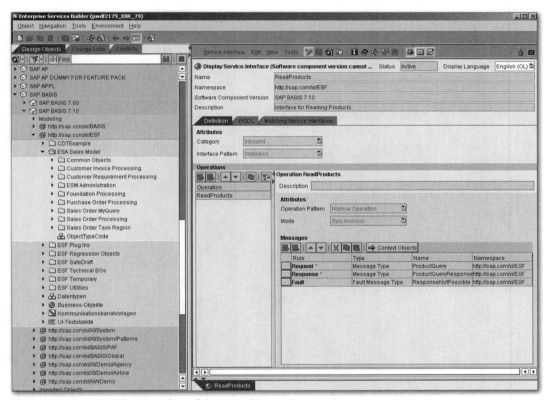

Figure 4.3 Graphical User Interface of the ES Builder

One of the major benefits of the ES Repository is that all the services in a development landscape are stored in one system—all the objects in all the software products and their versions. To manage these services efficiently, the repository is divided into several work areas. The main work areas are the software component versions and the namespaces. You use software component versions to group your development objects. Within

Software components

a software component version, you group your objects by namespaces. You can only uniquely identify an object in the ES Repository by specifying a software component version and a namespace. Software component versions and namespaces are required to create and change objects in the ES Repository. Within a namespace, you can also define folders to subgroup your objects. These folders are particularly useful for grouping objects in a namespace into specific projects. Each object in the repository is uniquely identifiable by its name and the namespace in which it was created.

ES Browser The central development tool for managing the repository contents is the *Enterprise Services (ES) Browser.* This browser displays the development objects in the previously-described hierarchy of software component *P* namespace *P* folder as an object tree. Figure 4.4 illustrates this.

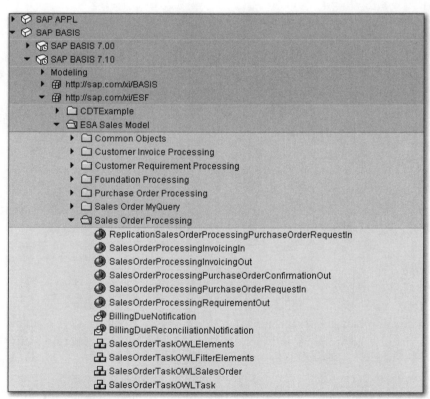

Figure 4.4 The ES Browser

The ES Browser is where you start modeling enterprise services. You can use it to create objects in software components and to load and change existing objects.

4.1.2 Modeling Component

The modeling component enables the distributed, company-wide modeling of business processes and offers administration and analysis functionalities. Its user-friendly functionalities allow a quick start with professional business process management and enable even less experienced modelers to quickly get up to speed. The intuitive user interface and the many automated process design procedures provide optimal support for users. The modeling component offers the utmost flexibility in modeling, analysis, and optimization of business processes. The modeling component provides comprehensive functionalities for managing scripts, templates, and filters, providing users with a powerful configuration, analysis, and management tool. One major benefit of the modeling component in the ES Repository is its ability to extend the available model types. This allows the modeling component to be tailored to the modeling process. This tool thus meets company guidelines, rather than company guidelines having to be tailored to fit the tool. This functionality was used to implement the SAP modeling process for enterprise service–based applications in the system, as introduced in Chapter 3, Model-Driven Business Process Development.

To create the models described in Chapter 3, the ES Repository offers the following model types:

Model types

- ▸ Integration scenario model
- ▸ Process component model
- ▸ Process component interaction model

Figure 4.5 shows a process component model in the ARIS modeling tool in the ES Repository.

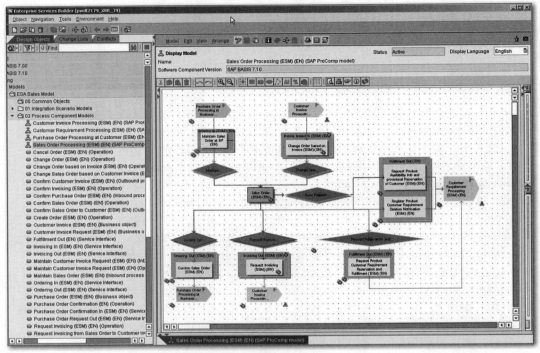

Figure 4.5 Process Component Model

Navigation

On the left is the ES Browser, which displays all the models in a software component. From this view, you can navigate to the modeling tools for each model type. The integration scenario model is the point of entry to a number of other refined models. These relationships among the model types are administered using the ES Repository. By clicking an entity in the integration scenario models, you navigate to the next—more refined—model. For example, you can go from here to a process component model or a process component interaction model. You can also navigate in this way when you start the design phase, to model the service interface and its data types from the process component model. To do this, you navigate from the process component model to the service interface object editor in the Enterprise Services Builder, and from there to the data type editors. Figure 4.6 shows the service interface editor.

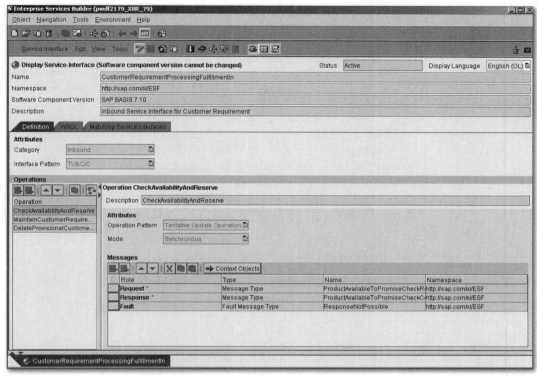

Figure 4.6 The Service Interface Editor

4.1.3 Tools

The following functions support developers in defining design objects:

▶ **Where-used list**
You can use the where-used list to show object usage to find out about object dependencies.

▶ **Search functionality**
Reuse is very important for modeling services. In the development environment, you can search the repository for design objects. This allows developers to locate all the available data types needed to define their services.

▶ **Consistency check for entities and models**
The development environment lets you perform a consistency check on each design object. An object is consistent if all its object refer-

ences point to objects in the repository. The results of an object check are displayed in the object editors via dedicated logs.

▶ **Documentation/Print design objects**
The ES Repository lets you document each design object. The documentation editor supports HTML. The editor can also use the metadata of a design object to generate and print documentation.

▶ **Release status**
On an application platform, where any number of consumers need to implement applications using the available services, it is vital to have some way of setting the release status for a design object. In the ES Repository, you can set this status with the object properties for all object types. The ES Repository distinguishes between the following statuses:

   ▶ Not released

   ▶ Conditionally released

   ▶ Released

   ▶ Obsolete

   ▶ Release reset

4.1.4 Software Logistics

Change, version, and lock management

Another important central feature of the ES Repository is the software logistics tools. It includes tools for managing change logs using change lists, version management, and object lock management. The ES Repository offers special transport tools for distributing objects in complex landscapes and for shipping ES Repository content.

▶ **Object history**
There can be multiple versions of an object. A new object version is always created if the object is added to a change list (for example, when it is first saved). The object version is closed in the change list when the object is activated. If the changes to an object in the change list are discarded, that object version is revoked. The object history displays all the versions of an object that were added to the change list by being activated. You can open versions from the version history in the editor to compare different object versions or to retrieve and save object versions.

► **Change lists**

You can use change lists to manage changes to objects. You can display change lists in the navigation bar on the CHANGE LISTS tab. Figure 4.7 shows an example of a typical change list in service development.

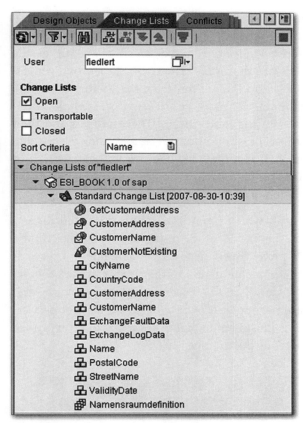

Figure 4.7 A Change List

When you open a change list, all the objects within this list are displayed. You can open objects directly from a change list. If a user is editing an object, that object is only visible for that user (status: IN PROCESS). This object will only be visible for all users when it is activated. If the user re-edits an active object, that object will be added to an open change list again when it is saved. A new object version is then created. If an object has not been activated, you can still undo all the changes made to it. The same applies to deleting objects.

4.2 Development Environment and Tools

When services are modeled centrally in the ES Repository, proxy generation and the subsequent service implementation is done locally within a backend system. Before a Web service proxy is generated, you decide in which system to generate the proxy. Then you start proxy generation locally in that system and the entities from the ES Repository are transferred into programming language constructs (for example, interfaces, classes, data types) in the local system. These proxies and their defining data are stored in the applications or application systems and are handled as a part of that, as if they had been created manually. This makes the actual application and service runtimes independent of the ES Repository.

Generation process There are two scenarios in which proxy generation is needed for service interfaces. First, on the provider side, using the WSDL description of a service interface, a proxy object needs to be generated to serve as the starting point for the implementation of the service in the provider system. In the second scenario, on the consumer side, a proxy object is needed to enable a consumer application developer to call a Web service. This generation process is illustrated in Figure 4.8 and will be explained in more detail in the sections that follow.

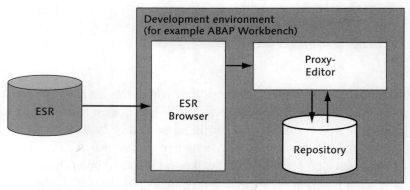

Figure 4.8 Proxy Generation Process

To support this generation process, the development environment on the provider platform offers an Enterprise Services Repository Browser (ESR Browser) to display the repository content. Figure 4.9 shows the development environment for ABAP proxy objects that is integrated into the ABAP Workbench (Transaction Code SE80).

ES Browser

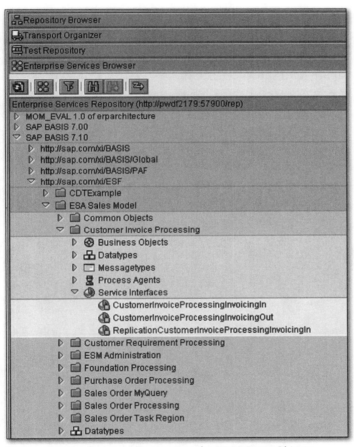

Figure 4.9 Development Environment for ABAP Proxy Objects

The ES Repository Browser has the same structure as the browser in the ES Builder. Here, too, objects are grouped by software components, namespaces, and object types. This offers developers in the implementation system the same view on the repository content as modelers have in the ES Repository.

Generation status One very useful function of the ES Repository Browser is the ability to manage the generation status of proxy objects. This allows you to see at any stage in development whether a repository object has already been generated in the provider system or whether a generated object is not identical to the object in the ES Repository. If it is not, the browser offers you the option of regenerating the object.

In addition to the overview of the repository objects, the main task of the browser is to offer functions for generating proxy objects. To this end, the development environment offers a special proxy editor for each object type. Figure 4.10 shows an example of a proxy editor for implementing service interfaces for the ABAP platform.

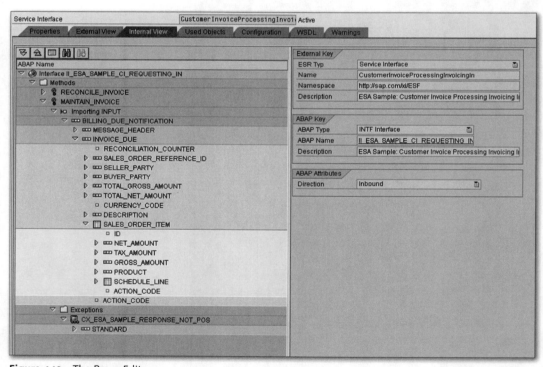

Figure 4.10 The Proxy Editor

The proxy editor interprets the WSDL of the service interface, converts **Proxy editor**
it into the appropriate constructs for the implementation platform, and
stores them in the corresponding development repository. Of particular
importance here is the mapping of the data types used in service interfaces to the corresponding representation on the target platform. The
data types are stored as XSD files in the WSDL of the service interface.
In Java, the XSD data types are generated into Java interfaces and classes
in accordance with the JAXB specification. On the ABAP platform, proxy
generation creates data elements and data structures in the ABAP Dictionary from the data types. Particularly in ABAP, this mapping gives
rise to further challenges due to the restrictive name length of the object
types in the ABAP Dictionary.

The following sections illustrate this process using a highly simplified
data type *address*. The XML Schema representation of this data type could
be created in the ES Repository as follows:

```
<xsd:complexType name="AddressElements">
  <xsd:sequence>
    <xsd:element name ="City" type="String" />
    <xsd:element name ="PostalCode" type="p3:PostalCode" />
    <xsd:element name ="Street" type="String" />
    <xsd:element name ="Building" type="p3:HouseID" minOcccurs="0" />
    <xsd:element name ="CountryCode" type="p3:CountryCode" />
    <xsd:element name ="Type" type="AddressType" />
    <xsd:element name ="ValidityStartDate" type="Date" />
    <xsd:element name ="ValidityEndDate" type="Date" />
  </xsd:sequence>
</xsd:complexType>
```

Listing 4.1 XML Schema Representation of the Data Type Address

From this data type, the DDIC structure is generated in ABAP, as shown
in Figure 4.11.

Component	Typing	Component Type	Data Type	Length
CITY	Type	SFDT_LANGINDP_MED_NAME	CHAR	40
POSTAL_CODE	Type	GDT_POSTAL_CODE	CHAR	10
STREET	Type	GDT_STREET_NAME	CHAR	60
BUILDING	Type	GDT_HOUSE_ID	CHAR	10
COUNTRY_CODE	Type	GDT_ESM_COUNTRY_CODE	CHAR	3
TYPE	Type	ESA_SAMPLE_ADDRESS_TYPE	CHAR	2
VALIDITY_START_DATE	Type	CDT_DATE	DATS	8
VALIDITY_END_DATE	Type	CDT_DATE	DATS	8

Figure 4.11 Generated DDIC Structure

Java interface

In Java, proxy generation provides a Java interface with methods to read and set individual elements:

```
package addr;

public interface Address {
  String getCity();
  void setCity(String value);

  PostalCode getPostalCode();
  void setPostalCode(PostalCode value);

  String getStreet ();
  void setStreet(String value);

  HouseID getBuilding();
  void setBuilding(HouseID value);

  CountryCode getCountryCode();
  void setCountryCode(CountryCode value);

  AddressType getType();
  void setType(AddressType value);

  java.util.Calendar getValidityStartDate();
  void setValidityStartDate(java.util.Calendar value);

  java.util.Calendar get ValidityEndDate();
  void setValidityEndDate(java.util.Calendar value);
}
```

Listing 4.2 Generated Java Interface

4.3   Services Registry

A Services Registry is vital if you need to run system landscapes with many services or service components (see Figure 4.12 for specific Services Registry tasks). Service consumers will ask such questions as:

Problem definition

▶ Which services are modeled or implemented and can be used as the basis for developing a consumer application?

▶ Which services can potentially be used or called directly to configure a consumer application?

A service provider will ask such questions as:

▶ Where can I publish my callable or potentially callable services so that they can be discovered by service consumers?

▶ Which service consumers use my service, that is, whom will I potentially invalidate if I change my service?

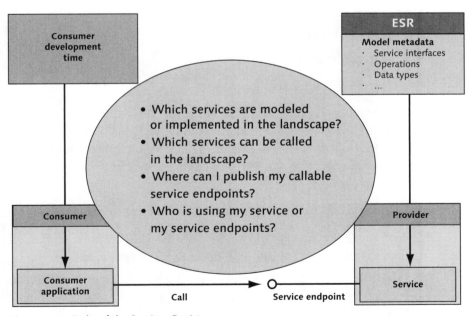

Figure 4.12 Tasks of the Services Registry

These questions are not easy to answer. Whereas the question concerning service models can be answered centrally by the ES Repository, the answers to all the other questions are only known by the respective (backend) systems. How can someone with a specific question be sure that he is accessing the correct (backend) system and does not forget to query all the relevant (backend) systems?

Normally, if you query specific (backend) systems directly, you will not receive a complete view about the whole landscape, or this way of querying may take a lot of effort to ascertain. It becomes more difficult, the bigger the system landscape is.

4.3.1 The Services Registry: The "Yellow Pages" of a Service Landscape

The solution to this dilemma is to query a *central location*, which can provide answers to all questions concerning:

▸ Model information

▸ Implementation information

▸ Configuration and runtime information

This location is the Services Registry.

For the Services Registry to be able to answer these questions, we must first ensure that the provider side is completely and consistently registered with the provider systems in the Services Registry. Only in this way, can you guarantee that a service consumer will be able to get all the relevant information.

Requirements

The Services Registry must meet two crucial requirements that:

1. Both the ES Repository and all the provider systems must publish all the consumer-relevant information to the Services Registry.

2. To enable all the enterprise service and Web service infrastructures to use the Services Registry (both for publishing and browsing), it must be *UDDI-based*.

UDDI is the universally established standard for Services Registries and is supported by all conventional infrastructures. Consequently, the Services Registry can be used regardless of on what platform the service or service consumer is being developed. Figure 4.13 illustrates this situation.

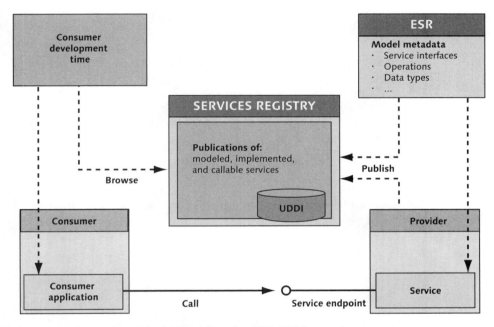

Figure 4.13 Interaction of Registry and the other SOA Middleware Components

If both the above-described requirements are met, the Services Registry is able to offer comprehensive assistance with the *development of a service consumer*.

The Services Registry should also support the *management of a service infrastructure*, that is, it should form the basis for:

Infrastructure management

▶ Configuration of a service landscape—of the services and the service consumers

▶ Handling change scenarios:

   ▶ A service provider must be able to use the Services Registry to find out which service consumers could be invalidated if a service is changed.

▸ The Services Registry must notify both service consumers and service providers of changes that are relevant for them.

▸ It must be possible to use the Services Registry to centrally define settings (for example, security settings) that apply to the entire system landscape, and replicate those settings to the participating systems.

Additional requirements

Consequently, as well as the already described requirements, the Services Registry meets the following additional requirements:

▸ It allows registration of service consumers, including the information about which business functionality the consumers want to use.

▸ It notifies service providers and service consumers about changes that are relevant for them. This is based on the notification functionality offered by UDDI version 3 (V3).

▸ It allows management of central settings and the replication of this information to participating systems.

These additional functionalities of the Services Registry are summarized in Figure 4.14.

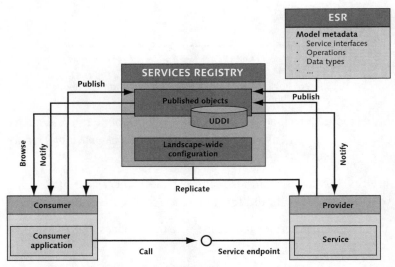

Figure 4.14 Notification of Changes with the Services Registry

4.3.2 Architecture

The architecture of the Services Registry follows these main principles:

Wherever possible, use UDDI entities and concepts defined using UDDI

Specifically, this means:

▶ All publications and registered content are described using entities defined in UDDI V3.

▶ The publication of service models, services and service endpoints adheres to the rules of UDDI Best Practice for WSDL.[1]

This ensures that pure UDDI-based components can work with the Services Registry. Special tools are not required.

Compatible extension of UDDI where it is absolutely necessary

UDDI has gaps in some areas and does not focus on certain concepts that are of great importance for a Services Registry. These areas include:

▶ **Support for classifications**
UDDI supports publishing and discovery of Web services, based on technical content contained in a WSDL document. However, in business scenarios, this technical information does not represent criteria for describing and discovering a service. In reality, services are classified or searched for by a service consumer using different business criteria. For this reason, the Services Registry offers support to enhance publications using classifications in order to precisely define the (business) context in which the service is offered. This makes it much easier to find services, as it is sufficient to use the (business) context to find a service, and it is no longer necessary to search using technical details. These classifications extend the rules of the UDDI Best Practice for WSDL while retaining compatibility, so to not invalidate registry users that are exclusively bound to the UDDI standard.

---

1 *http://www.uddi.org/bestpractices.html*

▸ **Registration of the consumer side**
UDDI concepts are used exclusively to define publication of the provider side. However, it is beneficial for consumers to be registered in a Services Registry as well, because the entire service landscape is then known for central components (such as a configuration framework) at a dedicated location. This also makes it possible to process change scenarios through the Services Registry, as not only the service consumers and services are known, but so are the relationships between them.

▸ **Basis for the configuration of a service landscape**
UDDI is restricted to only offering functionality for registration and notification. However, a central Services Registry can also form the basis for the configuration infrastructure of a service landscape. This means configuration entities that are relevant for multiple systems can be maintained there and distributed to the systems. Also, the configuration and change processes in the individual systems can be initiated centrally through the Services Registry and even placed in the correct sequence to prevent inconsistencies.

Offering an easy-to-use API

To allow as many potential users as possible to use the Services Registry, access must be as simple as possible. For this reason, the dedicated Registry API (UDDI-independent access) must be kept as simple as possible. This calls for:

▸ **UDDI abstraction**
The registry API offers, for example, elementary operations to publish service models, services, and endpoints and thus hide the complexity of UDDI, as publishing causes many entities to be created on the UDDI level.

▸ **Minimal technical barriers to use**
The Registry API is itself provided as a Web service. This ensures that it can be used at a technical level on all common platforms, and its use is not restricted to a particular programming language.

▸ **A local consumer API for users on SAP platforms**
To provide the maximum abstraction of technical details to known

Services Registry users, dedicated, local consumer APIs are offered for the SAP platforms (ABAP and Java). These APIs offer an additional abstraction from the registry Web service and enable users to work in an object-oriented way with the logical entities in the registry.

This local API is used in the SAP Java and ABAP development environment as well as in the ES Repository to provide user interfaces within each development environment.

Provide a self-contained functional spectrum

To present a functionally complete component, the Services Registry not only offers its functionality, but also supports dedicated user interfaces for publication, search, and configuration.

Figure 4.15 provides an overview of the architecture of the Services Registry and illustrates the fundamental concepts.

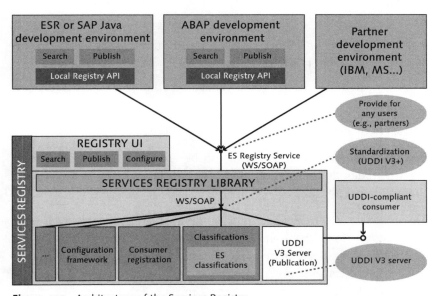

Figure 4.15 Architecture of the Services Registry

The *Services Registry Library* is a central component of the Services Registry. Its purpose is to offer registry users a simple interface and to delegate internal access to data sources in the registry. The Services Registry

Services Registry
Library

Library therefore abstracts from the fact that data is maintained within the UDDI V3 server or is managed in the additional components. A Web service interface is also used for this internal communication between the Services Registry Library and the other components. This allows any number of UDDI servers from different vendors to be used within the Services Registry. The only stipulation to the UDDI server is that it is compatible with version 3. This means UDDI servers that are potentially already in use in the system landscape can be reused for the Services Registry.

4.3.3 Publish and Search with the Services Registry

Now that we have described the fundamental purpose of a Services Registry and its basic concepts, you will see how publishing and searching work in the registry.

To understand what we mean by publishing, it is important to answer two questions:

▶ *What* is published? What data is stored in the registry, and in accordance with what rules?

▶ *How* is publishing done? What publishing options does the infrastructure offer?

The sections that follow address these questions.

What is published to the Services Registry?

We can make an essential distinction between the publication of the service model, the service, and the service endpoints. Figure 4.16 shows the individual phases.

Publishing the service model

The publication of a service model is intended to show service consumers what functionalities a service provider offers and give them sufficient information to allow them to implement their consumer application using these services. Consequently, the publication of a service model must include all the information that is relevant for development time.

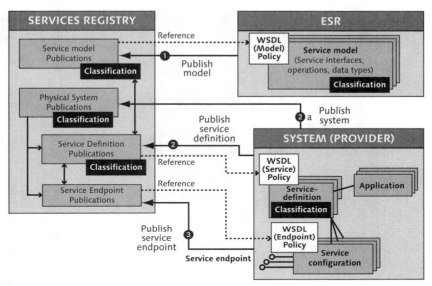

Figure 4.16 Publication to the Services Registry

The service models that are modeled in the ES Repository are composed of the following metadata:

▶ **Interface of the service**
This is the signature, operations, parameters, and data types used.

▶ **Behavior (design-time configuration of the service)**
In addition to the actual interface, each service has a behavior that defines the constraints for a call. The behavior determines whether the service is stateless or stateful, reliable or nonreliable, or security critical or not security critical. The definition of the behavior affects the configuration of the service, as it allows the infrastructure to automatically derive the technical configuration for the specific behavior. This situation is covered in greater detail in Sections 8.1.2, Description of a Service via Metadata, and 8.2.1, Releasing of Applications and Scenarios via the Application Administrator.

▶ **Classification of the service**
Classification assigns the service to different contexts that subsequently allow that service to be found easily. These classifications include:

► The definition of the business context through the assignment of the services to a deployment unit, a process component, and a business object. The classification thus defines a hierarchy through which a service can be discovered.

> **How is "business context" defined?**
>
> Whereas the business object is the direct anchor point that provides a particular business functionality, the process component groups together multiple business objects, making a reusable component from which business processes can be assembled. In turn, a deployment unit groups semantically related process components.

► The definition of technical contexts, such as the release status of the service (service released publicly, released internally, not released)

The metadata of the interface description, the behavior, and the classification are published to the Services Registry in accordance with the rules of the UDDI Best Practice for WSDL. Some of this data is stored directly in the registry, whereas other data is simply referenced by the registry:

► The following data is stored directly in the Services Registry:
  ► The name and short description of the service model
  ► The flag indicating that the published entity is a service model
  ► The classification of the service, that is, the values of the different classification criteria
  ► References to other metadata, detailed below

► The following are referenced from the Services Registry:
  ► Metadata for the interface and behavior description
    This metadata description is made available by the ES Repository through WSDL (for the description of the interface) and WS Policy (for the description of the behavior). WS Policy describes information in a standardized way that could not be expressed through WSDL. These WS Policy expressions are integrated into the appropriate places within the WSDL document. As a result, the WSDL

document contains both the description of the service interface[2] and the WS Policy expressions that describe the behavior. The reference, that is, the URL, to the corresponding WSDL/WS Policy description in the ES Repository, is stored in the Services Registry.

▶ Documentation of the service
The Services Registry also contains the reference, that is, the URL to the documentation of the service. This documentation is normally stored in a document management system.

To allow the Services Registry to be used for scenarios in which services are not built using the ES Repository (for example, services that were developed on another platform), publishing the service model is optional. In such situations, publishing the service definition performs the task of publishing the service model, as it also contains all the metadata of the service model.

The publication of a service definition shows that a service can be used, that is, that the business functionality offered through the service can be used in production. Consequently, the service is published from the provider system, ideally after the application has been configured, in other words, after customizing is done.

Publication of the service definition

The publication of a service definition essentially contains the same information as the publication of a service model and, in addition, metadata about the physical system providing the service.

Therefore almost the same situation applies for the publication of the service definition as for the publication of the service model; that is, interface description, behavior description, and classifications are published in accordance with the same rules. The publication of the service definition differs from the publication of the service model in the following ways:

▶ The publication carries a flag indicating that the service definition can be called and that it is not a service model.

▶ The WSDL and the WS Policy document that describe the interface and the behavior are generated by the providing system and not by

---

2   The WSDL document only contains the <wsdl:portType> part, but not the <wsdl:binding> of the <wsdl:service> part.

the ES Repository. For this reason, the publication in the registry contains the reference, that is, the URL, to the WSDL/WS Policy description in the provider system.

▶ The publication of the service definition is additionally classified with the information about by which (physical) system the service is provided. Unlike the publication of the service model, the publication of the service definition has a specific system reference. Before the service publication can be classified with the providing system, that system must first be published to the registry.

The publication of the service definition does not require the service model to have been published first. Rather, the publication of the service model should be seen as complementing the publication of the service definition to make available the necessary development-time metadata to consumers, regardless of the fact that the service is already being provided by a specific system.

Publication of a system

Each backend system that provides services must be made known in the Services Registry. The system is published to the Services Registry when the first service in a system is published to the registry. All the subsequent service publications reference this system publication.

The system publication is composed of the following information, which is stored directly to the registry:

▶ The call address, that is, the HTTP host and port of the system.

▶ The list of deployment units and process components that are provided by the system. This is expressed through the same classifications as for the service models and service definitions. The information about which deployment units and process components are provided by a system is inferred from which deployment units and process components the services that are published for this system belong to.

Publication of the service endpoint

The aim of publishing the service endpoints is to provide consumers with information about which services can actually be called and to give them all the metadata needed to configure the service consumers. For this reason, the endpoints are published after the service has been configured on the provider side.

The publication of the endpoints establishes the relationship to the service definition, which can be called through the endpoint. It also makes available the metadata needed to call the service definition. Again, some of this data is stored directly in the registry; other data is referenced from the registry.

- The following data is stored directly in the Services Registry:
  - The name and the short description of the endpoint
  - The call address of the service
  - Information about which service definition the service endpoint belongs to and by which system it is provided. This is done by classifying the publication of the service endpoint with the publication IDs of the service definition and the systems.
- The metadata that describes the configuration of the service endpoint is referenced from the registry.

This metadata contains the call address of the service and information about, for example, which security settings to use and how to configure reliable communication. The description of the metadata is generated by the providing system and is composed of a WSDL or WS Policy document:

- The WSDL description comprises the part relevant for the runtime[3] and a reference to the WSDL document of the published service interface.
- The metadata that cannot be described through WSDL, but that is nevertheless relevant for the configuration of the service consumers, is defined through WS Policy expressions that are integrated into the WSDL document. These WS Policy expressions define such things as which specific security mechanisms to use or which protocol and which settings to use for reliable communication.[4]

---

3   The WSDL description includes the <wsdl:service> part and, referenced by that, the <wsdl:binding> part.

4   Reliable communication can, for example, be conducted using the WS Reliable Messaging protocol with specifications version 02-2005 with the settings Acknowledgement_Intervall = 5 Minutes and Retry_Intervall = 1 hour.

That completes the publication of the provider side. When describing the aims of the Services Registry and architecture, we mentioned that the service consumers are also registered in the Services Registry. We will not explain how this publication is done and which data is included here. We will return to this matter in Section 8.3.1 after we have looked more closely at the relevant entities on the consumer side.

Now that we know the rules by which the different entities on the provider side are published, we should explain what publishing options SAP NetWeaver offers.

1. **Integrated publication**
   The publication is done implicitly within service development. This support includes the publication of the service definition and the service endpoints:

   ▶ As part of the application configuration, you can automatically publish the application's service definitions to the registry after the application has been configured.[5]

   ▶ When a service endpoint is created for a service definition that has already been published, SOA middleware automatically ensures that this service endpoint is also published.

2. **Publication from the ES Repository**
   The ES Repository lets you explicitly publish service models to the Services Registry.

3. **Publication from the administration environment of the (SAP) system**
   In the SAP system, administrators can initiate publishing for particular service definitions and service endpoints through a dedicated publication environment. The following functionality is offered for this:

   ▶ You can define which service definitions or service endpoints are relevant for publication. You can do this either by specifying the names of the service definitions or by using the classification systems to define which classification values have content that is relevant for publication. You can specify publishing rules, such as

---

5 This functionality is only available with a particular NetWeaver Release. Until then, in these cases you should use option 3, that is, the publication environment of the SAP system.

"Publish all the service definitions for deployment units A and C," or "Publish all the service definitions for process components P1, P2 and P3."

▶ When these rules have been defined and publication was initiated, the publication environment ensures that all the relevant service definitions and existing service endpoints are initially published to the Services Registry.

▶ Next, the publication environment ensures that if changes are made in the system, the publications in the Services Registry are updated. For example, if a service definition that belongs to a published service is deleted, its service definition publication, together with all its endpoint publications, are deleted from the registry. In the same way, when a new service endpoint is created, or when an existing endpoint is deleted or changed, its publication is updated accordingly.

4. **Publication through the publication interface of the Services Registry**
If you need to publish service definitions or service endpoints that were not created with an SAP platform, or that originated from an older SAP system,[6] the Services Registry offers a special user interface. An administrator can specify the relevant data, such as the address of the WSDLs and classification of the service. This data is used by the infrastructure to publish in accordance with the above-described rules.

Unlike Option 3, this procedure does not automatically ensure that the publication is automatically updated if changes are made to the service definition or the service endpoint. Instead, the administrator must make these changes manually.

4.4 Integration Server

The target scenario for providing or consuming services requires both provider and consumer to conform to the service paradigm and both to know each other; that is, the service consumer has developed its application directly based on the service offering.

---

6 In an SAP system based on SAP NetWeaver 2004 or SAP NetWeaver 2004s.

In many cases, these assumptions do not strictly apply. Typical examples are:

- ▶ The service consumer and the service provider are decoupled; for example, they were developed in different companies. They are not coupled until configuration time, or even until runtime, at which time dedicated rules and technologies are used to build a relationship between them.

  In these scenarios, the consumer and provider frequently reference different service interfaces. In these cases, an additional mapping is needed to map the different service interfaces to each other.

- ▶ The consumer or the provider do not conform to the service paradigm: In cases where either the consumer or the provider is a legacy system that does not have service technology, adaptors must be used to bring the parties together, that is, to establish a protocol conversion between the Web service protocol and the protocol of the legacy system.

SAP NetWeaver PI   The SAP product for implementing these integration scenarios is *SAP NetWeaver Process Integration* (PI). SAP NetWeaver PI is a special flavor of SAP NetWeaver. It builds on the above-described components of SOA middleware and enhances them with additional functionalities that are needed to implement the integration logic. These include previously mentioned functionalities, such as mapping, routing, and adapters, as well as a business process runtime to execute automated business processes.

This SOA middleware–based process integration ensures that the differences between purely service-based scenarios and integration scenarios can be kept to a minimum: from a service perspective, SAP PI Integration Server behaves like a normal SAP application system; that is, it uses the ES Repository and the Services Registry and has the same service runtime as the (backend) systems.

Integration   For this reason, for integration scenarios, the same approaches can be
scenarios   used for the development of a service provider or a service consumer, as described in Chapter 6, Developing an Enterprise Service, and Chapter 7, Developing an Enterprise Service–Based Consumer Application. In these situations, SAP PI Integration Server takes on the role of the service

provider or the service consumer for the party that cannot conform to the service paradigm.

This situation is summarized in Figure 4.17.

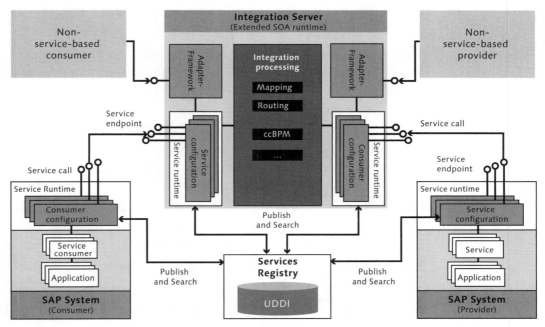

Figure 4.17 Fundamental Architecture of Service-Based Integration Scenarios

The SAP PI Integration Server is an extended version of SOA runtime. It has the following features:

Integration Server features

▶ It contains all the functionalities of the service runtime within the application systems. This means that all processing logic at runtime is based on the Web service paradigm and supports the Web service standards necessary for executing business processes.

▶ For situations in which communication does not take place through Web service technology, the SOA runtime uses the Adapter Framework to transform the proprietary communication technology into the service paradigm. The Adapter Framework offers a wide variety of dedicated adaptors.

▶ It is built to separate the communication layer from an internal processing layer, which executes mapping, routing, and process logic. This means the integration logic can be executed regardless of which communications technology was used to send the call to the SAP PI Integration Server.

Integration Server in the role of service provider

When the SAP PI Integration Server takes on the role of service providers, the following points are important:

▶ For each of these services, one or more service endpoints are generated in the service runtime. These service endpoints are fully described through WSDL and WS Policy (see Section 8.1.2, Description of a Service via Metadata).

▶ These service endpoints (the describing WSDL/WS Policy document) are published to the Services Registry, where they can be discovered by service consumers in the same way as service endpoints that are provided directly by (backend) systems.

▶ At runtime, the service runtime handles the processing of the communication protocol and, if necessary, calls the integration processing to execute additional services such as mapping or routing.

Integration Server in the role of service consumer

If the SAP PI Integration Server takes on the role of the service consumer, it uses the following:

▶ The Services Registry to identify the provider systems, which provide the required service or service endpoint

▶ The service runtime to generate configurations to call the relevant service endpoints and, while the call is being executed, to ensure that communication is service-compliant. In addition to calling Web services, the service runtime also supports calling functionalities through other communication protocols. Here, the Adapter Framework ensures that the proprietary communication protocol is converted into the service-oriented processing model.

Because the same concepts apply for integration scenarios in general and specifically for processing on the SAP PI Integration Server as for application systems, the sections that follow do not distinguish specifically between these scenarios. To find out more about the SAP PI infrastructure, we recommend the SAP PRESS books *SAP Exchange Infrastructure* by Jens Stumpe and Joachim Orb (SAP PRESS 2005) and *SAP Exchange Infrastructure* by Valentin Nicolescu et al. (SAP PRESS 2006).

In the first chapter, we looked at the approach to modeling on the application platform. Now, we will look in detail at the interaction scenario between two process components.

5 Interaction Models for SOA Middleware

Different interaction models can be implemented through services:

- ▶ Stateless asynchronous
- ▶ Stateless synchronous
- ▶ Tentative update and confirm or compensate (TU&C/C)
- ▶ Stateful synchronous

All of these these interaction models are based on a uniform set of runtime properties, which are configured differently in each interaction model.

Before we take a closer look at the runtime properties and interaction models, we first offer a definition of the fundamental paradigm of a service interaction and an explanation of the main components.

5.1 Fundamental Paradigm and Processing Flow

When two applications want to communicate with each other through services, they usually use *service proxies*. The main tasks of service proxies is to abstract communication details, such as XML and SOAP, and provide the applications with an interface that contains only business data and operations in the form of normal method calls and classes in the programming language used.

Service proxy

In the following, the proxy used by the consumer application is referred to as the *consumer proxy*. The proxy that is implemented by the provider application to provide a service is referred to as a *provider proxy*.

Consequently, consumer and provider applications work only with proxies, which consist of an interface, methods, and data structures. The proxies and the service runtime in SOA middleware ensure that SOAP messages are generated to be exchanged between the components.

Consumer proxy   If a method is called through a *consumer proxy*, the proxy uses the service runtime to ensure that a SOAP/XML call is generated from the passed data and sent to the provider in the expected way. If this method returns a response, the proxy reconverts the SOAP/XML response to data structures in the programming language used, and these are then available to the application program to continue processing.

Provider proxy   If a service is called on the provider side, the *provider proxy* uses the service runtime to ensure that the inbound SOAP/XML call is mapped to a method call in the provider proxy. Specifically, the relevant data structures in the programming language are initialized based on the XML data. If the method call returns a response, the provider proxy again converts it to a SOAP/XML message, which is returned to the caller as a response message.

To illustrate the service paradigm, the following sections describe in greater detail the steps for processing a call (see Figure 5.1).

5.1.1   Consumer Side

The steps on the consumer side are as follows:

1. When the consumer application is started, a consumer transaction is also started.

2. In the consumer application, the generated consumer proxy is instantiated, and all subsequent calls intended to go to this service can use this instance. The service call is made through the method call in the proxy instance.

3. The service runtime then ensures that the method call is converted to a SOAP/XML message and sent to the service provider. It ensures that the data structures in the method call are passed to the XML Schema

representation of the corresponding data types in the SOAP message.

4. If the service returns a response, the service runtime converts the received SOAP/XML response to the data structures of the proxy and returns the data as a result of the method call to the consumer application.

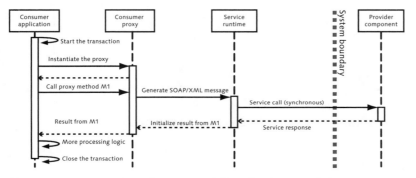

Figure 5.1 Processing Steps for a Service Call on the Consumer Side

5.1.2   Provider Side

The processing steps on the provider side are as follows:

1. When a SOAP/XML message is received on the provider side, the service runtime starts a new provider transaction. This ensures that the consumer and the provider remain decoupled, which would not happen if the consumer transaction was propagated to the provider side.

   Provider transaction

2. Next, the service runtime transfers the SOAP/XML message to a method call in the provider proxy and calls this method. The service runtime first instantiates the provider proxy and then calls the method of this instance with the data from the SOAP message. The data is transferred from its XML Schema representation to the data structures of the programming language.

3. When the provider proxy method has been processed and has returned a result, the service runtime transfers this result of the proxy call to a SOAP/XML response and returns it to the consumer.

4. Then, it closes the provider transaction.

Figure 5.2 illustrates this process

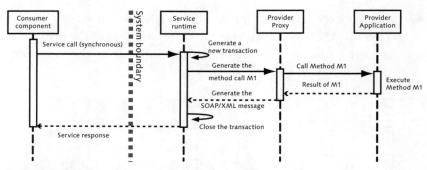

Figure 5.2   Processing Steps of a Service Call on the Provider Side

5.1.3   Summary of the Processing Sequence

Figure 5.3 shows an overview of the steps on the consumer side and the provider side.

It should be noted that this graphic only applies to a scenario with SAP software. If non-SAP consumers or a non-SAP provider are used, the internal processes may be different.

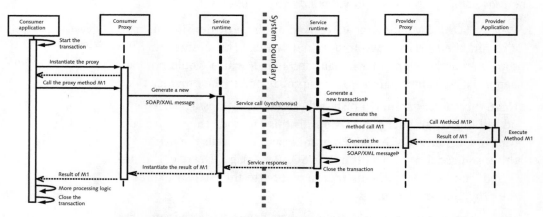

Figure 5.3   Overview of All of the Steps

5.1.4   Runtime Properties During Interaction

Now that we have explained the fundamental paradigm of service communication, the following sections explain the runtime properties, and then look at which configurations these properties have within the interaction models.

We distinguish between the following properties:

▶ **Message exchange pattern (MEP)**
MEP defines whether only parameters are passed with a service operation and whether the call returns no data (i.e., one way), or data can be both passed with an operation and returned by the operation (*request response*). For example, service calls that perform checks are modeled using a request response pattern, because the consumer needs the result to continue processing the application logic. Service calls that are composed of more complex business processes, such as order creation, are typically modeled as one way, because the consumer (so as to not impact performance) cannot or does not want to wait for the result, preferring instead to be notified later as part of a higher-level business process.

One way in contrast to request response

▶ **Transactionality**
If a scenario is transactional, then either all the service calls sent in a transaction are processed (if the transaction is completed successfully) or none of the calls are processed (if the transaction is terminated unsuccessfully).

▶ **Caller blocking**
This property is mainly relevant for the service consumer side. If a service call is blocking, the execution of the consumer program is interrupted until the result of the service call has been reported by the provider. If the call is not blocking, the processing within the consumer program is continued immediately after the call has been submitted.

This property is closely connected to the MEP: If the response from a service is relevant for the consumer, meaning the service operation was modeled using the request response pattern, then the consumer application will be blocked until the result of the service has been received. If, conversely, the service does not return a result (meaning the operation was modeled using one way), then the consumer application can continue processing immediately after the call has been submitted, without having to wait for the call to be processed on the provider side.

▶ **Reliable communication**

If a service operation is designated *reliable*, the communication infrastructure ensures that the call is exchanged exactly once between the consumer and the provider. In addition, the infrastructure can also ensure that the sequence of multiple reliable calls is adhered to (i.e., exactly once in order). In SOA middleware, the standard protocol *WS-Reliable Messaging* is used to ensure interoperability among heterogeneous platforms.

▶ **Commit handling**

This property is mainly relevant for the service provider side. If commit handling is supported for a service operation, then the communication infrastructure ensures that the transaction is committed after the service implementation has been executed. This causes the application data processed within the transaction to be persisted to the database. If the execution of the service implementation terminates with an exception, the infrastructure ensures that the transaction is rolled back.

▶ **Session handling**

Session handling controls whether there can be dependencies between different service calls or whether each service call is executed in isolation.

If session handling is supported for a service interface, then a session is generated on the provider side when the first call is processed. This session remains open for multiple service calls and is explicitly closed by the consumer. In this session, data in memory can be shared and exchanged between service calls, which allows structured service calls.

If session handling is not supported, a new session is generated for each service call on the provider side and closed again when the call has been processed. This ensures that each service call is processed in isolation.

5.2   Asynchronous Scenarios

Asynchronous communication is chosen particularly in scenarios in which consumers and providers will be decoupled. Here, the transaction on the consumer side is not dependent on the transaction on the provider side, which means the consumer can continue processing its application logic immediately after the call has been submitted.

5.2.1   Configuration of the Runtime Properties for Asynchronous Scenarios

Whether communication will be executed asynchronously is defined on the level of the operations of a service interfaces. If communication takes place through an asynchronous service operation, the above-defined runtime properties are configued as follows:

▶ **MEP**   One way
The MEP is one way, because the decoupling of the consumer from the provider transaction makes the consumer side independent of the execution of the service call on the provider side, and there is no waiting for a result. However, if information is subsequently needed about the result of the asynchronous service call, this is modeled using a separate service call, which is used either by the consumer to query the status from the provider or by the original provider to proactively return the status to the original consumer.

▶ **Transactionality**
With regard to transactionality, the behavior on the consumer side differs from the behavior on the provider side:

  ▶ On the consumer side, the behavior for sending calls is transactional, which means all the service calls submitted in a consumer transaction are not passed to the service runtime to send until the transaction has been completed successfully. If the transaction terminates, all the calls are deleted.

  ▶ On the provider side, the behavior for processing calls is not transactional, which means the transactional context of the consumer is not retained. Each service call is processed in its own transaction, so each service call that is received in the right order by the provider is passed to the application. If the application was executed successfully, the transaction for this call is closed (see description of commit handling).

▶ **Blocking the caller**
In asynchronous scenarios, the service call on the consumer side is nonblocking, which means the consumer program continues processing immediately after the call has been submitted. As already described, the actual service call is not sent to the provider until the consumer transaction has been completed.

▶ **Reliable communication**
In asynchronous scenarios, communication is always reliable, which means that the infrastructure must ensure that a message is exchanged exactly once between the consumer and the provider. Only in this way can the consumer really be decoupled from the provider, as the consumer can rely on the call reaching the provider, and therefore the provider application does not have to confirm this explicitly via a service result to the consumer application.

If the sequence of submitted calls is important to the consumer (for example, to ensure the call sequence within a transaction), then the consumer can configure the service runtime explicitly.

▶ **Commit handling**
On the provider side, commit handling is done in the infrastructure, which means that whether a transaction is confirmed or rolled back depends on the success or failure of a service call.

▶ **Session handling**
Session handling is not supported, as it would prevent complete decoupling of the consumer from the provider.

5.2.2 The Consumer Side in Asynchronous Processing

On the consumer side, the sequence is as follows:

1. The consumer application uses a consumer proxy to call a service operation. To this call are passed the input parameters that the provider needs to execute the service call.

2. The call is registered in the consumer's service runtime but is not immediately sent to the provider. When a call is registered, the service runtime generates the XML representation of the input parameters of the call.

    Registration

3. When the call has been registered, control is returned to the consumer application. Consequently, the service call is nonblocking, because the consumer application can now continue processing without waiting for the service to be executed on the provider side.

4. The consumer application can now, within the same transaction, trigger further service calls of this type, which are also registered in the service runtime.

5. When the consumer application successfully completes its transaction the service runtime triggers the next steps to send the registered service calls. This is done to ensure the transactional behavior. If the transaction has been successfully completed, the service runtime passes all the registered calls to the reliable messaging layer, which handles the reliable transfer.

    If a transaction fails, all the registered calls are discarded.

6. The first step within the reliable messaging layer is to persist the calls. If there is a system crash, this ensures that the calls are not lost. When the call is persisted, the reliable messaging layer can guarantee the reliable transfer. This step completes the processing that was triggered by the application transaction.

    Reliable Messaging layer

7. To send the registered calls to the provider, the reliable messaging layer opens a new transaction. In this transaction, the service runtime is initialized with the persisted call data, and it generates a SOAP message that it can send to the provider. The standard protocol WS-Reliable Messaging is used as the exchange format for reliable transfer. It extends SOAP communication with additional information and interactive steps, allowing the consumer and the provider to establish reliable communication.

    WS-Reliable Messaging

8. If the service call is received by the reliable messaging layer on the provider side, the provider's reliable messaging layer sends the consumer's reliable messaging layer a confirmation (in the form of a WS-Reliable Messaging acknowledgment) that it has received the call.

9. If the consumer's reliable messaging layer receives this confirmation, it can consider the call to have been transmitted successfully. If it does not receive a confirmation, it reschedules the call to be sent later.

To illustrate the asynchronous interaction model, Figure 5.4 summarizes the steps taken during processing of an asynchronous call for the consumer side.

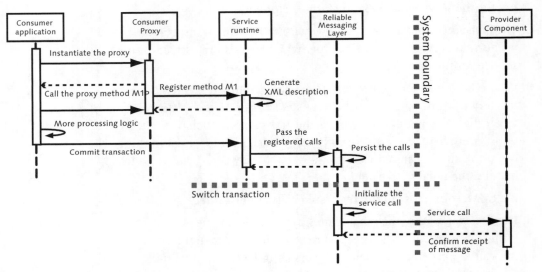

Figure 5.4 Steps in an Asynchronous Scenario on the Consumer Side

5.2.3 The Provider Side in Asynchronous Processing

The following steps are performed on the provider side:

1. If a service call is received on the provider side, the call is first checked to establish whether it requires reliable messaging. If it does, the SOAP message of this call is passed to the reliable messaging layer, which interprets the call and persists it to ensure that the call can be processed reliably.

Persistency
2. If persisting is successful, the provider's reliable messaging layer sends the consumer's reliable messaging layer a confirmation (in the form of a WS-Reliable Messaging acknowledgment) that it has received

the call. Then the provider's reliable messaging layer schedules the execution of the provider proxy and closes the transaction with which it received the call.

3. The reliable messaging layer starts a new transaction to execute the application on the provider side based on the received call. In this transaction, the service runtime is initialized based on the persisted call data. Then the service runtime ensures that the corresponding operation of the provider proxy is called.

4. The subsequent steps depend on the execution of the provider proxy:

   ▶ If the execution is successful, the service runtime ensures that the transaction is closed successfully and notifies the reliable messaging layer of this status. The reliable messaging layer can now delete this call from its work list and trigger the execution of the next persisted call.

   ▶ If the execution fails, the service runtime ensures that the transaction is rolled back and notifies the reliable messaging layer of this status. The reliable messaging layer then ensures that the execution of this call is scheduled for later, or it error flags the call, which means an administrator must decide what should happen next.

Figure 5.5 summarizes the steps on the provider side.

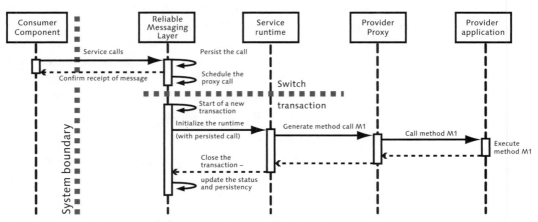

Figure 5.5 Steps for an Asynchronous Scenario on the Provider Side

5.2.4 Summary of the Steps for Asynchronous Scenarios

In an SAP-to-SAP scenario, the above-described steps can be combined. Figure 5.6 descibes this view.

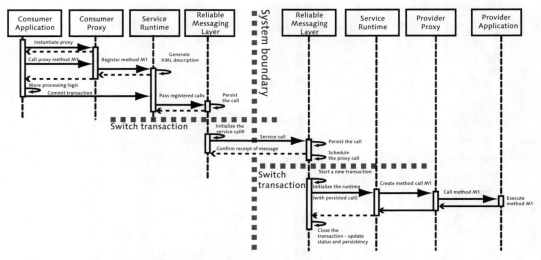

Figure 5.6 Summary of All of the Steps for Asynchronous Scenarios

Same sequence In many scenarios, the above-described asynchronous communication is not sufficient. Special mechanisms are needed to retain the sequence of changes to business object instances in scenarios, in which, for example, these changes are made through asynchronous service calls between systems, without these object instances being locked. If changes to a business object depend on preceding changes to the business object, then *sequencing* is needed. The calls must be processed in exactly the same sequence on the provider as they were submitted by the consumer. If this is not done, the following could happen:

▸ A change call is received, but the business object that needs to be changed does not exist, because the create call has not been received.

▸ A delete call is received before the create call is received.

▸ A second change call is received before the first change call is received.

The following sections describe two concepts supporting sequencing scenarios within SOA middleware.

5.2.5 Sequencing through In-Order Processing

One way of ensuring the sequencing of asynchronous calls is in-order processing of reliable calls (i.e., Exactly Once In Order), in which the service runtime ensures that the calls are processed by the provider in the order in which they were submitted by the consumer. The application on the consumer side only needs to indicate that it requires sequencing. The communication infrastructure then takes all further steps to ensure the correct sequence on a technical level.

In-order processing is guaranteed because the consumer assigns calls, for which dependencies to preceding calls exist, to the same sequence. A sequence thus represents a grouping of multiple service calls within which the sequence of calls is preserved. This is ensured by the reliable messaging infrastructure, which uses the WS-Reliable Messaging protocol to ensure that all calls in a sequence are passed to the provider application in the right order. Sequences are managed by the service runtime, and the application can access the sequences to assign calls to them.

In-order processing with reliable messaging also ensures that the individual calls in a sequence are numbered consecutively in ascending order. This has several positive side effects:

- If the sequence is broken (see Figure 5.7), the number of missing calls can be determined based on the number of the next available entry in the sequence. This information can be used for notifications.

Figure 5.7 Interrupted Sequence with In-Order Processing

- If an unprocessed call in a sequence is deleted, processing does not automatically continue. This increases security, because the correct conditions may otherwise not exist to process subsequent calls.

Exactly once in order

Sequence

▶ A further benefit is that, on the consumer side, the calls in a sequence can be sent in parallel, as they only need to be sorted on the provider side. This improves throughput and, in turn, performance.

The following sections describe how in-order processing is supported by the service runtime in greater detail. The steps are very similar to asynchronous processing, so we will focus on the additional steps. To illustrate this, the steps for processing two calls whose sequence needs to be preserved are described.

Consumer Side

Processing on the consumer side takes place as follows:

Sequence object
1. Unlike purely asynchronous processing, after instantiating the consumer proxy, the consumer application also generates a sequence object to indicate that in-order processing is required. This sequence object is used to bring all the calls from the consumer proxy in sequence. An identifier or name can be assigned to identify the sequence over time (for example, over multiple transactions).

2. For each call of the consumer proxy methods (assigned to the sequence object), the service runtime registers these calls in their initial sequence in the sequence object.

3. If the transaction is closed by the consumer application, the service runtime passes both the registered calls and the sequences used to the reliable messaging layer.

4. The reliable messaging layer then starts to send all the collected calls in the sequence via a new transaction. The WS-Reliable Messaging sequence needed to transfer this data is either newly generated or reused if a WS-Reliable Messaging sequence for the sequence object already exists.

Sequence ID
If the sequence is newly generated, the reliable messaging layer and the provider first agree on a WS-Reliable Messaging sequence in which to exchange the calls. The sequence ID is included in the WS-Reliable Messaging header data in all SOAP messages and gives the provider a means of identifying which messages need to be put in order.

116

5. Once a sequence is defined, the consumer consecutively numbers all the calls in ascending order in accordance with their registration in the sequence. In the previous example, the call from M1 is given the number 1 and the call from M2 is given the number 2 (because the sequence was new).

   This numbering is sent together with the sequence in the SOAP message.

6. The consumer's reliable messaging layer then sends the SOAP message for the call of M1. Let's assume that the message is lost due to a technical issue (for example, the provider is not available). Because the consumer's reliable messaging layer consequently does not receive a confirmation of receipt, it schedules the call to be sent again after a certain delay.

7. Then the consumer's reliable messaging layer sends the SOAP message for the call of M2. This call contains the information that indicates that it is the second call in the sequence.

> **Note**
>
> The message-send sequence on the consumer side is unimportant, because the messages are sorted on the provider side.

8. The provider's reliable messaging layer receives this call and returns the confirmation of receipt to the consumer.

9. When the time delay has elapsed, the consumer again sends the SOAP message for the call from M1.

10. The call is received by the provider's reliable messaging layer, and a confirmation of receipt is returned to the consumer.

Confirmation of receipt

When it receives this second confirmation of receipt, the consumer knows that all the calls in the sequence were transmitted successfully and that it can stop processing for the sequence. However, the sequence is not automatically terminated. In fact, the opened sequence can be used again at a later time. Terminating a sequence must be initiated explicitly.

Figure 5.8 summarizes the steps on the consumer side.

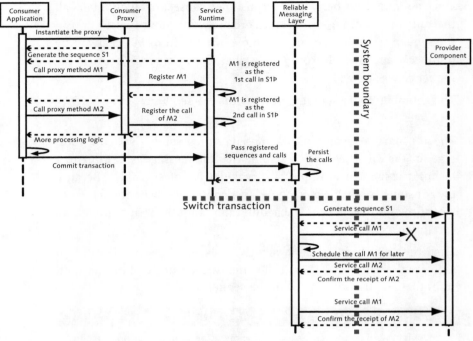

Figure 5.8 Steps for In-Order Sequencing on the Consumer Side

Provider Side

The steps on the provider side are as follows:

1. First, a sequence between the consumer's reliable messaging layer and the provider's is established. If it is a new sequence, it is created at the request of the consumer. The provider's reliable messaging layer then generates a reliable messaging sequence and notifies the consumer. If the sequence already exists, the consumer uses the existing reliable messaging sequence.

   The reliable messaging sequence is sent in all SOAP messages and gives the provider the means to identify which messages need to be put in order.

2. As the example shows, the provider's reliable messaging layer then receives the service call for M2, which is the second in the sequence. It persists this call and returns a confirmation of receipt to the consumer. Based on the administration data, the provider's reliable messaging layer analyzes whether it has received this call in the correct

sequence and whether it can initiate the provider proxy call. In our example, the reliable messaging layer notices that the first call in the sequence is missing, so it stops processing. Figure 5.9 summarizes the steps on the provider side.

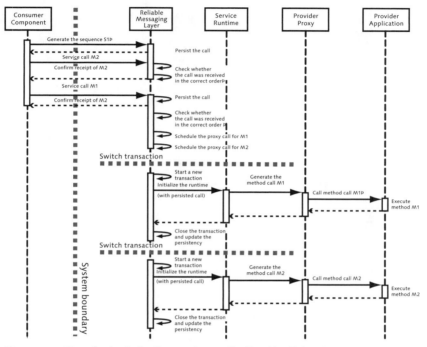

Figure 5.9 Steps for In-Order Sequencing on the Provider Side

3. Some time later, the provider's reliable messaging layer receives the service call for M1. It persists this call and returns a confirmation of receipt. The reliable messaging layer also identifies that this call as the first in the sequence, so it schedules the provider proxy call for M1.

   The reliable messaging layer also detects that it has already received the second call and schedules the call for M2—to be executed only after the call for M1 has been completed.

4. First M1 and then M2 are executed in accordance with the previously described sequence for asynchronous communication. Note that the calls are executed in different transactions to ensure their independence.

Sequence context

> **Note**
>
> To enable a sequence to be identified for a period of time, each of these sequences is assigned to a *sequence context*, which contains the data that needs to be changed in a particular sequence. A sequence context is identified by its name, which can be used to gain access to the sequence.
>
> Typical examples of sequence contexts are a business object instance and a business object node instance.

Summary of the Steps

Figure 5.10 shows the overall picture of the SAP-to-SAP scenario.

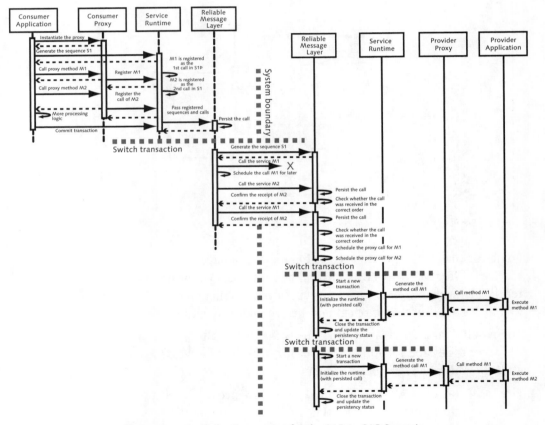

Figure 5.10   In-Order Sequencing for the SAP-to-SAP Scenario

Limitations of In-Order Sequencing

With in-order sequencing, the correct call sequence can be guaranteed on a technical level by applying the exactly once in order semantics. The advantage of this is that on the application layer, no additional precautions must be made beyond normal locking.

If, however, a problem occurs in an in-order scenario with a call that is already registered in a sequence, the whole sequence will be delayed until the problem has been resolved. This may lead to a process termination, which will not be visible on the application layer, which means the application layer has no way of resolving the issue, as the starting point is not known in that layer.

Potential process termination

5.2.6 SAP Sequencing

SAP has developed a special model to optimally support asynchronous scenarios. This model adheres to the previously described general properties of asynchronous coupling through reliable messaging and defines additional semantics exclusively on the application layer.

Application layer

The reason for having a sequencing model on the application layer is that, on its own, in-order processing is not enough if errors due to lost or corrupt calls cause inconsistencies that prevent subsequent calls from being executed successfully.

It is precisely this problem that SAP sequencing addresses by defining an interaction model for the efficient exchange of calls (particularly changes) and a reconciliation algorithm. One aim is to circumvent the necessity for sequencing that uses technical in-order processing through the communication infrastructure in as many situations as possible. In the following sections, we look at this more closely after first offering a more detailed explanation of the limitations of pure in-order processing.

Reconciliation

Although the implementation of in-order processing using a sequence with multiple sequentially numbered entries improves the ability to discover errors and behavior in error situations, it does nothing to resolve error situations in which the sequence itself has errors. In situations such as these, the sequence needs to be restarted, which requires the reconciliation of the consumer and the provider to achieve a common, consistent state before changes can be transmitted again. This process is described next.

Restarting Sequences

Errors due to lost calls or call errors in a sequence cause inconsistencies and even prevent subsequent calls from being processed. To resolve situations such as these, it is necessary to restart the sequence, which takes three steps:

1. **Invalidate calls from preceding sequences.**

   To establish a common synchronization point between the consumer and the provider of the calls, we must ensure that from the synchronization point on, all the preceding calls that have not been processed are invalidated.

   If this is not done, calls that were assumed to be lost and arrive late, or calls with errors that were corrected manually, would be processed, even though their effects were already reflected in the current synchronization point.

2. **Reconcile the instance in the business object that was processed in the sequence.**

   Synchronization point This leads to the common synchronization point between the consumer and the provider and provides the basis for subsequent calls. To establish this synchronization point, the consumer and the provider each exchange their current view on data in the processed business object instance. This allows them to identify the time from which it is possible to continue the process in a consistent state.

3. **Continue the service calls in a new sequence.**

A sequence can be restarted in the following situations:

Automatic restart
▶ Automatic: If the provider detects a lost call or a call with errors. We can distinguish between the following situations:

   ▶ If the key of the business object instance can be extracted from the failed call, the provider can immediately request a restart for the sequence for this business object instance.

▶ If only the ID of the failed call can be extracted, the provider can request the consumer to identify the sequence for the call.

In these situations, the sequence restart can be initiated by the provider.

▶ Manual: If a user has noticed an obvious deviation or a deviation is detected by a consistency check. In these situations, the restart can be initiated either on the consumer side or on the provider side.   Manual restart

▶ As a precaution, at regular intervals, if possible parallel to regular calls. The restart is initiated by the consumer.

The following sections look at the three steps required to restart a sequence: invalidation of calls from preceding sequences, reconciliation, and the continuation of processing in a new sequence.

Invalidation of Calls from Preceding Sequences

Calls that were assumed to have been lost but then arrive at the provider side with some delay, or calls with errors that were corrected manually must be invalidated if a reconciliation has taken place and the sequence has been restarted.

For it to be possible to invalidate calls in a sequence, these calls must be identified so that it is clear to which sequence they belong. To do this, a *reconciliation counter* is used. The reconciliation counter consecutively numbers the reconciliations that precede the starting of a sequence. All the calls that belong to a particular reconciliation contain the number of that reconciliation; the next reconciliation raises this number and invalidates all the preceding calls.   Reconciliation counter

This situation is illustrated in Figure 5.11: The change of +2 is identified by the reconciliation counter 1 and must therefore be ignored when reconciliation 2 has set a new synchronization point.

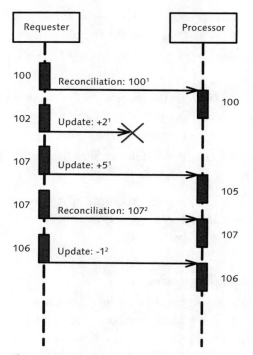

Figure 5.11 How the Reconciliation Counter Works

A reconciliation defines a synchronization point between the consumer and the provider to render both into a consistent state again. To achieve this, no changes are transferred via the reconciliation call. Instead, the reconciliation call contains all the data for the business object instance in its current state. This allows the call to resolve inconsistencies that may occur due to delta changes being lost. In addition, the reconciliation counter is increased to start a new sequence. For each sequence, the initial value of the reconciliation counter is 1. With each reconciliation, the counter is increased by 1 (see Figure 5.11).

The reconciliation call is modeled as an additional operation in the service interface.

Rules   Calls that are sent by a reconciliation algorithm are executed based on the following rules:

▶ A reconciliation call invalidates all the previously made calls on the provider side that have not been processed. The invalidated calls must therefore be ignored on the provider side once the reconciliation call is successfully processed. In the example in Figure 5.12, change +5, which is flagged with reconciliation counter 1, must be ignored, because reconciliation 2 has set the current value to 107.

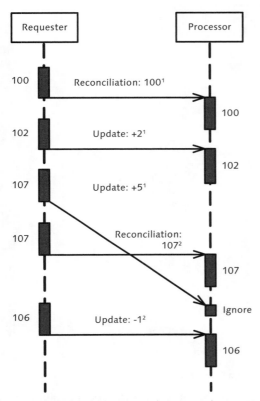

Figure 5.12 How the Reconciliation Mechanism Works (Continued)

▸ All the calls that were sent after the reconciliation call must be processed by the provider after the reconciliation call has been processed—but before subsequent calls are processed. This situation is illustrated in Figure 5.13.

▸ All the calls that were sent after the reconciliation call can be processed by the provider before the reconciliation call is processed. However, they must be recorded and executed again when the reconciliation call has been processed. In the example shown, the change -1 in reconciliation 2 must be processed again after this reconciliation has set the synchronization point to 107.

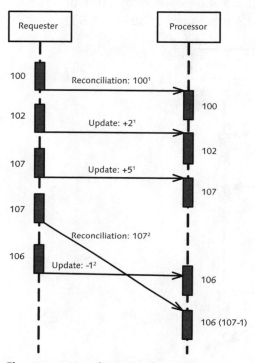

Figure 5.13   How the Reconciliation Counter Works (Continued)

Continuing Processing in a New Sequence

To place the calls in sequence again, starting with the reconciliation, a new sequence object must be created in the third step. This action allows the sequence to be restarted correctly, because the old sequence object is still locked because calls were lost or failed and should be deleted as soon as possible. The first call in the new sequence contains the actual reconciliation call that transfers the entire business object instance. Figure 5.14 shows an example of a sequence being restarted.

Figure 5.14   Sequence Restart

In this example, the first sequence is started with an initial reconciliation call, and the reconciliation counter is set to 1. The subsequent calls 1.1 and 1.2 are executed successfully. Then call 1.3 causes an error and stops the sequence. Because of this, calls 1.4 and 1.5 cannot be processed.

Consequently, a reconciliation of the business object is necessary to establish a new synchronization point that will start a new sequence and set the reconciliation counter to 2. Further calls that are based on this reconciliation have the same reconciliation counter (2) and are renumbered in the new sequence (calls 2.1 and 2.2).

New synchronization point

The decision about how the consumer handles this situation is made on the application layer. Essentially, the consumer has the option of restarting the sequence (the entire business process) — that is, performing steps 1.1–1.5 with the new reconciliation counter 2 — so they are numbered 2.1–2.5. Alternatively the consumer application can decide to continue the sequence after the synchronization point (1.2) with the new reconciliation counter (2.1–2.3). This decision is largely dependent on the requirements of the application and not on technical constraints.

5.2.7   Avoiding Sequencing

In scenarios in which changes to business objects are processed, in addition to the reconciliation option, optimization is also possible. Dependencies between changes typically require sequencing, but not every change depends on the preceding change. Also, many changes that have dependencies can still be made in a different order because they are interchangeable.

Change groups

This leaves two ways of avoiding sequencing in order to process as many changes as possible in parallel and in turn to minimize the effects of lost and failed changes to subsequent changes when multiple changes need to be combined to attain a consistent state:

▸ Minimize the sequence context
▸ Make changes interchangeable

Minimizing the Sequence Context

Changes can be divided into groups of changes for which dependencies only exist to previous changes in the same group, but where there are no dependencies between changes from different groups. Each group defines a *sequence context*, which defines the changes that need to be reordered within a sequence. Sequence contexts are defined in accordance with the following rules:

► **Definition of a sequence context based on instances, not on types**
The instances of a business object are typically independent of each other, so it is not necessary to define a sequence context on the level of the business object (type). For example, changes to an order request only affect that particular order request and no others.

► **Separation of concerns in an instance**
Some business object instances can be divided by separating areas of responsibility into different sequence contexts: changes to one part of the instance can be independent of changes to another part of the instance. For example, changes to the delivery address for an order can be made independently of changes to order items.

Note that a sequence context is also specific to a particular recipient of the changes (i.e., service provider). Consequently, sequencing only takes place with changes between one component and another. The same change can be sent to multiple recipients, but then no sequencing takes place between the different recipients.

Making Changes Interchangeable

Most changes must be executed in the sequence in which they were requested, because subsequent changes rely on preceding changes having been executed. In this way, the results of preceding changes can be the precondition for subsequent changes. For example, a change that modifies a business object node requires that this node actually exists, which in turn is the result of a preceding change that created the node.

Changes, if they are defined proficiently, can be made interchangeable, so that they do not require sequencing. The following rules can be applied to this process:

► **Use delta values for changes to elementary fields**
Instead of changing elementary fields using absolute values, where each change overwrites the preceding change, making it necessary to

adhere to the correct change sequence to arrive at the correct results, express changes using delta values. For example, an inventory change can be expressed as an increase of 20 instead of setting the current inventory amount to 50.

The application logic must take specific precautions to manage temporary values that would not have existed if the correct sequence had been adhered to. For example, it must be possible to reduce the inventory by 10, even if it was already 0, because a previous increase of 20 is only processed on the provider side after the reduction.

▶ **Use binary status changes as delta values**
Changes to binary status values can be processed in the same way as changes to elementary fields. Instead of setting the current status from *false* to *true* or vice versa, the status can be raised or lowered. A positive status value represents *true*, and a negative status value represents *false*.

For example, the status *archivable* indicates that the business object can be moved to a backup medium. If the status is reset, because the business object was temporarily reactivated, but was then set to *true* again, the activation can easily be done in a subsequent change: the business object remains on the backup medium and can be processed with lower performance, but when the delayed change has been processed, the business object is still in the archive, as desired.

▶ **Express changes by adding and deleting**   Adding an item
Instead of changing an existing item or row directly, this operation can be done by adding a new item or row to the existing item and simultaneously deleting the existing item or row. This approach can even be used to express changes to complex data types. Strings can be expressed to be made interchangeable. For example, an item in an order request can be changed by inserting a new item instead of the item to be changed and deleting the original item.

However, even when using interchangeable changes, data inconsistencies can still be caused if calls are lost. To restore consistency in such situations, a reconciliation between the consumer and the provider is sometimes needed.

5.2.8   Modeling the Behavior for Asynchronous Scenarios

Stateless

Asynchronous communication is always modeled in the same way, regardless of whether exactly-once processing, sequencing through in-order processing, or SAP sequencing is being used. In each case, the service interface must be stateless. This interface is used to model one or more operations, which are set to asynchronous.

Only with SAP sequencing do you need to ensure that the reconciliation call is modeled as an additional operation in the service interface.

No output parameters

The modeling environment ensures that an asynchronous service operation can only have input and fault parameters - no output parameters - because an asynchronous call does not return results directly to the consumer. A detailed description of how asynchronous operations are modeled in the ES Repository can be found in Section 6.1.3, Modeling Services in the Enterprise Services Repository.

Whether only exactly-once processing is used or whether in-order processing is used as well is not modeled explicitly. Instead, it is decided programmatically in the consumer application. With in-order processing, an explicit sequence object is used in the consumer application. This sequence object ensures that the calls are placed in order.

During modeling, you should ensure that all the calls that need to be placed in order are modeled as operations in the same service interface. This makes it easy for the service runtime to identify which calls have dependencies and which do not.

In a stateless service interface, asynchronous operations can also be combined with synchronous operations, for example, to allow read accesses.

5.3   Synchronous Scenarios

Applications

Synchronous coupling is typically preferred over asynchronous coupling in the following cases:

► In scenarios in which the consumer application needs a result from the provider side to be able to meaningfully continue its execution.

These interactions are usually read calls; sometimes write accesses are needed as well.

▶ In scenarios in which the transaction control is on the consumer side. These are stateful scenarios in which a session between the consumer and the provider is established and in which the consumer decides when the session and thus the transaction is closed. This interaction model is typical for user interface scenarios.

5.3.1 Configuring the Runtime Properties of Synchronous Scenarios

If communication takes place through a synchronous service operation, the above-defined runtime properties are configured as follows:

▶ **Message exchange pattern (MEP)**
The MEP is typically a request response, because synchronous scenarios are characterized by the fact that the consumer expects a result from the provider's service call in order to be able to meaningfully continue processing.

▶ **Transactionality**

  ▶ Synchronous calls on the consumer side are not transactional, because they are sent to the provider immediately after they are submitted in the consumer program, regardless of whether the consumer transaction is closed successfully or not.

  ▶ The calls on the provider side are also not transactional. Typically, each individual call is executed in a separate transaction.

However, transactionality can be ensured on a higher level. One approach for this is tentative update and confirm or compensate (TU&C/C), which is described later.　　　　　TU&C/C

▶ **Caller blocking**
In synchronous scenarios, the service call on the consumer side is blocking, so the consumer program only continues processing when the result of the service call has been returned by the provider and is available in the consumer program.

- **Reliable communication**
  In synchronous scenarios, communication is not reliable, because there is a close dependency between the consumer and the provider, which does not make it absolutely necessary to use reliable communication.

- **Commit handling**
  On the provider side, no commit handling is used in the service runtime, because synchronous calls are meant to be used primarily for read operations.

  There are two exceptions to this rule:

  - If a higher-level transaction concept (such as TU&C/C) is used, then commit handling is also supported in the service runtime.

  - If an application still wants to commit data in a read call (for example, applications logs), then it can programmatically initiate commit handling.

- **Session handling**
  As a closer relationship between the consumer and the provider is established in synchronous scenarios, session handling can optionally be used.

The overall process for a synchronous service execution is illustrated in Figure 5.15.

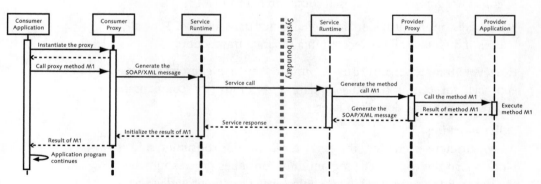

Figure 5.15 Overall Process of Synchronous Service Execution

In this process, the decisive factor is that processing in the consumer application is interrupted until a call on the provider side has been processed and the result is available to the consumer.

Synchronous scenarios, for which the consumer immediately needs the result of the service call from the provider, are generally not reliable. When the consumer does not receive a response from the provider, it does not know whether the provider has received the call or whether the response has been lost.

In these situations, the consumer cannot automatically decide whether to resend the call (in case the provider has not received the call) or whether to request the result of the call again (in case the response was lost).

For this reason, whenever possible, you should avoid using synchronous calls if data is written on the provider side. However, as scenarios do exist in which synchronous write operations are needed, you should use a higher-level transaction concept to have secure, synchronous write scenarios. One such transaction concept is described below.

The following sections examine three synchronous scenarios:

▶ **Stateless read**
The classic case of a synchronous read interaction, as described above

▶ **TU&C/C**
The higher-level transaction concept that allows synchronous write scenarios

▶ **Stateful write**
Write scenarios in which transaction control is on the consumer side

5.3.2 Stateless Read

Stateless read scenarios are the recommended variant for synchronous scenarios. In these scenarios, the service interface contains one or more operations that are synchronous in the sense described above.

On the service provider side, a new session context (and implicitly a new transaction) is opened for each service operation call and closed again when the call is completed. This ensures that there are no side effects between multiple calls from different service operations.

Modeling

Stateless read scenarios are modeled by creating a stateless service interface and defining one or more of its operations as synchronous.

When synchronous service operations are modeled, the modeling environment allows you to specify both input, output, and fault parameters, because a synchronous call returns a dedicated result to the consumer.

Section 6.1.3 Modeling a Service Interface provides a more detailed description of how synchronous operations are modeled in the ES Repository.

In a stateless service interface, synchronous operations can also be combined with asynchronous operations, for example, to allow write accesses.

5.3.3   Tentative Update & Confirm or Compensate (TU&C/C)

Higher-level transaction protocol

A higher-level transaction protocol is needed to allow reliable processing for synchronous write scenarios and with optimal decoupling (using stateless service calls).

There are different approaches for this:

▶ One option is to use a two-phase commit protocol. This is a commonly used model for distributed transactions. Although in theory it meets the requirements for these scenarios, past experience has shown that it does not scale in real-world business applications. It forces a close technical coupling of the components involved in the transaction to the extent that critical resources (for example, database connections and work processes) are bound to each component until the distributed transaction is closed.

A further disadvantage is that conflicts are manifested on a technical level, which makes them difficult to resolve by a business user, who would be familiar with the business meaning of a conflict.

▶ The alternative is to use the TU&C/C protocol, which addresses transactional coupling on a business level. This protocol bypasses the disadvantages of the two-phase commits, because it allows both a loose technical coupling of the components and also allows conflicts to be resolved on a business level. Using this protocol requires special application knowledge, so it cannot be handled exclusively by the communication infrastructure (service runtime).

The TU&C/C protocol assumes a particular trust relationship between the involved components or applications, because it defines a contract that must be strictly adhered to. For this reason, TU&C/C is suited to communication in trusted environments, such as a system landscape in a company, but it is not suited to communication with anonymous users on the Internet.

Only in trusted environments

The TU&C/C concept is based on the process of a reservation and subsequent confirmation or cancelation. For example, if a travel agency requests a flight reservation using a synchronous call, the airline makes a temporary change (i.e., tentative update) to the available free seats for the flight. This change is temporary, because the airline must assume that the reservation may be canceled later and because there is no binding reservation yet, but also because the airline cannot give this seat to someone else if it has confirmed the reservation.

Example

The reservation can be changed several times before the final booking is made through another synchronous call, which leads to another change to the preceding temporary change. When the travel agency has decided what to do with the reservation, it uses an asynchronous call to send either the confirmation or the cancelation. This results in a confirmation or a cancellation of the reservation that was created through the preceding synchronous calls.

In the context of TU&C/C, this is known as a *contract*. It is based on the following agreements:

Contract

▶ The consumer is obligated to send a confirmation (confirm) or a cancelation (compensate) as soon as it has completed its own transaction. This is independent of how the transaction was closed. This includes not only explicit commits or rollbacks, but also any type of error that would cause the termination of the transaction, such as a system crash.

▶ The provider is obligated to convert the temporary changes (i.e., tentative update) into final changes if the provider receives a confirm call. In the same way, the provider will discard the temporary changes if it receives a compensate call, regardless of what has happened on the provider side in the meantime. This also includes fatal error situations, such as a system crash.

If no temporary changes were made on the provider side, the compensate call is ignored.

This contract means that the consumer can be sure that the provider will bring its transaction to the same conclusion as the consumer transaction. The consumer must only ensure that it sends the confirm call as soon as the consumer transaction has been completed successfully and that the execution of this call and the closing of the transaction are transactional. The same applies to sending a compensate call if the transaction fails.

The provider can be sure that the consumer will notify the provider of the completion of the consumer transaction and that the provider will not need to take any action on the temporary changes until the provider is explicitly requested. Specifically, the provider may not set a timeout that would lead to the temporary changes being automatically canceled after a certain time has elapsed. By doing this, the provider would be in breach of the contract, because the provider is obligated to convert the temporary changes into permanent changes if a confirm call is received. The provider would no longer be able to do this if the temporary changes have been deleted.

Breach of contract

As there is always the possibility that the contract will be breached—be it due to human intervention or a software error—compliance with the contract must be monitored:

▶ If the provider receives neither a confirm nor a compensate call for a very long time, the status of the consumer transaction that caused the temporary changes on the provider side must be analyzed:

  ▶ If the consumer transaction has failed, then to restore data consistency, the tentative updates can be deleted on the provider side without an explicit compensate call.

  ▶ If the consumer transaction was completed successfully, the conflict must be resolved manually. It is normally not sufficient to convert the temporary changes into permanent changes, because the lost confirm call could contain additional data, which would be missing on the provider side.

- ▶ In all other cases, the consumer transaction can continue and be checked again at a later time.
- ▶ If, upon receiving the confirm call, the provider cannot convert the temporary changes into permanent changes, or if, upon receiving the compensate call, cannot cancel the temporary changes, then this situation is flagged as an error and must be resolved manually.

The TU&C/C contract requires that the consumer application send either a confirm or a compensate call as soon as the consumer transaction has terminated, regardless of how it terminated. To guarantee this behavior, even in the worst case of a system crash while the transaction is running, the compensate call in the consumer component is registered in the service runtime before the first service call of a tentative update is submitted. If the transaction for any reason subsequently fails, the already prepared compensate call is sent by the service runtime. If the transaction is completed successfully, the consumer application passes the confirm call to the service runtime. The service runtime then executes this confirm call and simultaneously invalidates the compensate call.

TU&C/C in SOA middleware

> **Note**
>
> To ensure that the calls reach the provider as stipulated by the contract, both the compensate call and the confirm call are sent asynchronously with exactly-once semantics.

The steps in a successful TU&C/C transaction are described in more detail below:

Steps in a transaction

1. The consumer application instantiates a consumer proxy for its TU&C/C-based transaction.

2. To ensure that the transaction can be rolled back, the first operation is to call the compensate method in the proxy instance. The consumer application passes data for this call, including the transaction ID and an ID of the consumer application. The provider may need this data to roll back the transaction.

3. The service runtime will not send the call immediately. Instead it registers the call in its XML representation in a similar way to a "normal" asynchronous call. However, this registration is different in that if the transaction is abnormally terminated, the call will be sent through the

reliable messaging layer—not if the transaction is completed successfully. For this reason, the registered call is also immediately persisted, so that it is not lost if the transaction fails.

4. After the call has been successfully registered, the service runtime guarantees that the compensate message will be sent reliably (exactly once) to the provider if the transaction fails.

Tentative update 5. Next, the consumer application calls one or more tentative update methods in the consumer proxy instance. These methods are executed synchronously and result in temporary changes on the provider side. All of these tentative update calls are also given the transaction ID and the ID of the consumer application, so that the provider can flag the changes and identify them for a subsequent confirm or compensate call.

> **Important**
>
> Even though the changes are temporary, they are immediately persisted by the provider and not retained in memory. This ensures that the entire transaction is stateless, that is, each call can be processed in a separate session to guarantee that the service calls are executed independently.

6. If the consumer application has successfully completed its transaction, its last action is to call the confirm method in the consumer proxy. The proxy then triggers the registration of the call in the service runtime.

Transactional confirm and compensate action 7. In the service runtime, the following transactional actions must be performed to ensure a consistent state:

▶ The confirm call is persisted and registered in the reliable messaging layer for immediate sending

▶ The Compensate call is deleted

The transactional execution of these two actions is important, because if anything should fail in this step, the replacing of the compensate call with the confirm call would be undone, and the compensate call would be executed.

8. If replacement is successful, the reliable messaging layer triggers the sending of the confirm call. If the call arrives at the provider, the provider converts the temporary changes into permanent changes.

> **Note**
>
> Figure 5.16 provides a simplified representation of the steps for an asynchronous call of the confirm message.

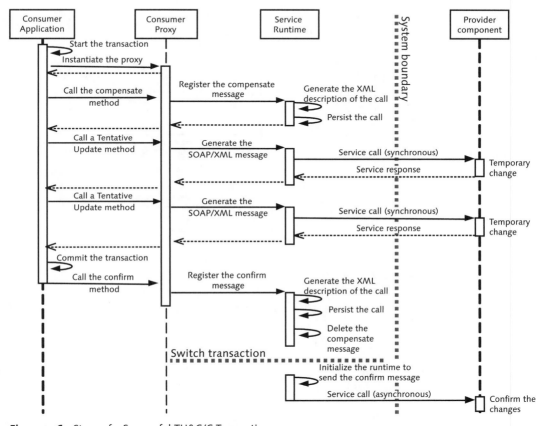

Figure 5.16 Steps of a Successful TU&C/C Transaction

If the transaction is rolled back by the consumer application, or if a system crash occurs, the service runtime ensures that the compensate call is reliable, that is, sent exactly once. This situation is shown in Figure 5.17. The steps for the asynchronous sending of the compensate call are also simplified here.

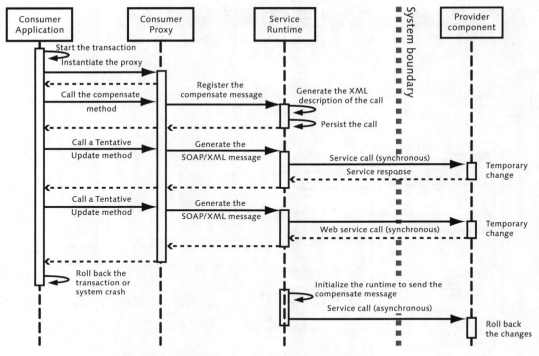

Figure 5.17 Steps for a Terminated TU&C/C Transaction

Modeling When the service interface is modeled in the ES Repository, a dedicated TU&C/C interface pattern is offered. A TU&C/C service interface is automatically set to stateless.

If a service interface is configured as a TU&C/C interface, the modeling infrastructure ensures that:

▶ The modeler defines exactly one compensate operation. This operation is automatically set to asynchronous.

▶ The modeler defines at least one confirm operation. These operations are also automatically set to asynchronous.

▶ The modeler defines at least one tentative update operation. This operation is set to synchronous. When the inbound service interface is modeled on the provider side, the modeler also designates that commit handling is supported for this operation in the service runtime (similar to asynchronous operations). If the operation is executed successfully, the service runtime commits the transaction; if an error occurs, the service runtime rolls back the transaction. This ensures that the tentative update calls are written directly to the database and that the provider does not need to retain the state in memory.

Section 6.1.3, Modeling a Service Interface, provides a more detailed description of how a TU&C/C Interface is modeled in the ES repository.

5.3.4 Stateful Write and Update

As mentioned earlier, in some scenarios, the transaction control is on the consumer side, for example, in user interface scenarios. In these situations, the first call establishes a session between the consumer and the provider. This session allows a common state to be managed for multiple service calls. This session is generated when the first call is processed on the provider side, which keeps it open until it is explicitly closed by the consumer or a timeout is exceeded.

This session can be used on the provider side to retain and modify data in memory for the duration of multiple service calls. Specifically, instances of provider proxies can be reused for multiple calls.

To ensure that the consumer sends all the calls to the same session, the provider includes a session ID in the service response to the first call. The consumer includes this session ID in subsequent calls.

Session concept

This session concept allows a transactional coupling to be established between a consumer and a provider.

The service interface for these scenarios includes:

- Business methods through which data can be manipulated on the provider side. On the provider side, all manipulations through these business methods are performed in memory.

- Methods that successfully commit a transaction or that roll back a transaction:

  - If a commit method is called, the provider persists all the data that was modified in memory by preceding calls of business methods. In addition, the service runtime automatically ensures that the provider transaction is closed (committed).

▶ If the rollback method is called, the provider discards all the data in the memory. In addition, the service runtime ensures that the provider transaction is rolled back.

Interaction model In the interaction model, the transaction begins with the first call of a business method by the consumer. On the provider side, a new session and a new transaction are generated. The response returned by the provider includes the session ID, which the consumer includes in subsequent calls. At a specific time, the consumer decides whether to close the transaction successfully or not. If the transaction is closed successfully, the consumer calls the commit operation in the service interface; if the transaction is terminated unsuccessfully, the consumer calls the rollback method.

Figure 5.18 shows the steps in this stateful transactional model when a transaction is completed successfully.

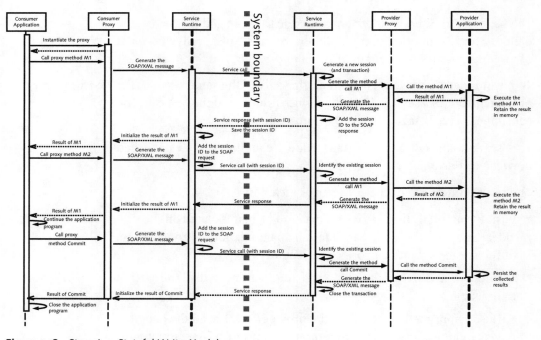

Figure 5.18 Steps in a Stateful Write Model

This chapter will take a closer look at the design and implementation phase, which is where the service interfaces and their data types are defined in the ES Repository and implemented on the implementation platform. We focus on the ABAP platform as the target platform for the provider side.

6 Developing an Enterprise Service

In the previous two chapters, we looked at the main components of SOA middleware and their interaction models. In this chapter, we will examine how to use these components to define and implement an enterprise service, and publish it so it can be used in a consumer application. For developers of provider applications, the ES Repository, the Services Registry, the provider system, and the configuration framework must interact closely. Service providers should aim to offer functionality that is as easy as possible for consumers to consume. In particular, service providers should ensure the following:

▶ The elements of a service, such as data types, parameters, and operations, should be standardized as much as possible. This increases the probability that all the parties to a business process can work directly with the service. If no standard exists, then a mapping will usually be needed between the data structures of the consumer and the provider, because both consumer and provider will work with their own structures.

Standardization also ensures that the service consumer does not have to work with provider-specific details.

▶ Reuse between data types and operation signatures should be maximized. For example, the result structure for a service call that selects the details of a business object should be identical to the input parameters of the service call to change that business object. This ensures

Requirements

that a consumer application that reads and then changes business object data reuses the same data type for both service calls.

▶ It should be as easy as possible for consumers to discover services suitable for them. Consumers should not need to know the names of services; it should be possible to search for services using the business context.

To allow you to optimally comply with these points, SOA middleware offers the procedure for developing a service provider:

▶ Model the service in the ES Repository

▶ Generate and implement the enterprise service proxy in the provider system

▶ Publish the service in the Services Registry

The development procedure can be divided into seven steps:

❶ Model the services in the ES Repository (ESR)
Enterprise service development is model driven. All the entities relevant for the service are modeled independently of any programming language. These entities include the service interface, the service operations with their parameters, and the data types referenced.

In the following, we will call the entity built here the *service model*, because it already contains all the implementation-independent metadata of the service.

❷ Publish the service model
A service model contains all the metadata a service consumer needs to implement an application. Therefore, the service model is published to the Services Registry to provide service consumers access to these models.

❸ Generate the service definition in the provider system
This step implements the services in the provider system. Based on the service model metadata, a representation is generated in the respective programming language. In the following, this entity is referred to as a *service definition*. It contains the generated programming language constructs (normally an object-oriented interface with

methods and parameters) and other metadata, which we will examine in the following chapters.

❹ Implement the service definition

The application developer implements the generated service definition. This either creates completely new application functionality, or the application developer maps the service interface to existing application logic.

❺ Publish the service definition

For a consumer, implemented service definitions are the basis for developing a consumer application. They also tell the configuration framework which services can be configured so that they can be called by a consumer. For these reasons, service definitions are also published to the Services Registry now.

❻ Configure the service definition

To allow a service to be called by a consumer, the technical settings for the runtime environment must be made. These settings include security settings and the call address. This is done when the service definition is configured. Consequently, this step creates services with their *service endpoints*. Service endpoints are the entities that can be called by a service consumer.

The service configuration is done by a configuration framework, which can centrally configure all the services and service consumers in a system landscape. Therefore, the configuration framework also accesses the Services Registry to ascertain all the entities that are potentially relevant for configuration (Figure 6.1 phase ❻a) and initiate the configuration process in the relevant (backend) system (Figure 6.1 phase ❻b)

❼ Publish the services and service endpoints

After the service endpoints have been created, they are published to the Services Registry, since they are the primary points of reference for the configuration of the service consumer.

Figure 6.1 summarizes these steps to develop enterprise services.

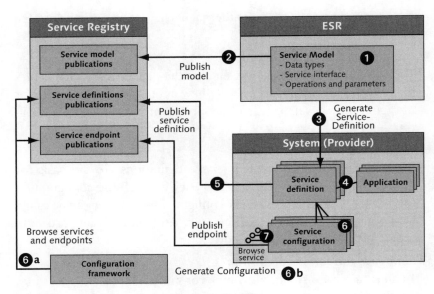

Figure 6.1 Steps to Develop an Enterprise Service

6.1 Modeling a Service Interface

A Web service scenario should always begin by modeling the services. This ensures that the interface is both optimally abstracted from implementation details and, as much as possible, that it contains known and standardized elements to make their use by consumers as easy as possible.

Three modeling areas

Modeling a Web service consists of the following three areas, which are covered in greater detail in the sections that follow:

- Modeling the data types
- Modeling the interface
- Modeling the behavior

First, however, some administration tasks must be done in the System Landscape Directory and the ES Repository. We will look at these in the next section.

6.1.1 Organizing the ES Repository Content

Before you can start modeling design objects in the ES Repository, you must first create the technical administration objects that are needed to manage the ES Repository content and specifically to ship it as a product. From the perspective of software logistics, a product is a shipping unit, which can exist in multiple versions, and is composed of one or more software components, which can also have multiple versions. The *System Landscape Directory* (SLD) stores the information about the software component versions that a particular product version needs. A software component version is a shipping unit for design objects in the ES Repository, and, as such, is used to group the objects. Within a software component, you also group your objects by namespaces. You can only uniquely identify an object in the ES Repository by specifying a software component version and a namespace. Software component versions and namespaces are therefore required to create and edit objects in the ES Repository. There are two types of software components in the ES Repository:

Software logistics

- ▸ Local software components
- ▸ SLD-based software components

Local software components are objects that are defined free-style in the ES Repository, and are used to group objects that are not intended for shipping. The name of the software component is assigned when it is created in the ES Repository. Normally, a local software component only contains objects used for testing. The objects can therefore not be transported using the ES Repository's transport tools.

Local software component

SLD-based software components are used to group objects that are intended to be shipped as part of a product. This type of software component is defined in the SLD and then imported into the ES Repository. Names are assigned centrally in the SLD and used when the objects are imported into the ES Repository. The objects can be included in a transport list and prepared for shipping using the Change Management System tools. Figure 6.2 shows the editor for a software component in the ES Builder.

SLD-based software component

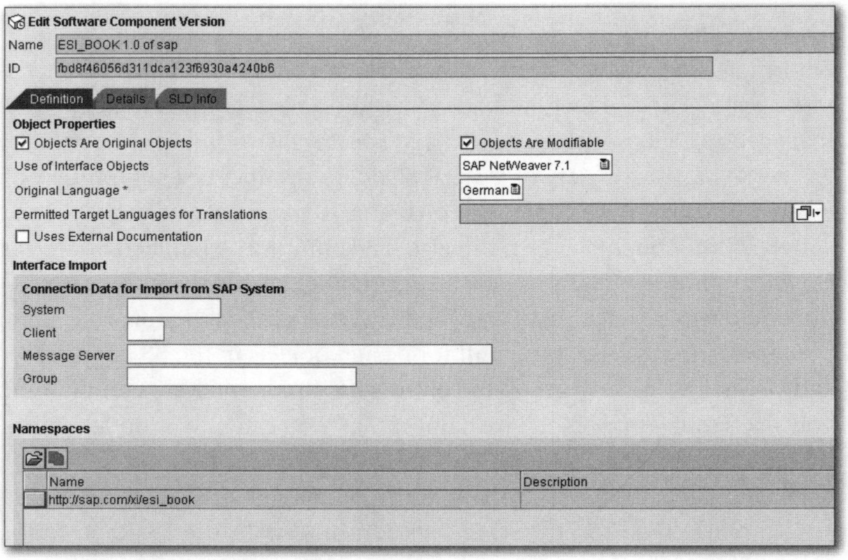

Figure 6.2 Editing a Software Component

Declaring
dependencies

Software component versions can build on each other. The software component version on which another software component version is dependent is known as the *underlying software component version*. The benefit of declaring dependencies is that you can immediately use the design objects of the underlying software component for modeling. The relationships between software components are also maintained in the editor in the ES Repository.

Namespaces

You can also use the Software Component (SWC) editor to create the namespaces to model the service interfaces. ES Repository namespaces are used to prevent naming conflicts with other objects with the same name, since no duplicate object names for an object type can exist in the same ES Repository namespace. An ES Repository namespace is an entity in the ES Repository in which the object names are unique. Using naming conventions when the namespaces are defined prevents namespaces from overlapping. All the namespaces shipped by SAP begin with the prefix *http://sap.com/*.

When a software component and its namespaces are created, the ES Browser displays the elements as shown in Figure 6.3.

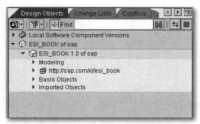

Figure 6.3 Software Components and Namespaces in the ES Browser

When the software component and the required namespaces are cre-   Creating objects
ated, the prerequisites for modeling service interfaces are in place. Using
the ES Browser (see Figure 6.4), you can now create design objects in
the namespace. Using the context menu in a namespace node in the ES
Browser's tree view, you can open the object gallery of the ES Repository object. In this window, you can specify the object type and the basic
object properties.

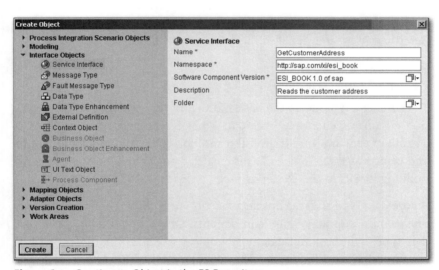

Figure 6.4 Creating an Object in the ES Repository

When the object has been created, you navigate automatically to the
corresponding editor to edit the object. We explain this in detail in the
following sections for the object type's data type and service interface.

6.1.2 Modeling the Data Types

When modeling data types, we distinguish between two development scenarios in the ES Repository:

▶ **Defining a free-style data type**
Here, you define a data type in accordance with the subset of XML Schema constructs prescribed by the ES Repository. In this way, you define simple and complex types based on the primitive types defined by XML Schema, such as xsd:string, xsd:integer.

▶ **Defining a data type in accordance with CCTS**
Here, you define aggregated data types using the core data types (Date, Code, Amount, etc.) prescribed by the specification. Thus, in this modeling approach, you abstract the type modeling from the XML Schema type system.

As reuse of data types and the semantics-driven modeling of data types are of utmost importance for service development based on an application platform, the CCTS-compliant modeling approach for data types is described in greater detail in the following sections.

Defining a Core Data Type

The core data types form the basis of the SAP type system on the application platform. When new core data types are created, they originate as a result of semantic and technical restrictions (for example, length limits and value range restrictions). This creates a powerful library of semantic building blocks in the ES Repository.

A core data type always consists of a content component and optionally one or more supplementary components. One simple example of a core data type is the Amount data type. You can use an Amount data type to semantically describe an amount of money, which is determined by a sum of money and a currency unit. The sum in this example is the content component, and the currency unit is a supplementary component. Figure 6.5 shows how you define a semantic restriction for the data type Amount as a core data type in the enterprise services data type editor.

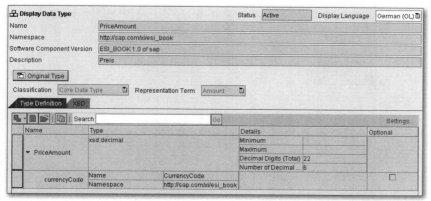

Figure 6.5 Creating a Core Data Type

The basic semantics of a data type are described by a *representation term*. By defining the representation term, the editor decides which supplementary components are available. The modeler then decides which of the components are needed for the data type. The modeler also sets up the data type of the content component. However, there are restrictions here too, which are checked by the editor using the representation term. With an Amount data type, the content component must be defined with an xsd:decimal type or a derivative type (for example, xsd:int). Using xsd:string is not permitted. Other restrictions to the value range are also changed in the core data type editor. In the above example, the accuracy of the content component was set to six decimal places. Additional restrictions can also be made to the value range, such as setting a minimum or maximum.

Representation term

Defining an Aggregated Data Type

The core data types are a good starting point for modeling data types. However, using only core data types, you cannot define complex interfaces for service interfaces. To this end, the ES Repository provides aggregated data types, which are built on aggregated data types or core data types. When you model aggregated data types, you can only create elements that reference core data types or other aggregated data types. An element also indicates how often it is used in an instance. Attributes

Metamodel

and references to free-style data types or XML Schema data types are not permitted. The metamodel for the data types is shown in Figure 6.6.

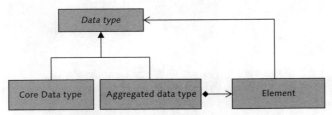

Figure 6.6 Metamodel for ES Repository Data Types (Simplified)

Figure 6.7 shows how core data types can be used to build an aggregated data type for an address.

Name	Type	Occurrence	Description
▼ CustomerAddress			
City	CityName	1	City
PostalCode	PostalCode	1	Postal Code
Street	StreetName	1	Street
CountryCode	CountryCode	1	Country
ValidityStartDate	ValidityDate	1	validity from
ValidityEndDate	ValidityDate	1	validity to

Figure 6.7 Aggregated Data Type in the ES Repository

6.1.3 Modeling a Service Interface

The next step after modeling the data types is to model the *service interface*. The service interface starts the defining an enterprise service and groups all the entities that semantically belong to a service.

Service operation One or more *service operations* can be defined within a service interface. Operations should be grouped in a service interface that are either semantically related (for example, operations that operate on the same business object or are part of the same business process) or technically related. An example of this is the need to preserve, on the provider side, the sequence of service calls initiated by a consumer. This sequence can only be preserved for operations in the same service interface.

One or more parameters can be defined for each service operation. There are three types of parameters here: input, output, and fault parameters. Input parameters must be passed by a service consumer, and output parameters are returned by the service provider as the result of a service call. Fault parameters are returned by the provider if the service call fails. Each parameter contains a reference to a previously modeled data type.

Parameters

In the ES Repository, you can define input and output parameters using two modeling paradigms:

▶ **Document style**
Here, the focus is on modeling an XML/SOAP message that is exchanged at runtime between the consumer and the provider. Consequently, you define the interface using message types that are also modeled in the ES Repository as separate entities. Each message type represents an XML/SOAP message and has one link to a data type that determines the structure of the message. A message type can be reused in multiple interfaces.

▶ **RPC style**
Here, the focus is on modeling the method or procedure call. The operation signature is defined in a similar way to calls in programming languages, such as Java, which means one or more input parameters and one or more output parameters are modeled explicitly.

The scenario determines which of the two modeling paradigms for parameters is preferred. Whereas in B2B scenarios, communication is typically defined through the exchange of messages, communication in user interface or composite scenarios normally takes place through method calls.

How a service interface is modeled can also vary depending on the scenario:

Differences in modeling

▶ In point-to-point scenarios, the service interface is determined by the service provider. Thus, the service interface is first modeled on the provider side. This interface is called an *inbound service interface*.

The consumer uses this definition to define its *outbound service interface*. With point-to-point scenarios, it is important that the interfaces are absolutely identical, which is ensured if they are defined using this procedure.

▶ There are also scenarios in which the consumer wants to define its outbound service interface independently of the provider's service interface. This is also supported by the ES Repository: the outbound service interface can be defined without an inbound service interface on which to base it. In these scenarios, point-to-point communication is no longer possible, because the structures of the consumer and provider service interfaces are typically different from each other. A central broker must be interposed to map the two interfaces to each other. This *brokering* functionality is provided by the SAP Process Integration.

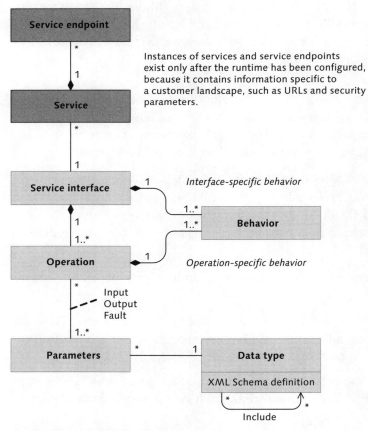

Figure 6.8 Enterprise Services – Metamodel

In addition to the interface aspect of a service interface, which is defined by the operations and their parameters, it is important for a user to know the behavior of a service, to provide all the information about how a service can be used. The behavior of a service interface indicates which interaction model the service implements. On the operation level, the behavior also shows which role the operation has in the service interface. At the end of this section, we will look more closely at modeling the behavior. The above-described properties result in a metamodel for enterprise services, as shown in Figure 6.8.

Service behavior

Figure 6.9 shows the service interface editor in the ES Repository with an example of a synchronous read service. The task of the service modeled here is to find the address of a customer using the customer name.

Service interface editor

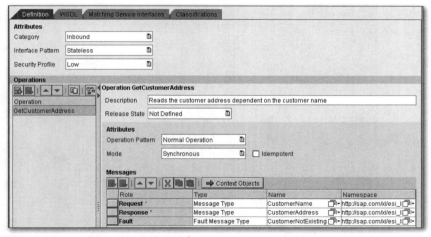

Figure 6.9 Modeling a Service Interfaces

For this service, an operation GetCustomerAddress is needed. You can see this operation in the editor to the left in the operation overview. From this overview, you can create more operations if the scenario requires. The interfaces for the operations are defined on the right side of the editor. The interface structure is determined by the modeled behavior of the operation. For example, with asynchronous communication, it is not possible to specify a response message. In our example of a synchronous service, the interface of the operation is determined by a request message, which contains the name of the customer, and a

Operation

155

response message, with which the address of the customer is sent to the service consumer.

Fault message
A fault message CustomerNotExisting is also defined. This fault message is returned to the caller if the customer does not exist in the provider system. In the service interface editor, you only assign the message objects to the interface. The message objects themselves are handled as separate ES Repository objects. This allows the message objects to be re-used for multiple services. This is especially important in a situation where the response message of one service is the request message of another service. The message objects are edited in the ES Repository using the *Message Editor*, which is where you edit the data type assignments. Figure 6.10 shows the modeling for the response message in our example, which is determined by the data type *Address*.

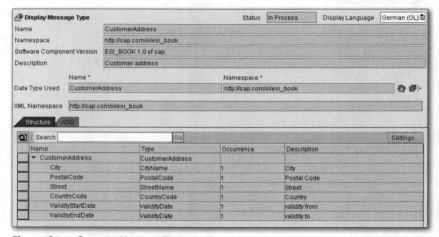

Figure 6.10 Create a Message Type

Having modeled the service interface, we will now take a closer look at modeling the behavior. The behavior of a service is shaped by different interaction models, through which Web service communication can take place. For example, there are *asynchronous models*, in which the consumer and the provider are completely decoupled and *synchronous models*, in which a relationship between the consumer and the provider is established, because, for example, the consumer needs the result of the service call on the provider side. We already examined the interaction models and their properties in Chapter 5, Interaction Models for SOA Middleware.

To simplify behavior modeling, the ES Repository provides predefined *interface* and *operations patterns* for the supported interaction models. This ensures that the services modeled in the ES Repository have a standardized behavior.

Interface and operations patterns

On the level of the interface patterns, the ES Repository provides three patterns: *stateless*, *TU&C/C*, and *stateful*.

The stateless interface pattern is used to model either asynchronous write scenarios or synchronous read scenarios. The asynchronous and synchronous operation patterns are used for this.

Asynchronous communication is always modeled in the same way, regardless of whether only exactly-once processing, sequencing through in-order processing, or SAP sequencing is used. In a service interface, one or more operations are modeled using the operations pattern asynchronous. Only with SAP sequencing do you also need to ensure that the reconciliation call is modeled as an additional operation in the service interface. The modeling environment ensures that an asynchronous service operation can only have input and fault parameters, and no output parameters, because an asynchronous call does not return results directly to the consumer. Figure 6.11 shows the how an asynchronous operation is modeled in the ES Builder.

Asynchronous communication

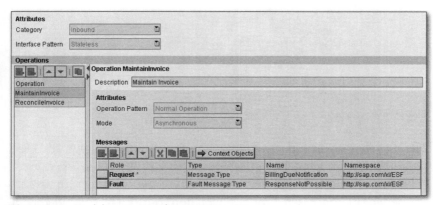

Figure 6.11 Modeling an Asynchronous Operation

You do not model explicitly whether only exactly-once processing or in-order processing will also be used. Instead, this is decided programmatically in the consumer application. With in-order processing, an explicit sequence object is used in the consumer application to place the calls in order. At the modeling stage, you should ensure that all the calls that must be in sequence are modeled as operations in the same service interface. The service runtime can then easily detect which calls have dependencies on each other and which do not.

In a stateless service interface, asynchronous operations can also be combined with synchronous operations, for example, to allow read accesses.

Stateless read

Stateless read scenarios are modeled in the same way as asynchronous write scenarios, creating a service interface with the stateless interface pattern. One or more operations are then assigned the synchronous operations pattern in this interface. Figure 6.12 shows the modeling steps for a synchronous operation in the ES Builder.

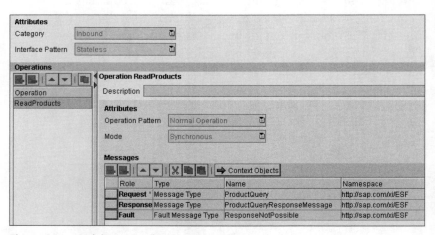

Figure 6.12 Modeling a Synchronous Operation

The modeling environment allows you to specify input, output, and fault parameters when modeling synchronous service operations, because a synchronous call returns a dedicated result to the consumer. In a stateless service interface, synchronous operations can also be combined with asynchronous operations, for example, to allow read accesses.

To model secure, synchronous write scenarios, the service interface is assigned the interface pattern TU&C/C. A TU&C/C service interface is automatically set to stateless.

If a service interface is assigned a TU&C/C interface, the modeling infrastructure ensures the following:

▶ The modeler defines exactly one *Compensate* operation. This operation is automatically set to asynchronous.

▶ The modeler defines at least one *Confirm* operation. These operations are also automatically set to asynchronous.

▶ The modeler defines at least one *Tentative Update* operation. This operation is set to synchronous. When modeling the inbound service interface on the provider side, the modeling infrastructure also defines commit handling as supported in the service runtime (similar to asynchronous operations) for this operation: if the operation is executed successfully, the service runtime "commits" the transaction; if an error occurs, it rolls the transaction back. This ensures that the tentative update calls are written directly to the database and the provider does not need to retain the state in memory.

Figure 6.13 illustrates the modeling of a TU&C/C service interface.

This service interface is used to check the customer requirements in the business process Sell from Stock (see Chapter 3, Model-Driven Business Process Development). When the order has been received, a check is performed to see whether the ordered products are available in that quantity in stock. If the required quantity is available, a temporary (tentative) reservation is created in the stock. This step is performed through a synchronous Tentative Update operation. If the order process is completed successfully, the asynchronous Confirm operation triggers a conversion of the reservation into a shipment. If the order is aborted, the asynchronous Compensate operation rolls back the reservation.

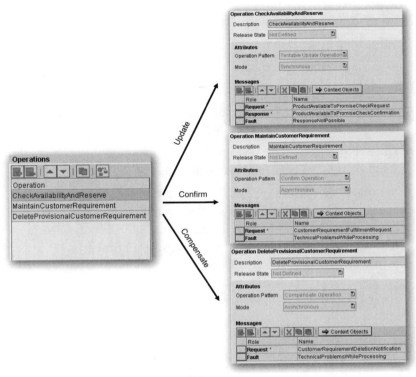

Figure 6.13 Modeling of a TU&C/C Interface

Stateful write/update

The ES Repository also provides a special interface pattern to model the stateful write/update scenario. When this interface pattern is used, the service interface is set to stateful. In addition, and the ES Repository ensures that at least one business operation and both a Commit and a Rollback operation are defined.

6.1.4 Working with Change Lists

One main task of the ES Repository is to manage the ES Repository objects. There are also tools to manage changes to objects. All the changes for a user that are made with the ES Builder to the ES Repository objects are collected in a change list. This makes it possible to easily manage changes to multiple ES Repository objects. The change lists that exist in the ES Repository are displayed by the change list browser. Figure 6.14

shows this browser with the change list of the objects that were created for the GetCustomerAddress service.

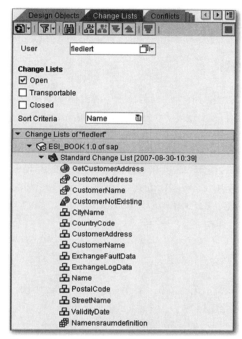

Figure 6.14 Working with Change Lists

A change list also ensures that an object is not changed unintention- **Locking objects** ally at the same time by multiple users. Thus, an object in a change list is locked to changes from other users. An object can only be locked in one change list. Consequently, no more than one changed version of an object can exist. This precludes the use of complex merge logic for competing changes. In addition, the changes to an object in a change list are only visible to the owner of that change list. All other users see the version from before the object change. Only when the object is released are the changes globally visible in the ES Repository. This release is also important for the implementation of a service, as only released object changes are respected in proxy generation. A change list can also be used to easily reset a change, because when an object is added to a change list, a new object version is always created automatically. This versioning is automatically done by the ES Builder, without user intervention. When a change list is released, the changes to production ES Repository objects can be distributed to downstream systems. To this end, the change list browser lets you release the changed objects for transport. Then the objects can be processed using transport tools.

6.2   Service Implementation

Proxy generation and ABAP Workbench

In the preceding sections, we described how service interfaces are modeled in the ES Repository and which interaction models are supported. In this chapter, we want to explain how services are implemented in ABAP through proxy generation and using the ABAP Workbench. The first part of this section looks at proxy generation, which generates a service definition in the provider system from the WSDL description of the service interface. The second part examines the interaction models and special considerations during implementation.

6.2.1   Proxy Generation

Whereas the services were modeled centrally in the ES Repository, proxy generation and service implementation are done locally in a particular provider system. Before a service proxy is generated, the implementer decides in which system to generate the proxy. Then you start proxy generation locally in that system, and the entities from the ES Repository are converted into programming language constructs (such as interfaces, classes, and data types) in the local system. This generation process was covered in Chapter 4, Components of SOA Middleware. We will now take a closer look at it and the generation of the service definition for the example *GetCustomerAddress*. To perform the generation process in the ABAP system, the development environment provides an ES Browser, which you can use to display the ES Repository content. This browser is integrated into the ES Repository Browser in the ABAP Workbench, which makes for an efficient collaboration between generation and manual implementation of service definitions.

Figure 6.15 shows the development environment for ABAP proxy objects in the ABAP Workbench.

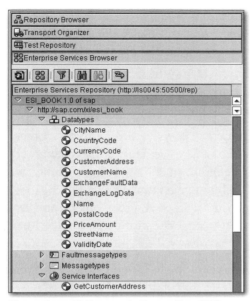

Figure 6.15 ES Browser in Transaction SE80

The structure of the browser tree display is identical to that of the ES **Hierarchical display** Repository Browser. Again, it shows a hierarchy of software components, namespaces, and ES Repository objects. One important feature of the object display in the provider system is the ability to manage the status of a proxy object. As modeling in the ES Repository is independent of proxy generation, you can set the following statuses for a proxy object:

▸ The object exists in the ES Repository, but no proxy object has been **Objects statuses** generated for it. The objects are developed in the ES Repository, and you can start proxy generation. This situation is shown in Figure 6.15 with our example.

▸ The object exists in the ES Repository, and a proxy object has already been generated. The proxy object and the corresponding ES Repository object are—from the perspective of metadata—identical, which means the object in the ES Repository has not been changed since the proxy was generated. This should be the normal status for a proxy object.

▸ The object exists in the ES Repository, and a proxy object has been generated for it. After the proxy object is generated, changes are made to the ES Repository object. There is a discrepancy between the metadata of the ES Repository object and the proxy object. This status should always be repaired by regenerating the proxy object.

▶ The proxy object exists in the provider system, but the ES Repository object has been deleted. This status should also be repaired to resolve the discrepancy between the ES Repository and the provider system.

Context-sensitive actions

Depending on the status, the browser allows you to perform different actions on objects. You can use the tools to generate a proxy object for the first time, regenerate it, or delete it. In the following sections, we particularly want to shed more light on generating newly developed ES Repository objects. In the ES Repository Browser, proxy objects are positioned on the object that you want to generate in the tree display. Then you select **Generate** from the context menu.

The tool to create proxy objects is then opened. Figure 6.16 shows the proxy editor for service interfaces.

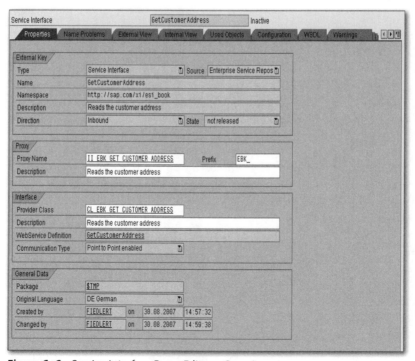

Figure 6.16 Service Interface Proxy Editor – Overview

You specify the name of the proxy object in the Properties window of the editor. The proxy editor proposes a value for all object names, which you have the option to overwrite. The name must conform to the ABAP conventions for object names, so only uppercase letters and a maximum length of 30 characters are permitted for object names.

Naming conventions

Another important function of proxy generation can also be seen in the PROPERTIES window: for each service interface, an interface and an implementation class are automatically generated during proxy generation. The signature of the interface is derived from the WSDL description of the service interface. The generated class implements this interface and serves as a basis for implementing the service functionality. When the service interface and the operations are mapped to methods in the generated ABAP interface, the tool also generates a name proposal. You can change this proposed name, as shown in Figure 6.17.

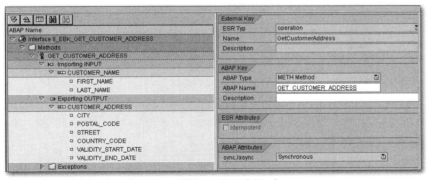

Figure 6.17 Service Interface Proxy Editor – Detail Display

This graphic shows that in ABAP, a method with an import parameter INPUT and an export parameter OUTPUT is generated from a synchronous service operation. An asynchronous operation is composed of only the import parameter. Note the mapping of the fault message to an ABAP object exception class, which is then also defined as an exception in the signature of the interface method. As a result, raising an exception in the implementation class of a service definition will trigger a fault message sent to the caller of the service.

Probably the most important mapping in proxy generation is the mapping of the data types to corresponding ABAP Dictionary objects. This

Mapping data types to ABAP Dictionary objects

mapping is critical because some of the types modeled in the ES Repository cannot be mapped to ABAP in a one-to-one relationship. The simplest example of this is the xsd:boolean type, which has no corresponding type in ABAP. Thus, proxy generation must offer the best possible data type for the target platform.

Table 6.1 is a summary of the mapping of ES Repository objects to ABAP objects:

ES Repository Object Type	ABAP Objects Object Type
Service interface	Service definition + Interface + Class
Service operation	Interface method
Simple data type	DDIC data element
Complex data type	DDIC structure
Fault message	Exception class

Table 6.1 ES Repository Objects and their Corresponding ABAP Objects

During proxy generation, the service interface behavior modeled in the ES Repository is also converted to the proxy definition. At configuration time and at runtime, this behavior is interpreted by the Web service runtime to guarantee the modeled behavior.

6.2.2 Proxy Implementation

To implement the provider side of an enterprise service, the application logic is stored in the generated provider proxy class. As the generated service proxy—through its methods, parameters, and data types—only reflects the business information, application developers do not need to concern themselves with communication-specific details. You have the option of either storing all the application logic directly in the provider proxy class or accessing existing application logic by calling function modules or other ABAP classes.

In some scenarios, it is not sufficient to work only with business-relevant information. In these scenarios, additional information is needed, or must be included, to be used in the service runtime to process the SOAP calls.

This communication-relevant information is, for example, used to control which calls in a sequencing scenario to process in sequence. Also, access to security information or the ID of the SOAP message is required to correctly process the application logic.

To work with this sort of communication-relevant information, we use *SOAP protocols*. SOAP protocols have access to special areas (SOAP headers) in a SOAP message, which are the basis for the communication-specific processing of the calls. SOAP protocols are divided into different areas, which are parsed when a SOAP message is processed. SOAP protocols exist for reliable messaging, security, session handling, and so on.

SOAP protocols

You can gain access to instances of the different SOAP protocols through the instance of a service proxy.

Implementing the Interaction Models: Special Features

In addition to the previously described general guidelines for using enterprise services, there are also special rules for implementing the interaction models. We will take another look at these special rules for specific interaction models.

On the provider side, transaction control takes place entirely through the service runtime. Therefore, no calls can be used in the implementation of the provider proxy that close or terminate the transaction. This is done only by the service runtime.

Asynchronous scenarios

In scenarios in which the sequence of the service calls must be preserved, you need to define which calls must be placed in which sequence in the program logic of the consumer application. This is done using the Reliable Messaging SOAP protocol, which allows you to generate sequence objects and assign calls to those sequence objects. The service runtime then uses these sequence objects to ensure that the calls in a sequence are processed in exactly the same order as was registered in the sequence. These rules also apply to asynchronous scenarios.

Sequencing through in-order processing

For the implementation of SAP sequencing scenarios, both the rules for asynchronous scenarios and the rules for in-order processing must be applied. In addition, you must ensure that the operations needed for the reconciliation algorithm are defined and implemented.

SAP sequencing

TU&C/C   For implementation of the provider side of a service, in accordance with the TU&C/C model, you should ensure that the Confirm and Compensate operations are implemented so that they end successfully and do not raise any exceptions.

For the implementation of Tentative Update operations, you should ensure that the temporary changes are persisted for each call and not retained in memory, as the model is stateless and data in memory is not available for subsequent calls. The service runtime on the provider side handles transaction control for each call; after each call has been executed, the transaction control decides whether the transaction is completed successfully or rolled back.

6.3   Classifying and Publishing a Service

The aim of classifying a service is to make it easier for a service consumer to detect the service using particular contexts, without needing to know the name of the service. Usually, the consumer searches for a service through a business context. This business context was defined in the ES Repository when the business process was modeled, as described in Chapter 3, Model-Driven Business Process Development. The following sections briefly summarize the most important points.

6.3.1   Business Context as a Classification Criterion

Assigning components   When starting model-driven software development and modeling business processes, each service in the ES Repository is assigned to the following components:

▸ **Deployment unit or software component**
  Assigning a service to a deployment unit or software component defines the context in which the service is shipped. It also defines which additional functionality the service must always be run with on the same system. For the example service *GetCusomterAddress*, this would be the deployment unit *ERP Foundation*.

▸ **Process component**
  Which process component the service belongs to is defined in the deployment unit and software component. This identifies the sepa-

rate business subarea to which the service belongs. In our example, the process component is *BusinessPartnerDataManagement*. This situation is illustrated in Figure 6.18.

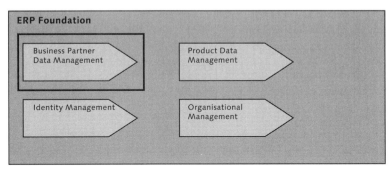

Figure 6.18 Deployment Unit ERP Foundation

▶ **Business objects**
The last step is to define the direct business anchor point of the service: the business object. This is illustrated in Figure 6.19, where, in accordance with the example, the service is assigned to the business object *Customer*.

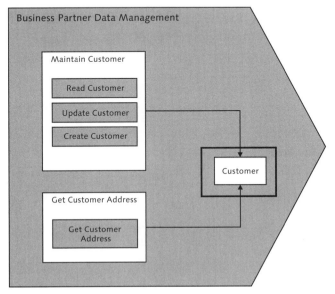

Figure 6.19 Process Component Model: BusinessPartnerDataManagement

6.3.2 Publishing from the Provider System

SOA middleware ensures that the business context modeled in the ES Repository, through proxy generation, is propogated to the application system, in which the provider proxy is implemented. This metadata is thus directly available and does not need to be defined separately by an application developer.

As well as the business context, the ES Repository is used to define additional classifications, such as the release status.

Figure 6.20 shows how this classification information is offered in the implementing system. Following the previous example, the service definition *GetCustomerAddress* is shown. This service definition was assigned to the deployment unit/software component ERP Foundation, to the process component *BusinessPartnerDataManagement*, and to the business object *Customer*. The graphic also shows that the service definition has the release status *Released*.

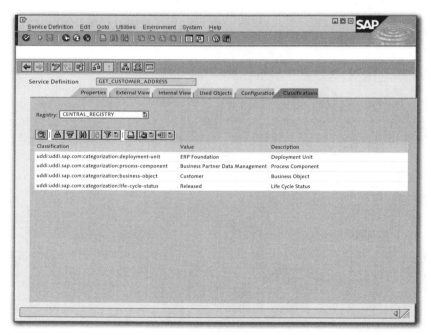

Figure 6.20 Classification of a Service

In addition to the classification information from the ES Repository, backend-specific information is included. When the service definition is published, the ES Repository classifications and the system-specific classifications are published as well.

The administrator can define which information is published in a system in each case.

First, the administrator can restrict the business context that is relevant for publishing. Normally, not all the deployment units, software components, or process components which technically belong to a system are relevant for publishing. Further, you should only publish service definitions for components that were set up for production use during customizing in the corresponding system.

Business context limitations

To define these active components, an administrator can display all the deployment units and software components, process components, and business objects in the system. From these, an administrator selects those that are relevant for publishing.

This situation is illustrated in Figure 6.21, which shows how the publishing-relevant content is defined on the level of the process components. We only consider the *CustomerInvoiceProcessing*, *SalesOrderProcessing*, and *BusinessPartnerDataManagement* process components to be publishing relevant.

The actual publishing is done by a job that is run regularly by SOA middleware (i.e., a background job). Every time this job is run, it checks whether any data is relevant for publishing. If any is, this data is automatically published to the Services Registry. Therefore, an administrator needs to configure this publishing job. The following is configured:

Configuring the publishing job

- Whether to apply the previously defined restrictions for publishing-relevant components or whether to publish all the content in the system
- Which objects to publish: only the service definitions or their service endpoints as well
- Whether to automatically republish if changes are made to the service definition

Figure 6.21 Defining Publishing Restrictions

Figure 6.22 illustrates this configuration of the publishing job. In this example, the publishing rule was defined to apply the previously defined publishing restrictions and publish both the service definitions and their service endpoints.

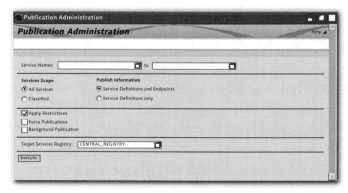

Figure 6.22 Configuration of Publishing

If the publishing job is configured and started, it is automatically executed at regular intervals. If new services, which meet the publishing rules, are then added to the system, those services are automatically published.

As the administrator publishes services decoupled from the configuration, it is important to regularly check the publishing status. If errors occur (for example, if there are problems with the connection to the Services Registry) an administrator can then explicitly restart publishing. To do this, SOA middleware provides dedicated tools to monitor the publishing results, as shown in Figure 6.23.

Monitoring publishing

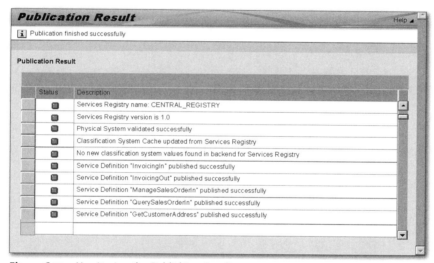

Figure 6.23 Monitoring the Publishing Results

When publishing is completed, a service consumer can find a service definition using the Services Registry. The service consumer is able to find a suitable service definition using its business context, as shown in Figure 6.24. Following the example, the service consumer identifies the service definitions that are relevant by using the deployment unit and software component *ERP Foundation*. There, the consumer finds the process component *BusinessPartnerDataManagement* and here, the business object *Customer*. In this business object, the consumer finds two service definitions that match the business context of the service consumer.

One of these is *GetCustomerAddress*, which was previously modeled and implemented.

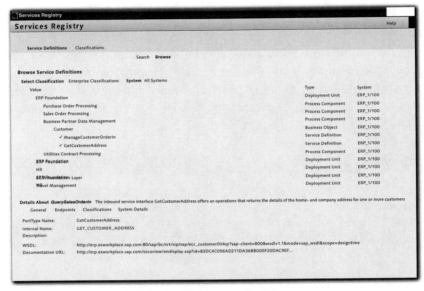

Figure 6.24   Result of Publishing to the Services Registry

In the previous chapter, we examined the development of a service provider. In this chapter, we look at how a consumer application comes into being, based on these services.

7 Developing an Enterprise Service – Based Consumer Application

This chapter first examines what an application developer must do to ensure that an application can be consistently configured and correctly run, and which tools SOA middleware provides to support this. Then we explain the general steps to develop a consumer application and illustrate the development process with concrete examples.

7.1 Challenges in Developing a Consumer Application

When developing an application that consumes a particular functionality through services, developers are faced with different challenges. To better understand these challenges, we will use an example: sales order processing. In sales order processing, customer requests for goods or services at a particular delivery time are processed. The request is sent to a sales division, which then handles the fulfillment of the contract. For this scenario, we need to develop an application that communicates with a CRM system (*Customer Relationship Management*) before the sales order is created. When the order is issued successfully, the application calls an accounting system to create the invoice. The application also needs to enable users to find existing sales orders, based on various search criteria, and to change and delete existing sales orders.

Example

The first challenge that faces the developers of this application is finding appropriate services to search and manage sales orders. Normally, an application developer will know the business context for which the

Finding a service

services are intended to be used, but the concrete service names and locations are often not known. Therefore, developers need support from SOA middleware in discovering appropriate services in service-oriented landscapes with hundreds or even thousands of services.

When a developer has found all the services needed, he can develop the consumer application and then either ship it to a customer or transport it from the development landscape to the production landscape. When the application is deployed or activated in a new landscape, an administrator must configure it, that is, link all the service endpoints with the application that will use them in the new landscape. While configuring the application, you must ensure that the consumer application also works consistently and correctly in the new landscape. It is therefore essential that all the services that are used by the consumer application and that reference the same application data also run on the same provider system.

SOA middleware tools for developers

To do this, SOA middleware provides tools that enable application developers to reduce the configuration options for administrators. This ensures that related services are always configured for the same provider system, even when there are multiple suitable provider systems. Application developers can group services used, and in this way they can signal to the administrator that the services in that group must run on the same system. For the sales order processing example, this means that for the following situations, the service call must be strictly bound to the same system:

- ▶ On the provider side, it is common practice to separate read and write APIs (services) to manage business entities. As a result, developers of a consumer application will probably find two services that allow them to manage sales orders: *Manage sales orders* and *Find sales orders*. The service interface for Manage sales orders contains operations that enable users to later process sales orders during the order creation process. The Find sales orders interface, however, has operations that can be used to search for sales orders and sales order items with different search criteria. To ensure that the entire consumer application (which combines all the above-mentioned functionalities) runs consistently, both of these services must run on the same provider system, so that they can access the same sales orders (using the same identifiers).

▶ A sales order can only be created in a CRM system if the person who is ordering something is already known as a customer in this system. Therefore, when someone is ordering something for the first time, the person processing the sale must first create a customer master record in the CRM system and can then create the order for the new customer. As both operations are executed as asynchronous service calls, it is vital that the SOA middleware ensures that the service call to create the customer is processed before the service call to create the new customer's order. Otherwise, the creation of the sale order would fail, because the CRM system did not know the customer specified in the order.

The consistency of this scenario is guaranteed by the *sequencing* mechanism, which ensures that service calls are executed *ExactlyOnceIn Order* (for more information, see Section 5.2.5, Sequencing through In-Order Processing). Here too, SOA middleware can only guarantee sequencing for these two service calls if both are executed in the same provider system, because access to the same data is required to preserve the sequence (*in-order* handling).

Sequencing

Figure 7.1 illustrates what would happen if an administrator configured the scenario incorrectly.

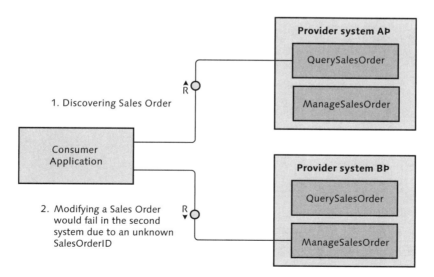

Figure 7.1 Consequences of Incorrect Configuration

The consumer application would be given a list of existing sales orders in provider system A. When the sales processor wants to change one of the sales orders, the consumer application would use the identifier of this order from provider system A and send the identifier to system B. The service call would fail at runtime, because the identifier would not be known in provider system B.

The correct configuration is shown in Figure 7.2

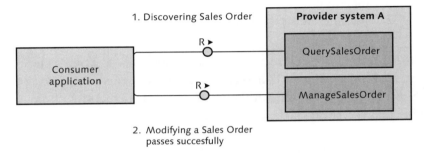

Figure 7.2 Correct Configuration of the Scenario

In the following scenarios, you must ensure that all used services are running on the same provider system:

▶ If different services access the same data

▶ If different services are combined in one transaction

▶ If different services are executed in a predefined sequence

▶ If different services are combined in the same session

Grouping services To assist administrators in configuring these scenarios correctly, developers must group these services together at the design time of the consumer application. If this grouping is not done at design time, the potentially incorrect configuration can only be detected much later at runtime.

Setting the business context In addition to grouping the services that must run on the same system, consumer application developers must specify the business context in which these services are intended to be used. Services are frequently provided for different business contexts, for example, for different industry sectors or countries, whereas a specific consumer application frequently references one particular industry sector or country. In our example, the

Manage sales orders service is provided for the food industry and the oil industry; the consumer application referenced in the example is specific to the food industry.

Depending on the actual business context, the signature of a service can be different from a similar service in another context. For example, the service interface can have fields that are relevant only for a particular industry or a particular country. A typical example of country-specific services is functionalities that are based on a country's tax law. Here, the challenge during application configuration is to select the service provider for the business context. Here too, developers can help administrators to choose only services from relevant contexts—as in our example with the *Manage sales orders* service for the food industry and not the service for the oil industry.

The challenges we have so far described concern situations in which consumer application developers can use metadata to define rules that guide an administrator through the configuration. Additional challenges exist throughout the lifecycle of services and consumer applications. Because consumer applications and services are loosely coupled, the service could be changed by the provider at any time. In these situations, it is important that SOA middleware identifies these changes as quickly as possible and that the consumer application is updated—ideally only by reconfiguration and not by changing the program code. If, for example, the *Manage sales orders* service is extended by adding a field, the challenge for the consumer application is to be able to use this new field—only by reconfiguring or customizing without changing the program code or re-deployment.

Challenges throughout the lifecycle

It is also important for SOA middleware to be in a position to support administrators, particularly in large service landscapes. This support can look like this:

SOA middleware tools for administrators

▶ Before a consumer application is activated or deployed, it is important to be able to check whether all the services needed by the application are available in the landscape. In this way, you can detect early whether the consumer application can be executed or not. The challenge here is to find this information in the new service landscape without activating or deploying the consumer application.

▶ When a consumer application uses many services, the challenge is to automate the mechanism for finding and selecting the correct service provider during configuration.

7.2 SOA Middleware's Solutions for these Challenges

SOA middleware offers three concepts to tackle the challenges described above:

▶ Services Registry

▶ Service groups

▶ Dynamic service call

7.2.1 Services Registry

To tackle most of the previously described challenges, a service-oriented landscape always contains a central Services Registry that provides information about all the services and service consumers in a landscape. We have already looked at the Services Registry in previous sections of this book:

▶ A description of the fundamental concepts and architecture (Section 4.3.2, Architecture)

▶ A description of the publishing rules and content of services and service consumers (Section 4.3.3, Publish and Search with the Services Registry)

▶ A description of the tool support in service publication with an example (Section 6.3, Classifying and Publishing a Service)

In this section, we will only examine which of the above-described problems the Services Registry resolves.

Central location   The Services Registry is the central location for discovering services at the development time of a consumer application. Based on the published metadata, the Services Registry offers application developers a multitude of search options, for example:

- By the modeled service name
- By the internal name of the service development object
- By the lifecycle status
- By the business context, which is described using classifications such as process component or business object

The Services Registry offers browsing and search functionality. In addition to searching by elementary search terms, you can combine multiple terms, for example, search for a service that processes sales orders and has the lifecycle status "released."

Following the example in which a developer needs a service to search and manage sales orders, the developer would identify the service using the browsing functionality in the Services Registry. To do this, the developer starts from the CRM area and navigates first to the process component Sales Order Processing and then to the business object Sales Order. In the business object, the developer finds the services to search and manage sales orders and displays some additional technical information about these services, for example, by which systems they are provided. On the basis of this information, the developer selects the service best suited to his application.

To optimally support developers in discovering services, SAP offers as part of all common development environments dedicated Services Registry browsing and search tools for developing consumer applications. Figure 7.3 shows an overview of this support in the development tools in the SAP NetWeaver Composition Environment (CE 7.1). | Browsing and search tools

By using the classifications, which are published together with a service, the Services Registry makes it possible to uniquely identify a service based on the context. Thus, if similar services for different contexts, such as industry sectors or countries, are provided, the publications for these services are enhanced with additional classifications for the industry sector or the country in addition to the basic classifications, such as process component or business object. | Contexts

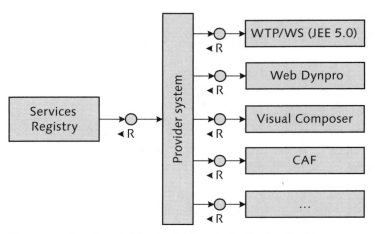

Figure 7.3 Overview of Browsing Options in the Services Registry

The Services Registry also provides functionalities to check—before a consumer application is activated or deployed in a particular service landscape—whether the application can actually run in that landscape, that is, whether all the services needed are provided in the landscape. This functionality is particularly helpful for composite applications, because a potential buyer of such a composite application can first verify that it can run in the landscape. This is illustrated in Figure 7.4.

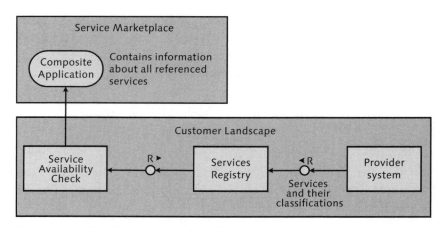

Figure 7.4 Availability Check for Composite Applications

The Services Registry also addresses the challenge of automatically con- figuring consumer applications, that is, locating the services and service providers that are needed for the consumer application to function consistently. In large landscapes, this is vital to maintain efficiency. For these scenarios, the Services Registry provides dedicated APIs, which, for a context you specify, return all the service metadata that is needed to configure the consumer application.

Configuration APIs

To resolve the last two challenges (i.e., check whether an application can run and automatic configuration of the application), the Services Registry alone is not sufficient. You also need a unified and structured description of the metadata for a consumer application that contains all the information about the services needed by the consumer application. This description is made using *service groups*, which we examine more closely in the following sections.

7.2.2 Service Group

For a consumer application at design time, service groups are used to set metadata on a logical level that describes which service provider or services the consumer application needs to run. A consumer application contains the metadata shown in Figure 7.5.

Logical metadata

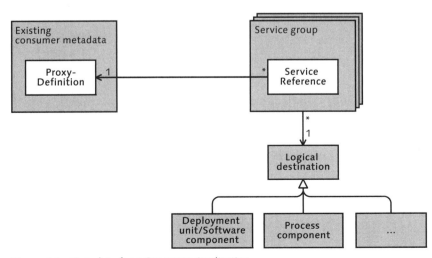

Figure 7.5 Metadata for a Consumer Application

Service bundling A consumer application contains one or more service groups, depending on whether a consumer application accesses one or more logical service providers. A service group is used to define the consumer-specific view on a logical provider. A service group is defined so that it contains all the service calls that must be made available by the same logical provider. All the service calls made available by the same logical provider are grouped together in the same service group, and service calls from different logical providers are grouped in different service groups. In this way, application developers can inform administrators about which services need to run in the same system. The possibility of configuring a consumer incorrectly can thus be eliminated, and unexpected distributed transactions, which could come about in such situations, can be avoided.

Components A service group is primarily composed of the following three components:

1. Definition of the logical provider system and of the context in which it will be used
2. The list of this logical provider's services to be called
3. The classification of the service group

These three components can be described as follows:

► **Definition of the logical provider system**
A service group contains a reference to a logical destination and defines the business context in which the logical destination will be used (for example, industry sector or country).

Logical destination The *logical destination* is an abstract entity. Logical destinations are used to divide a service landscape into higher-level, logical blocks, which consumers can reference. It is important to limit the number of logical destinations and to strictly regulate the creation of new logical destinations, as this will make reuse easier and make the logical system landscape easier to manage. Logical destinations represent the destination deployment unit or software component, the destination process component, an external service provider, or an organization.

> **Using Logical Destinations**
>
> When using SAP-defined services, it is recommended that you use the process components as logical destinations.

Logical destinations can offer functionality over multiple business contexts, such as industry sectors and countries. However, in an actual scenario or consumer application, normally only one context is relevant. In the service group, in addition to the reference to the logical destination, the provider's business context that is relevant for the service group is defined in more detail, specifically, which industry sector or which country the application is for.

SOA middleware can use this metadata to automatically bring the consumer and the provider together. On the provider side, when a service is published, information is always included about which deployment unit or software and process component it belonged to or for which context, that is, for which industry sectors or countries, it was provided. Also, the service publication contains additional information about the physical system that provides the service. Consequently, SOA middleware can use the Services Registry to find out which physical system provides the deployment unit or software component or process component for a business context that was referenced in the logical destination in a service group.

▶ **The list of this logical provider's services to be called**
Because a logical provider can provide significantly more services than are used in the consumer application, the service group contains a list of the services to be used in addition to the logical destination. This list is defined as a set of *service references*. Each of these service references points to a *proxy definition*. A proxy definition is the counterpart to a service definition, that is, it contains the identifier of the service interface to be called and the behavior of this interface. A proxy definition can contain either a generated consumer proxy class or a dynamic proxy call. Using this information, the consumer side can query the required information about the configuration of the individual service calls from the provider side. Also, the definition of the behavior makes it possible to perform smarter configuration on the consumer side.

These scenarios are explained in greater detail in the following sections.

► **Classification of the service group**
The service group should also be classified to allow the service consumers in the Services Registry to be browsed or searched. In this way, for example, the classifications for a service group can be used to find all the service groups that belong to a composite application or to analyze which service references are needed by a composite application.

Finally, based on the example of sales order processing, we will explain which metadata is in the consumer application to be defined (see Figure 7.6).

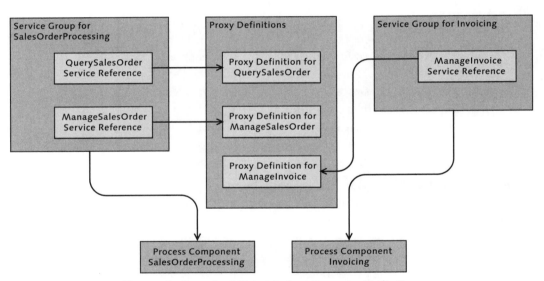

Figure 7.6 Example of Metadata for a Consumer Application

Example   In this example, the consumer application uses the services *Manage sales orders* and *Find sales orders,* which are provided by the Sales Order Processing process component. To ensure that the consumer application functions consistently, it is essential that both services are running on the same provider system and using the same customer master data.

Then these two services are grouped together in a service group that points to the logical destination Sales Order Processing. No further context restriction is needed in the service group, as in this case, no industry- or country-specific information is relevant. Additionally, if the order issue is successful, the consumer application will initiate the creation of an invoice in a separate accounting system using the service *Manage invoices*. Therefore, a second service group, which points to the logical destination Invoicing, is created for this service.

In this way, the Services Registry and the information from the service groups helps automate the configuration of the consumer applications by ensuring that the service endpoints that are suitable for a particular business context can be selected automatically. Without service groups, an administrator would have to manually identify all the services in the service landscape. It would not be possible to automate the configuration, which would significantly increase the risk of an incorrect configuration, because an administrator could select services that were not relevant for the business context.

7.2.3 Dynamic Service Call

Most of the previously-listed challenges are addressed by using the Services Registry and service groups. However, one big challenge remains: How can a consumer application adapt to changes made to the service by the provider; and what's more, how can this be done only by reconfiguration and not by changing the program code?

A service call can be executed through both a static and a dynamic call model. To select the most suitable call type for a particular scenario, you must first understand the benefits and disadvantages of each approach.

The *static call* is made through a generated consumer proxy. It conceals the complexity of the service call behind an API, which only passes the business data as parameters to the outside. Developers can use this proxy in exactly the same way as any other API.

Static call

A *dynamic call* is made through a *dynamic invocation interface* API, which allows the objects to be instantiated dynamically. The interfaces for the

Dynamic call

service calls are generated in memory during the initialization of the consumer application, based on the newest metadata on the provider side. You should choose this approach if a consumer at development time does not know the objects to call. As the DII is very generic, it is rather difficult to use directly in consumer applications.

Therefore, SAP integrated the DII into special frameworks, which do not rely on generated code but instead use dynamically loaded code. One such framework is Web Dynpro Foundation. Through its dynamic call model, Web Dynpro enables shipped applications on the customer side to be customized. In this way, customers can change their Web Dynpro applications by using only customizing—and not by changing the code—after importing a newer application system version. If, for example, a new field is added to the service interface and a customer wants to display this field in a consumer application, then the administrator on the customer side can make this new field visible declaratively in the Web Dynpro application. This is possible because the Web Dynpro Framework contains the information about the new field, as it is in a position to dynamically load the newest version of the service WSDL and identify the changes. For a statically generated proxy, it would have been necessary to at least regenerate the consumer proxy to be able to specify the new field.

7.3 Overview of the Development Process

Development of a consumer application involves the following three main activities:

▸ **Discover and import services**
Search for services to be called in the application and assign them to service groups.

▸ **Implement the consumers**
Generate the consumer proxy and use the proxy in the application.

▸ **Classify and publish the consumer application**
This makes it possible later to more easily find the consumer application in a configuration or monitoring tool.

7.3.1 Discover and Import Services

The first steps when developing a consumer application are to identify the logical provider system and then to discover services that offer the necessary functionality for the application. Normally, the application developer will know the business context in which the services are offered and not their specific names or locations. Therefore, application developers should use the Services Registry to navigate to the services through the business context. For enterprise services, navigation starts on the level of the deployment units and software components (for example, enterprise core components). Then, you can drill down to the actual services through process components (for example, sales order processing) and then through business objects (for example, sales order).

To be able to efficiently browse the Services Registry, that is, to use it to find only content that is potentially relevant for the consumer application, you first define the logical service provider. To do this, you first select the logical destination (for example, the process component *Sales Order Processing*), and then you refine the business context by specifying the relevant industry sector, country, and so on.

Defining a logical provider

Then the Services Registry is searched using the metadata defined for the logical provider systems, and it returns only the services and service endpoints that are suitable for the logical providers.

The second step is to select the services you want to use in your consumer application from the search results. If you want to use multiple services, you group them into service groups so that they will be deployed on the same physical system, and later in a customer or a productive landscape.

Selecting a service

7.3.2 Implement the Consumer

When you have identified and selected the services to use, you can start the implementation of the consumer application. How you do the implementation depends on whether or not you use a static or a dynamic service call. If you use a dynamic call, you can start using the dynamic invocation interface, because the SOA middleware only reads the necessary service metadata from the service provider later (at configuration time). If you use a static service call, the service metadata must be read from the service provider at development time, because a consumer proxy needs to be generated.

Metadata needed The metadata needed for a service call on the consumer side is the WSDL document for the service, which describes the interface, and the WS Policy document, which describes the behavior or the configuration of the service. With the static service call, when the proxy definition is generated, based on the WSDL and WS Policy documents, the mapping rules shown in Figure 7.7 are applied to the programming environment.

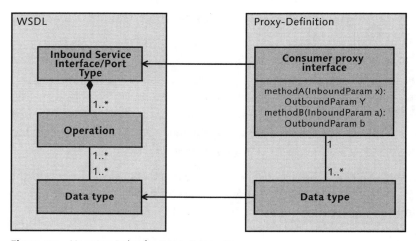

Figure 7.7 Mapping Rules for Proxy Generation

Consumer proxy interface A consumer proxy interface is generated for each service interface in the WSDL. The interface contains a method for each operation in the service interface. To call a service operation, the corresponding method in the consumer proxy is called in the same way as any other method in an object-oriented class would be called. In this way, SOA middleware conceals from the application developer the technical details of communication and the interaction with the provider.

Similar to the programming model on the provider side (see Section 6.2 Service Implementation), the methods of the generated proxy definition contain only parameters that represent the application data. The preferred service behavior is controlled using *SOAP protocols*. SOA middleware offers dedicated framework interfaces, for example, to control in-order processing for a reliable interaction or to make the security settings individually for particular service calls.

On the consumer side, we also need to explicitly distinguish whether the call is local or remote. Whereas with a local call, the caller and the called service share the same transaction and are thus closely coupled, with a remote call, the service is always in a separate transaction from the service caller. In this case, both parties are loosely coupled. Thus, if the transaction fails when the service is being processed, the caller can continue its transaction and if need be repeat the service call or use another service provider. Service calls are normally remote calls. This is also the case if the service consumer and the service provider are executed in the same system. Even here, the consumer and the provider are executed in different contexts and transactions, though SOA middleware does offer a communication protocol with optimized performance for these cases.

After the proxy definitions have been created, they can be used to make the service call. For this, the consumer proxy class must be instantiated. Instantiating a consumer proxy involves the same challenges as in classical object-oriented programs: there are scenarios in which an object-oriented class must be instantiated that implements an object-oriented interface for which there are multiple implementations. Developers must explicitly take precautions to define in which cases to use each implementation.

Instantiating the consumer proxy

Parallel to that are service-based scenarios in which the same service is either made available by multiple providers in a landscape or in which different endpoints exist for the same service implementation. In these scenarios, it also falls to the consumer application developers to build the program logic to enable the application to handle these potentially different service providers correctly.

Application developers must first decide how many logical providers they want to deal with:

Number of logical providers

▶ Only with, for example, a "pocket calculator" service.

▶ With multiple logical providers, the number of which is known at development time (for example, for a "copy" scenario in which data from one system A is read and written to another system B) using the same service interface, that is, the same proxy definition.

▶ With multiple logical providers, the number of which is not known at development time, for example, an exchange rate service. Here, developers do not know which service providers there are in the customer landscape, so they do not know with how many and with which banks a customer wants to work. The actual providers are apparent only when the application is being configured on the customer side. When the application is executed, one of the providers must be selected, based on the application context.

In the first two scenarios, it is sufficient to define a separate service group for each potential provider. The second scenario would require one service group each for the source system and the target system.

Service group to logical destination
In scenarios with multiple service providers that are unknown at development time, one service group is created for a specific logical destination. Later, during configuration, this service group is mapped to the actual service providers. At runtime, the consumer application is sent specific classifications that distinguish the individual provider systems from each other (for example, plant, business partner, etc.). Based on these classifications, the consumer application must dynamically decide which provider to use.

In all three scenarios, the service group is used as a *factory* in the program code to instantiate the consumer proxies. This determines to which service provider the service call is sent.

7.3.3 Classify and Publish the Consumer Application

Service groups can be supplied with enterprise service taxonomies or classifications in a similar way to services (on the provider side). This allows the consumer side to be assigned to a deployment unit or software component, a process component, and a business object. It also allows the business context to be enhanced with the industry or country context. These classifications can then be used by configuration or monitoring tools to, for example, find out which service groups belong to a composite or consumer application.

Some of these classifications that are relevant for service groups are made automatically by SOA middleware (for example, the software component). Others must be assigned manually by an application developer.

7.4 Developing a Consumer Application with SAP Development Tools

Using the examples of different SAP-supported development environments (SAP NetWeaver JEE 5.0, Web Dynpro for Java, and ABAP), this section illustrates the development process for a consumer application. We refer to the previous example from sales order processing and show how the implementation of the following scenario is supported in the two development environments.

The aim here is to develop a consumer application that enables a sales clerk to create, change, or delete sales orders for a customer. This requires functionality to search in the existing customer master, to create a new customer in the system (if the requesting party is not already a customer), and to edit a sales order for an existing customer. The application should be structured to allow users to search for a customer and to display existing sales orders for a selected customer through its user interface (UI). When a sales order is selected in the UI, details for that order are displayed. Also, the application should allow users to change sales orders or to create a new order. The basic UI floor plan looks like Figure 7.8.

Example application

Before you can start developing the consumer application, its range of functionality must be exactly defined, and the design time objects must have been created. First, you must define how many logical service providers the application needs to be able to handle. Note that all the services that are concerned with customer management must access the same customer database and the same customer identifiers. Consequently, all of these services must be grouped in the same service group. Exactly two service groups are needed for the consumer application:

Service groups

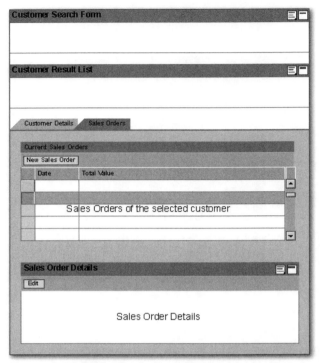

Figure 7.8 Floor Plan for the Example Consumer Application

▶ One that groups services providing the functionality to search for customers and to read customer details

▶ A second one that groups services providing the functionality to search and manage sales orders for a selected customer

The logical destinations that point to the provider of the functionality must then be assigned to both service groups. The units to be addressed are thus the process components of the provider.

Finding logical destinations

To find the logical destinations that need to be referenced in the two service groups, the Services Registry is the place to start. In this scenario, use is made of the knowledge that the required functionality is part of an ERP system. In an ERP system, two deployment units provide the required process components: ERP Core Component (ECC) and ERP Foundation. ECC includes the process component SalesOrderProcessing (to search and manage sales orders), and ERP Foundation includes the process component *BusinessPartnerDataManagement* (to search for customers and read customer details). Figure 7.9 shows this scenario in the Services Registry.

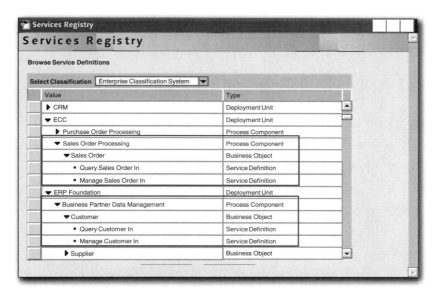

Figure 7.9 Browsing the Services Registry to Find Services for the Example Application

The second step is to find the available services and then to generate the proxy definitions for them in the development environment. In the Services Registry, we then search for appropriate services in the two selected process components *BusinessPartnerDataManagement* and *SalesOrderProcessing*. The process component *BusinessPartnerDataManagement* contains the business object *Customer*, and *SalesOrderProcessing* contains the business object *SalesOrder*. All the services that provide the required functionality are grouped under these two business objects. As shown in Figure 7.10, four services are needed to implement the consumer application: *ManageCustomerIn*, *QueryCustomerIn*, *QuerySalesOrderIn*, and *ManageSalesOrderIn*.

Service metadata   The Services Registry provides additional metadata for each service. This allows application developers to analyze whether the services really offer the relevant functionality and exactly how the services are used. Figure 7.10 illustrates this.

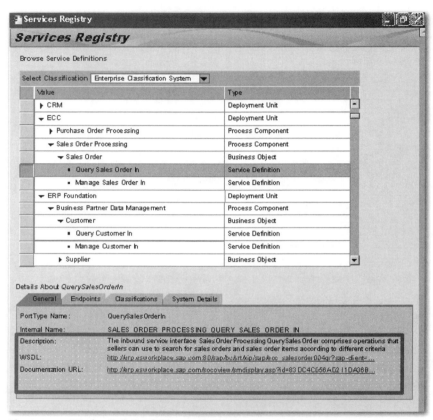

Figure 7.10   Display Details of a Service in the Services Registry

Documentation   One important part of the service metadata is the service documentation. This is not stored directly in the Services Registry; the Services Registry contains a link (in the form of a URL) to the documentation. The documentation itself is stored and edited in a documentation management system. Figure 7.11 shows an example of the documentation for the service *QuerySalesOrderIn*.

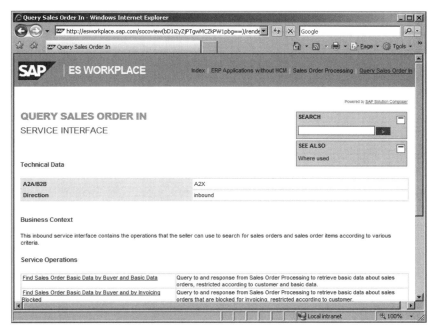

Figure 7.11 Display the Documentation for a Service

When the services to use in the consumer application have been selected, you enter the service references in the service groups. These service references point to the four proxy definitions to be generated for each of the four services. Figure 7.12 illustrates the metadata that is created.

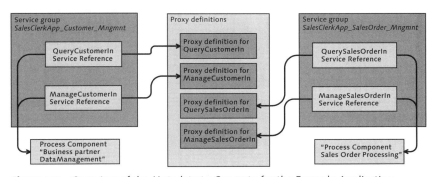

Figure 7.12 Overview of the Metadata to Generate for the Example Application

The next three sections show how this metadata is generated using the tools in the actual SAP development environments (JEE 5, Web Dynpro, and ABAP),

7.4.1 Consumer Development in SAP NetWeaver Developer Studio (JEE 5)

Java Platform, Enterprise Edition, (Java EE) is the industry standard for developing portable, robust, scalable, and secure Java applications. Based on the solid foundation of Java SE (Java Platform, Standard Edition), Java EE offers Web service support, component models, management and communication APIs, which make it the standard for the development of enterprise applications, service-oriented architectures, and Web 2.0 applications.

SAP NetWeaver Developer Studio supports the development of Java EE 5–compatible applications using a dedicated toolset. For the implementation of Web service consumers, developers of SAP extensions can profit from being able to define service groups together with logical destinations. These objects are extensions of the standard, which means that when this application is deployed on a non-SAP Java EE 5–compatible server, the application will still run correctly. However, administrators in these scenarios do not get the configuration support provided by service groups. They can configure the application incorrectly, for example, by having each proxy definition on a different system.

Servlets
For this example, let us assume that the sales processing application to be implemented is a Web application that is based on servlets. Several servlets are needed in this application:

- One servlet to search for customers
- One servlet to display and edit the list of sales orders for a selected customer
- One servlet to display and edit the details for a selected sales order

The servlets are only used to display data, whereas the data itself is read or written only through Web services from or to the application systems.

For this example, we will now examine the three activities *service discovery and import*, *classify the consumer application*, and *implement the consumers* for a Java EE 5–compatible consumer application.

Discover and Import Service

The first step in developing the consumer application is to create a *development component* (DC, see Figure 7.13), which represents an envelope around all the metadata and program parts needed for the application. A development component is always part of a software component, through which the shipment unit for a consumer application or composite application is defined.

Generate DC

For Java EE5 applications, a development component of the type *Java EE5* must be created. We will call this development component *SalesClerk*.

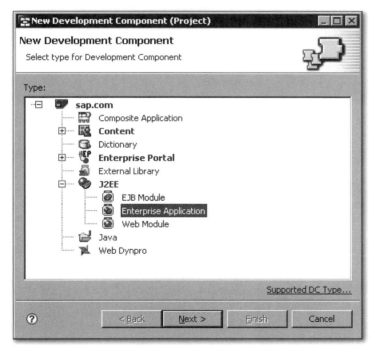

Figure 7.13 Creating the Java EE5 Development Component

Web modules   The development component is only an envelope that is used to create a deployable enterprise application archive (EAR), which is shipped to customers and can be executed on a Java EE5–compatible application server. The content of the application is in a separate development component, which is of type *Web Module*. This development component contains the web modules in the EARs. To create the *Web Module* development component, a subordinate development component of type *Web Module* is first created and named *SalesClerkWeb*. Then, a dependency is defined of the *SalesClerk* development component to the automatically exposed Web archive part of the *SalesClerkWeb* development component. As a result, while the *SalesClerk* development component is being built, the Web archive file that was created by building the *SalesClerkWeb* development component is automatically added. This is illustrated in Figure 7.14.

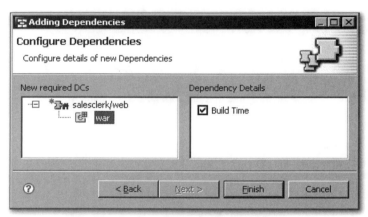

Figure 7.14   Creating a Dynamic Web Project

Importing services   After this step is completed, the first phase in the development of a consumer application—importing the services—can begin. This is done in the Java EE perspective using the *Import WSDL Wizard*. When you start this wizard, you first need to define the source through which the services will be imported. We recommend using the Services Registry. Figure 7.15 illustrates this situation.

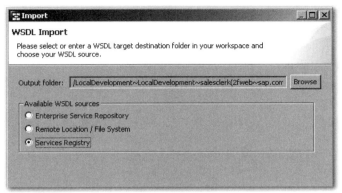

Figure 7.15 Select the Services Registry as the Data Source for the Import

In the next wizard step, you define the business context to which the services belong. This greatly simplifies the discovery of services, as the Services Registry can filter out only the services that really match the required business functionality out of a potentially very large number of services. The recommended business context, particularly for SAP provider systems, is the process component. In our example, functionality in the process component *SalesOrderProcessing* is needed in the consumer application, which is illustrated in Figure 7.16.

Defining context

Figure 7.16 Defining the Business Context

Then the Import Wizard uses the Services Registry to find all the matching services for the process component *SalesOrderProcessing*. These services are then offered to the application developer for selection. Figure 7.17 shows the result of the search. Each service operation is offered as a separate web service. The service operations that belong to the services *QuerySalesOrderIn* and *ManageSalesOrderIn* are visible. The service operation from *ManageSalesOrderIn* is first selected for import.

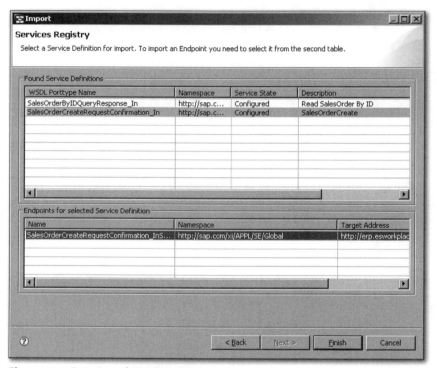

Figure 7.17 Overview of Matching Services

The next step is to assign the imported service to an appropriate service group. You can either create a new service group or re-use and existing service group.

Creating a service group

In our example, we assume that no service group exists. This is why the wizard is started to create a service group, as shown in Figure 7.18. In the next step of the service group wizard, you can select the classification to be used as a logical destination for the service group. You select the Process Component type and the value SalesOrderProcessing.

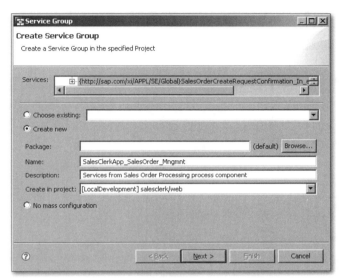

Figure 7.18 Overview of the Service Group to Create

After the wizard is closed, the service group is created and a service reference is added to it. As the service usage through the JEE5 programming model is a static call model, when the Import WSDL wizard is closed, the WSDL and WS Policy documents for the selected service are downloaded directly from the provider and stored locally in the project.

These steps need to be repeated to import all the services and to assign them to the two service groups *SalesClerkApp_SalesOrder_Mngmnt* and *SalesClerkApp_Customer_Mngmnt*.

Classifying the Consumer Application

All the service groups created for the application should also be classified, so that they can be published to the Services Registry and can be easily found there. Service groups can be classified because they are part of a development component, which is assigned to a composite application (i.e. Product) through its software component. Consequently, all

Composite application

the entities in a consumer application can be classified by the composite application classification system.

Figure 7.19 illustrates this scenario: The development component *Sales-Clerk* is part of the SALES software component. This software component belongs to the composite application *Sales*.

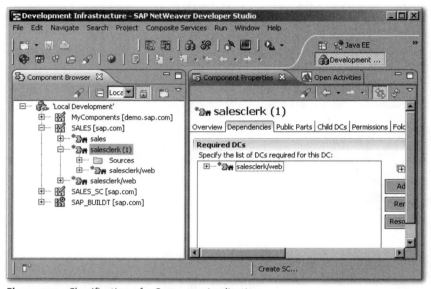

Figure 7.19 Classification of a Consumer Application

The most important entities in a consumer application have now been defined and created. Now we can implement the service calls in accordance with the static JEE5 call model.

Implementing the Consumer

The steps to implement the consumer involve generating the proxy definition including the consumer proxy classes and writing the program logic in the servlet.

Generating proxy definitions

To generate proxy definitions, use JEE5 tools. Right-click the imported WSDL document and select WEB SERVICES • GENERATE CLIENT. You can then use the wizard shown in Figure 7.20 to start proxy generation.

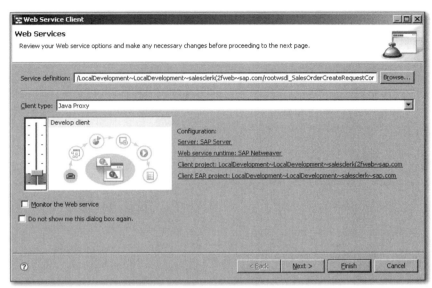

Figure 7.20 The Wizard for JEE 5 Proxy Generation

After the proxy definitions have been generated, the servlets are implemented. The program code to instantiate the consumer proxies is Java EE 5–compatible only. The proxy definitions are represented through generated Java classes that can be used directly within the servlet program code to initiate the service call. For each proxy definition, there is one generated *Factory* service class, one class for the service interface, and another class for each complex data type in the interface. Figure 7.21 provides an overview of the generated classes for proxy definition of the service *SalesOrderCreate*.

As we already mentioned, the JEE5 programming model is compatibly enhanced with SAP extensions only in a few cases. This is necessary in scenarios in which a service is provided by different logical destinations or in situations in which it needs to be decided in the consumer application in which provider system the service must be called. You can use help classes provided by SAP, which make it easier to coordinate calls for the same service to different providers. In our example, we do not use this option, because the consumer application is only intended to work with one provider system.

Figure 7.21 Overview of the Generated Artifacts for a Consumer Proxy

Implementing
servlets

The last step is the implementation of the servlets, which represent the customer data and the sales order data. To generate a servlet, right-click in the Java EE perspective on the *SalesClerkWeb* development component and select NEW • SERVLET. Then specify the required information, such as package and servlet name, and complete the creation wizard.

First, the servlet *CustomerSearchServlet* is created. This servlet enables users to enter different search terms and to display the customers found. When using servlets, developers have to create the layout and the navigation of the web application; this extends to generating the HTML code. The servlet itself must therefore manage actions such as initial loading, generating the input fields for the search, clicking the Search button, and displaying the search result.

The program code to call the service to search the customers with one click on the Search button, would look like this:

```
public class CustomerSearchServlet extends Httpservlet {

//the following code would initialize the service instance

//the WebServiceRef annotation is used on a field level

  @WebServiceRef(name = "QueryCustomerIn")

  BusinessPartnerDataManagementQueryCustomerInService
queryCustSvc;


private void showCustomers() {

    //intantiate the logical port for the service

    //SOA Middleware knows the ServiceGroup this

    //service is part of and thus the provider

    //of the service

    BusinessPartnerDataManagementQueryCustomerIn lp =
system.getPort(BusinessPartnerDataManagementQueryCustomerIn.
class);

    //initialize search criteria

    ...

    //invoke web service method

    lp.customerSimpleByNameAndAddressQueryResponse();

    //display result

    ...

  }


    //other servlet methods like doGet/doPost

    ...

}
```

Listing 7.1 Servlet CustomerSearchServlet

Running the servlet

As you can see in this code example, an application developer uses only JEE 5 APIs to instantiate the proxy. During the invocation of the getPort method, SOA Middleware determines the Service group the corresponding service is part of, instantiates the port, and returns it to the caller program.

For the other servlets, the program code is similar; its primary difference is that different methods or services are called.

When the entire consumer application has been fully implemented, it can be deployed on the SAP NetWeaver Application Server. The result, that is, the running application, is similar to that shown in Figure 7.22

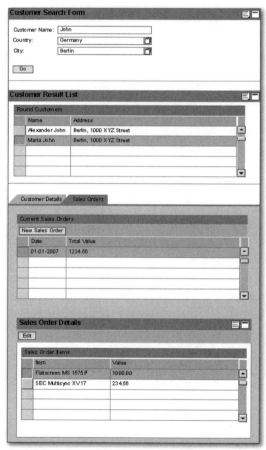

Figure 7.22 Overview of Running JEE 5 Application

Outlook: Extended Support for Service Groups

The above-described development process is based on the tool support that is available with SAP products from 2008. We will now look at what development process support is planned for future SAP products.

This extended support is intended to offer more comprehensive functionality to create and manage service groups. Whereas in the above-described development process, the service groups were only visible as part of the service import, in the future model, service groups will be the starting point for defining consumer applications. As they have the central role in correctly defining and grouping the functionality called in a consumer application, the service groups should be defined before the service import is done. The resulting changes to the development process are described in more detail in the following sections:

Similar to the above-described model, you first create the software components and development components. The second step is to define the service groups. In our example, these are the two service groups to manage the customers and sales orders. Here again, we are assuming that a suitable service group does not already exist, and we illustrate the creation of the new service group for managing sales orders. When creating a new service group, developers are supported by a wizard (see Figure 7.23).

Create software and development components

Figure 7.23 Creating a Service Group

Using this wizard, you first specify the name of the service group and select the CLASSIFIED PROVIDER option for the logical destination. Logical destinations for a service group can reference both classified and unclassified providers. Classified providers are all the providers that are described by a particular value in a classification system, for example, a

Classified providers

process component. Unclassified providers are typically external providers, for example, Amazon.com. Using classified providers allows you to later automate the configuration process, which is why we recommend that you set this option.

Then you select the classification value that represents the logical destination (see Figure 7.24). In our example, this is the process component *SalesOrderProcessing*.

Figure 7.24 Defining the Logical Destinations

When the wizard is completed, an empty service group has been created. In the service group editor, you can then, depending on the relevant context of the consumer application, define more restrictions to the logical destination. For example, you can specify the industry sector or country relevance (see Figure 7.25).

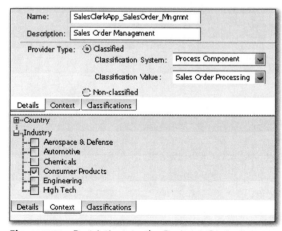

Figure 7.25 Restrictions to the Business Context

When the service group has been created, you can start adding the service references. You do this by importing the services that provide the required application functionality. Start the SAP Import WSDL Wizard by right-clicking over the newly created service group. The wizard lets you import service metadata from different locations (Services Registry, file system, URL). The wizard uses the standard way to find the service, so the SERVICES REGISTRY option is selected by default (see Figure 7.26).

Importing services

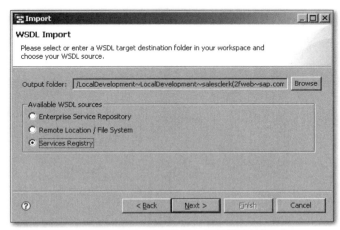

Figure 7.26 Importing a Service Using the WSDL Wizard

Search or browse the Services Registry to find the required services QuerySalesOrderIn and ManageSalesOrderIn, based on the above-described navigation. Because the WSDL Import Wizard was started in the service group context, the Services Registry filters out only services that are provided by the logical provider specified in the service group; that is, the registry displays only services that match the logical destination and the specified business context. For the service group in our example, these are all the services that are provided by the process component *SalesOrderProcessing* (see Figure 7.27).

Here again, when the wizard is completed, the WSDL and WS Policy documents for the selected services can be downloaded from the provider and saved locally in the project. Also, the matching service references to the service group are added.

These steps are then repeated to create the second service group to manage customers and to import its services.

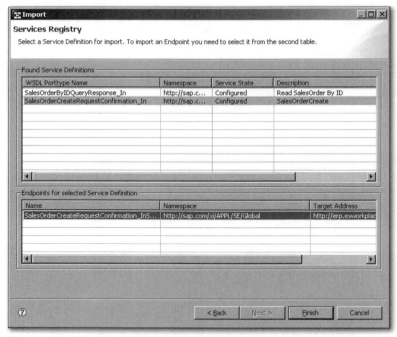

Figure 7.27 Overview of the Services Matching the Logical Destination

Service groups editor To get an overview of the imported services and their assignments to service groups, you can use the Editor for Service References. This editor also lets you reorganize the service references, for example, by moving them from one service group to another group (see Figure 7.28).

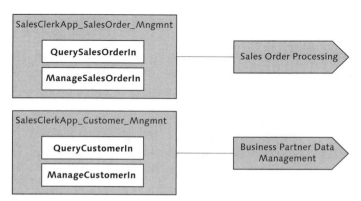

Figure 7.28 The Service Groups Editor

7.4.2 Consumer Development in Web Dynpro for Java

Web Dynpro is the SAP NetWeaver technology used to build UIs for business applications. The model-based approach supported by Web Dynpro lets you minimize manual coding, use graphical tools to design applications, and benefit from the reuse of UI components. The Web Dynpro model is based on the *Model View Controller* paradigm, which allows a clear separation of application logic and display logic. Web Dynpro also combines the strengths of the traditional SAP GUI approach with innovations based on Internet technologies to offer functionalities such as:

▶ Automatic help functionalities, based on the content of the ABAP Dictionary, for example, field-validation or error handling

▶ Tight integration into software lifecycle management, including infrastructure to perform installation, upgrade, administration, and monitoring

▶ Support for world-wide access for end users through Internet browsers, smart clients, or mobile devices

▶ Integration of any content into the UIs through hyperlinks

UI functions of Web Dynpro

Web Dynpro also offers dedicated support for development of UIs. In particular, Web Dynpro addresses the following challenges that face developers:

Development support

▶ **Central control for compliance with UI standards**
The use of specialized UI technologies in different development scenarios frequently ends up with a different look and feel or with noncompliance with standards, such as accessibility standards for users with physical disabilities.

▶ **Model-based UI development**
Rudimentary UI technologies that only offer support for code-based development frequently lead in the medium term to increased development costs. It becomes increasingly complex to maintain and extend applications based on these technologies.

▶ **Simplified development and build process**
The efficient management of Java development has already proved to be a challenge for many companies, especially when the projects are

big or increase in scope. It can be very difficult to establish and manage a process that balances local development work with global consolidation.

▶ **Separation of display logic from application logic**
When display logic and application logic are too closely coupled, there is a greater risk of business applications becoming inflexible and static.

To resolve these issues, Web Dynpro has the following capabilities. They are integrated into the Web Dynpro framework, making them directly accessible to developers. This distinguishes Web Dynpro from other frameworks, such as Java EE 5.

▶ Separation of the display logic and the application logic through clearly defined access to the data in the application system by including a service call. This service can be executed either locally or remotely. Typically, the connection to these systems is made through Web services, but it can also by made through another communication channel, such as adaptive remote function call (RFC).

▶ Structured and managed data access to application systems through Web services, RFCs, and other communication protocols.

▶ Division of large software projects into smaller, clearly organized components and their management through the SAP NetWeaver Development Infrastructure.

▶ Support for application design with graphical tools in SAP NetWeaver Developer Studio. You can use these tools to generate most of a Web Dynpro application, without having to explicitly implement program logic. This applies to the following parts of an application:

▶ Data flow between the frontend and the backend

▶ Layout of the UI

▶ Properties of UI elements of a UI

In addition to these declared parts of the application, the Web Dynpro toolset enables developers to manually insert sections of source code. These sections are included in the automatically generated source code sections and are not overwritten if the generated sections are regenerated.

▶ Integration of special technology to support small devices, interactive forms, and offline scenarios

▶ Testing and debugging Web Dynpro applications using integrated tools in the Java development environment

▶ Managing the complete software lifecycle using the SAP NetWeaver Development Infrastructure

If application are developed based on Web Dynpro, both the developers and later on the end-users can benefit: **Benefits**

▶ **Benefits for developers**

  ▶ You can concentrate on application design, keeping manual coding to a minimum. This minimizes subsequent maintenance costs, as the lifecycle of the application can be managed by the infrastructure.

  ▶ You are not dependent on a particular frontend technology, that is, your application can, for example, run in a browser or on a smart client.

  ▶ You can develop in small teams and still be sure that you will be able to integrate your components into a global project.

▶ **Benefits for users**

  ▶ You can work with consistent and user-friendly interfaces, which helps reduce training costs and increase productivity.

  ▶ You can be sure the application is compatible with frontend technology and accessibility standards.

  ▶ You can use the frontend technology (for example, browser or smart clients) that best suits your scenario.

As we mentioned before, each Web Dynpro application is structured in accordance with the *Model View Controller* programming model: **MVC model**

▶ The *Model* forms the interface to the back-end system and enables a Web Dynpro application to access the application data it needs.

▶ The *View* handles the data presentation in the Web browser.

▶ The *Controller* is placed between the View and the Model. It handles the transfer of the application data from the Model to the interface elements of the View that display the data. The Controller also processes user input and passes it to the Model.

After this brief overview of the basic ideas and concepts of Web Dynpro, the following sections show how our example application for managing sales orders can be implemented using Web Dynpro. Here too, we can distinguish three actions in consumer development: service discovery and import, classification of the consumer application, and implementation of the consumer.

Service discovery and import

The first step is—similar to the procedure for developing a Java EE5 application—to create the development component in SAP NetWeaver Developer Studio. Here, it is a Web Dynpro development component named *SalesClerkWD*. It is the assigned to a software component.

The following steps are also similar to the Java EE5 development process:

▶ The required services must be identified and imported, and then the *Web Dynpro models* must be created. A Web Dynpro model is the counterpart to a consumer proxy in the Java EE5 programming model. It handles the execution of the service calls and provides the Web Dynpro application with access to the service operations and parameters.

▶ During the service import, the required services are assigned to the service groups. If necessary, the service groups are created in this step.

Unlike the Java EE 5 development process, using Web Dynpro, the service import and the generation of Web Dynpro models is one atomic action. Consequently, the generation step is assigned to the phase service discovery and import, whereas the phase implementation of the consumer only encompasses modeling the Web Dynpro application.

To perform these steps, application developers must call the *Web Dynpro perspective* in SAP NetWeaver Developer Studio. In the SalesClerkWD development component, right-click the MODELS node and select the option CREATE MODEL. Then select the type of the Web Dynpro model. Following our example, select the option ADAPTIVE WEB SERVICE MODEL, because we want to include service calls. Note that a model must be created for each service. For each model, you must specify a name and a package; then you can start to import the service. First, generate a model for the service to search customers (service *QueryCustomerIn*).

In this scenario too, the service import is done using the *Import WSDL Wizard*; that is, all the steps described below are similar to the Java EE5 scenario. This leads to a significantly lower learning curve for application developers, as they only need to learn once how the service import works. Developers can then apply this knowledge both to Java EE5 development and to Java Web Dynpro development.

Importing services

When you start this wizard, the Services Registry is again selected as the source of the import (see Figure 7.29).

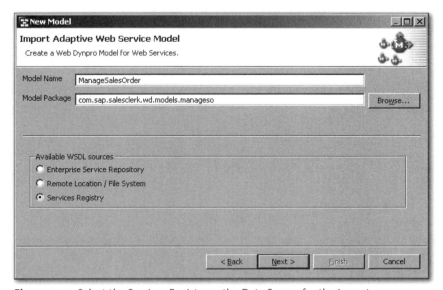

Figure 7.29 Select the Services Registry as the Data Source for the Import

Defining context   The next wizard step is to define the business context to which the services belong. The Services Registry is used to filter out only the services that really do match the required business functionality. In our example, functionality of process component *BusinessPartnerDataManagement* is needed in the consumer application.

Figure 7.30 illustrates this.

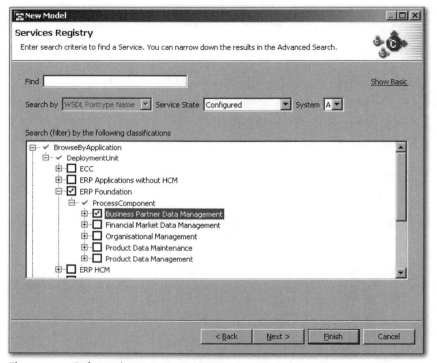

Figure 7.30   Defining the Business Context

Then the Import Wizard uses the Services Registry to find all the suitable services for process component *BusinessPartnerDataManagement* and offers them to the application developer to make a selection (see Figure 7.31).

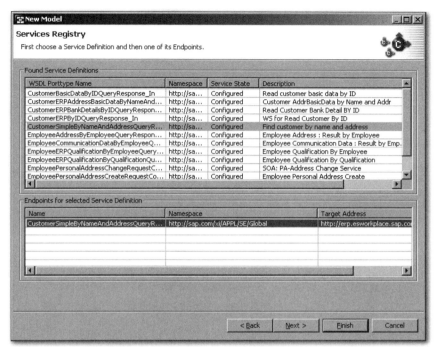

Figure 7.31   Overview of the Matching Services

The next step assigns the service to a service group. Here again, we are assuming that no service group exists. Therefore, the wizard initiates the creation of a service group, as shown in Figure 7.32. The wizard offers the default values for the logical destination of this component group as the type Process Component and the value *BusinessPartnerDataManagement*.

Assigning services

After you have defined the properties of the service group *SalesClerkApp_Customer_Mngmnt*, you can close the Import Wizard. This causes the Web Dynpro infrastructure to generate the Web Dynpro model and to generate the service group and the reference to the imported service QueryCustomerIn to be added.

These steps must be repeated:

▸ Generate the Web Dynpro model for the service *ManageCustomerIn* and add the reference to the service group *SalesClerkApp_Customer_Mngmnt*.

219

▶ Generate further Web Dynpro models for the services *QuerySalesOrderIn* and *ManageSalesOrderIn*, create the service group *SalesClerkApp_ SalesOrder_Mngmnt*, and add the two service references.

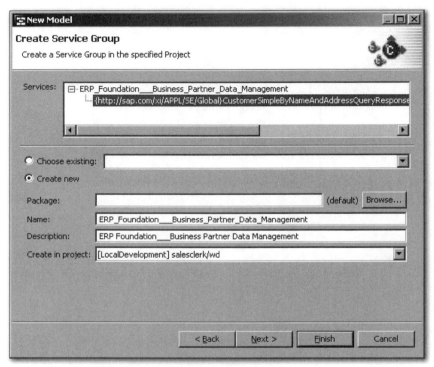

Figure 7.32 Overview of the Service Group to Create

Note
In the future, with the Web Dynpro scenario, extended support will be offered for the development process—similar to the Java EE5 scenario. This is identical to the support outlook described in Section 7.4.1 Consumer Development in SAP NetWeaver Developer Studio (JEE 5). The required service groups will be created explicitly before the services are imported. To do this, the same extended service group editors and wizards will be used, as described in the outlook for Java EE5 development.

Classifying the Consumer Application

Similar to the Java EE 5 development process, the consumer application should be specially classified for all service groups in the application so that it can be published to the Services Registry and easily found there.

Service groups can also be classified using the classification system *Composite Application*, as they are part of a development component that is part of a composite application through its enveloping software component.

Composite
Application

Figure 7.33 illustrates this situation: The *SalesClerkWD* development component is a part of the SALES software component, which belongs to the composite application Sales.

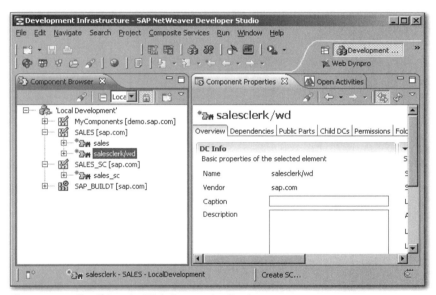

Figure 7.33 Classifying the Web Dynpro Application

Implementing the Consumer

If all the models have been generated and all the service groups created and classified, a Web Dynpro component is created to contain the actual program logic. To do this, right-click the COMPONENTS node in the Web

Dynpro project. You must assign a name to the component; in this example, we will call it *SalesClerkComp*. In this component, an empty Default window is created and given the name *SalesClerkComWindow*. No default view is created since the application will contain multiple views and the UI layout will be defined later.

Model-driven development Next, the model-driven development of the Web Dynpro application can start. This procedure is divided into the following steps:

▶ Model the layouts of the UI, including the required views

▶ Define the navigation between the different views

▶ Model the data exchange between views or in a view

▶ Generate the individual UI elements and bind these elements to the data to process

▶ Include the service calls

These steps are described in greater detail in the following sections.

Modeling the Layout of the UI

To model the UI, open the Window editor. In accordance with the interface design, select a grid layout with three rows and one column and make the following changes:

▶ In the first cell, create a new view *CustomerSearchCriteriaView*, which will later contain the search terms to find matching customers.

▶ In the second cell, create an empty view and then a second view *CustomerSearchResultView*, which visualizes the list of the found customers. This makes the empty view the default view, because the search result will not be displayed until the user clicks the Search button.

▶ In the third cell, create another empty view and then a tabstrip layout with two tabs. These views are given the names Details and Sales Orders, because they are intended to visualize the details for a selected customer and the sales orders as follows:

　▶ In the Details tab, create a new view *CustomerDetailsView* to display the customer details.

► Add a grid layout to the second tab, Sales Orders, with two rows and one column to display the list of sales orders and their details. In the first cell of this grid layout, add another view with the name *SalesOrdersView*. In the second cell, create an empty view and then the view *SalesOrderDetailsView*.

Figure 7.34 illustrates the above-described interface layout.

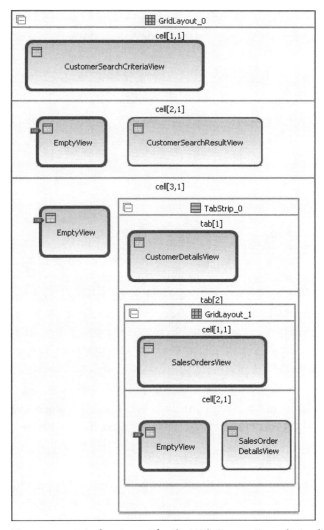

Figure 7.34 Interface Layout for the Web Dynpro Example Application

When this phase is finished, the basic layout of the consumer application is completely defined—without any source code being written.

Defining the Navigation between the Views

Plugs   The next phase defines the navigation between the views that users will see when running the application. This is done using the *inbound* and *outbound plugs*. Whereas inbound plugs define the potential starting points in a view, the outbound plugs can be used to call a subsequent view. Consequently, the navigation between views is defined by connecting an outbound plug in the first view with an inbound plug in the second view through a navigation link (see Figure 7.35).

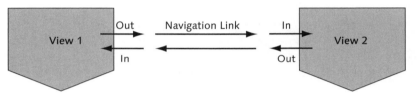

Figure 7.35   Relationship between Outbound and Inbound Plugs

For our example application, the following plugs are defined:

▶ For navigation between the interface to search for customers and the display of the list of found customers, an outbound plug *SearchOut* is created for the view *CustomerSearchCriteriaView*, and an inbound plug SearchIn is created for the view *CustomerSearchResultView*. Then a navigation link is defined between the two plugs. This navigation is initiated if a user clicks the Search button in a view *CustomerSearchCriteriaView*.

▶ An outbound plug *ToEmptyviewOut* is also created for the view *CustomerSearchResultview*, and a navigation link is defined between the empty view and the third cell. This plug is executed if no customer can be found and causes the details of a previously displayed customer to be hidden again.

▶ In addition, we also need a navigation link from the list of found customers to the detail display for a selected customer. We need another outbound plug *DetailsOut* for the view *CustomerSearchResultView*, an inbound plug *DetailsIn* for the view *CustomerDetailsView*, and a navigation link between both. In addition, a second inbound plug *DefaultIn* is created for the view *SalesOrdersView* and is connected to the *DetailsOut* plug. The *DetailsOut* plug is executed when a customer is selected and causes the details for the customer and a list of sales orders to be displayed. The reason two navigation links were defined starting from the *DetailsOut* plug is that the views *CustomerDetailsView* and *SalesOrdersView* are located in a tabstrip layout. Depending on how the *DetailsOut* plug is called, Web Dynpro is notified of which of the two views to display in the selected tab.

► Finally, you need to ensure that the details for a sales order are displayed when it is selected. For this, two additional outbound plugs, *ToEmptyViewOut* and *DetailsOut*, are needed for the view *SalesOrdersView*. The *ToEmptyViewOut* plug is connected to the empty view, which has the task of hiding the view *SalesOrderDetailsView* if no sales orders are available. Also, the *DetailsOut* plug is connected to the DetailsIn plug of the view *SalesOrderDetailsView* to include in the navigation the detail display for a sales order, starting from a previously selected order.

The result of the navigation definition is shown in Figure 7.36

Using only the Web Dynpro tool, that is, without manually writing source code, we have defined almost the whole navigation between the views. The only things remaining to add are the rules for executing the outbound plugs, based on user interactions, such as clicking a button or selecting a customer or sales order. This is done manually by adding one line of program code. For example, to execute the plug *SearchOut* by clicking the Search button, we must define an action, connect it to the button event, and then implement the action so that it calls the plug.

Defining user interaction

To perform this step, first open the view *CustomerSearchCriteriaView* and then add a button UI element to its layout. Then, in the properties for this button element, select the *OnAction* event and create a new action. This action is given the name and the display text Search. Then, to implement the action, save the following line of program code: `wdThis.wdFirePlugSearchOut()`. This causes the *SearchOut* plug to be executed and initiates the navigation for the view *CustomerSearchResultview*. Now, the navigation between the input interface for customer search and clicking the Search button to display the search results has been completely defined.

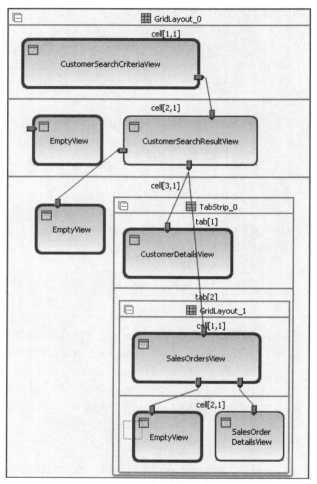

Figure 7.36 Overview of the Navigation Definition for the Web Dynpro Example Application

Similarly, you need to define more rules for other supported user interactions.

Modeling Data Exchange

Before we include the service call to search for customers and define the search result display, we want to first model a step to define how the input data for the search is handled. In particular, we need to define how this data gets from the view *CustomerSearchCriteriaView* to the view *CustomerSearchResultView*, because the service call is executed in the view *CustomerSearchResultView*.

To implement a data exchange like this between views, we use *data binding*, which binds properties of UI elements to the *context* of the view controller. This is necessary to be able to transport data to these UI elements or from these UI elements. To do this, the name of the context is assigned to each property of a UI element that is relevant for data exchange.

Data binding

A context is a structured repository for storing controller data. Each view always has its own controller, which stores the local data for this view in a separate context, the view context. A UI element can then be bound to this view context, provided that it belongs to the same view. However, the lifecycle or visibility of a view context is too limited to store data that needs to be used over multiple views.

In these situations, the *default context* of a Web Dynpro application comes into play. The default context belongs to the controller of the Web Dynpro component. Its lifecycle depends on the lifecycle of the whole component. The default context can be made visible to a particular set of view controllers while preventing access to it from other view controllers. This visibility concept means the data does not need to be explicitly copied between two contexts. Instead, the relevant elements in the two contexts can be mapped to each other. This step is called *context mapping*. Whenever an element in a view context is mapped to an element in the component context, the data in the (global) component context is stored, but not the data in the (local) view context.

Standard context

To define the exchange of the input data for the search between the two views, perform the following steps:

Data exchange

▶ Because data must be exchanged between different views, the data is managed in the component context of our Web Dynpro component *SalesClerkComp*. The structure of the data to exchange is defined by the input parameters of the service operation for the customer search. In the component context, a reference to the previously generated Web Dynpro model for this service operation is saved to make the generated data structure known in the component context. The actions required are summarized in Figure 7.37.

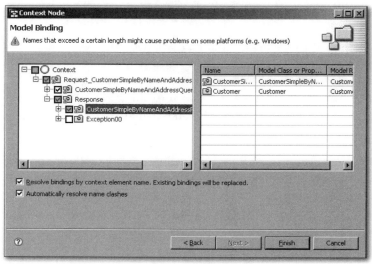

Figure 7.37 Defining the Component Context

▶ A new node for the controller context is added in the editor for the component controller. This node contains a binding to a generated Web Dynpro model.

▶ The generated model class for the service operation to execute the customer search is assigned to this node. This assignment makes the input data structure *NameAndAddress* available for this service operation for data exchange between views. The return structure of the service operation is assigned to the context node and is available to other views as a structure Response.

▶ Because the data from the data structure *NameAndAddress* is needed in the views *CustomerSearchCriteriaView* and *CustomerSearchResultView*, a mapping to this structure must be created in both views. To do this, nodes are created in both view contexts and mapped to the corresponding node in the component context.

Creating the UI Elements

After the data exchange between the contexts has been defined, we must create the UI elements needed for the customer search and map them to the corresponding attributes in the context node. To do this, open the layout of the view *CustomerSearchCriteriaview* and apply the Form Template. For this layout, input fields for the context attributes customername, country, and city are added to the input data structure. As a result, these UI elements are mapped to the corresponding context attributes so that if a user clicks the Search button:

▶ Web Dynpro automatically stores the values in the input fields in the above context attributes

▶ The Web Dynpro program (the different views) can read the data entered

For this to work, the executable model object must also be instantiated and bound to a context. This should be done when the Web Dynpro component is being initialized. The following source code should be added to the `wdInit()` method of the component controller:

Model object

```
public void wdDoInit()

{

  //@@begin wdDoInit()

    // create a new model instance (1)

    QueryCustomerModel model = new QueryCustomerModel();

    // create model objects (2, 3)

    Request_CustomerSimpleByNameAndAddressQueryResponse_

     In request = new Request_

       CustomerSimpleByNameAndAddressQueryResponse_

         In (model);

  CustomerSimpleByNameAndAddressQueryMessage_Sync value =

    new CustomerSimpleByNameAndAddressQueryMessage_Sync

      (model);

    // associate model objects (4)

    request.set
```

```
        CustomerSimpleByNameAndAddressQueryMessage_Sync
          (value);
        // bind executable model object to context node (5)
        wdContext.nodeRequest_
          CustomerSimpleByNameAndAddressQueryResponse_In().
            bind(request);
      //@@end

    }
```

Listing 7.2 Source Code for the wdInit() Method

Adding the service calls

Execute method The last step is to integrate the service call to find the customers. The call should be executed if the inbound plug *SearchIn* is called in the view *CustomerSearchResultView*. This happens when a user clicks the Search button and the outbound plug SearchOut of the view *CustomerSearch-CriteriaView* is executed. The call is initiated by calling the `execute` method for the corresponding model class:

```
  public void onPlugSearchIn
(com.sap.tc.webdynpro.progmodel.api.IWDCustomEvent wdEvent )

    {
      //@@begin onPlugSearchIn(ServerEvent)
        try {
wdContext.currentRequest_CustomerSimpleByNameAndAddressQuery
Response_InElement().modelObject().execute();
        } catch (Exception e) {

          ...

        }
      //@@end

    }
```

Listing 7.3 Calling the Execute Method

After the service has been called, the result of the call is written to the Response node of the context. From there, the results can then be read.

The following steps must be performed for the remaining views to fully implement the entire consumer application:

▶ Define the data to be exchanged in the context.

▶ Define the UI elements and bind them to the corresponding context attributes.

▶ Add the service calls.

The application can now be deployed on the local development application server. This step automatically configures it and makes it executable. Automatic configuration is possible because:

Automatic configuration

▶ SAP NetWeaver Developer Studio is integrated with the local development application server.

▶ Suitable provider systems are already known, as the service groups contain the logical providers.

Because the service groups for the SalesClerk application were classified using the classification Composite Application, they can be easily found in the Services Registry, for example, to change the application configuration (see Figure 7.38).

Finding the application

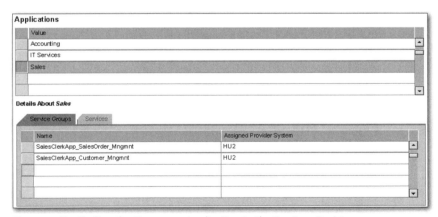

Figure 7.38 Finding the Consumer Application in the Services Registry

At runtime, the user interface looks like Figure 7.39.

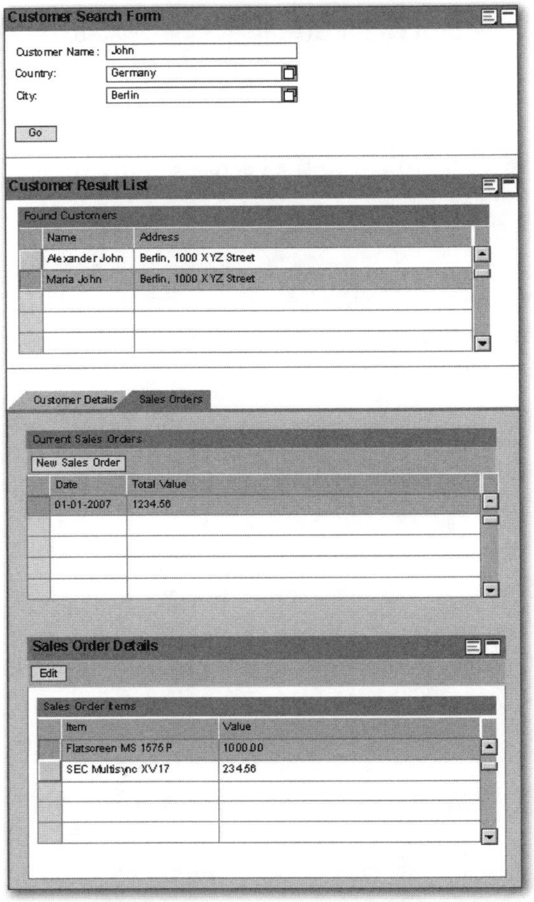

Figure 7.39 The Running Web Dynpro Application

7.4.3 Consumer Development in ABAP

The development of the example consumer application in ABAP follows the three actions of service discovery and import, classification of the consumer application, and implementation of the consumers. In this example, to retain simplicity, we do not discuss implementation details about the consumer application. Instead, we only describe how the objects relevant for the scenario, that is, proxy definitions and service groups, can be created and used.

Discovering and Importing Services

In ABAP, the first step is to generate the proxy definitions for the service and then bundle them in the relevant service groups. This makes sense because in ABAP, static consumer proxies are always used, that is, only generated proxy definitions can be used in service groups.

A consumer proxy definition is generated using the ABAP Workbench (Transaction SE80). Select the option to create an *enterprise service* object. A wizard is started, and Service Consumer is selected as the object type (see Figure 7.40).

Generating proxy definitions

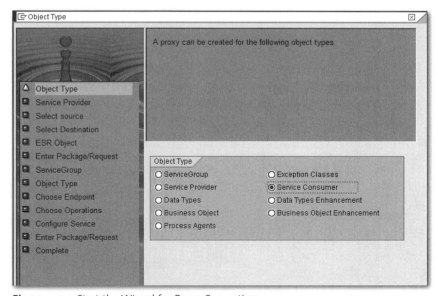

Figure 7.40 Start the Wizard for Proxy Generation

Here, we show how the proxy definitions can be generated using an alternative option to specify the relevant WSDL documents. Instead of using the Services Registry, the WSDL URLs are specified. This is the simplest option in scenarios in which the location of the WSDL document has already been identified. In the wizard, select the option URL/HTTP Destination (see Figure 7.41).

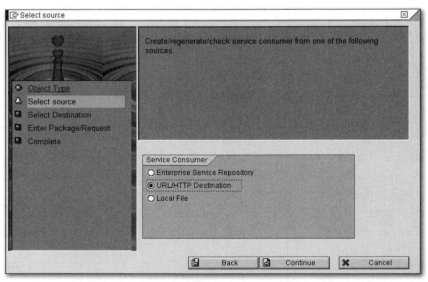

Figure 7.41 Selecting the WSDL Document through its URL

Then you specify the URL of the WSDL document and select the ABAP package, in which to generate the proxy definition, and the prefix for the objects to be generated, to avoid naming conflicts (see Figure 7.42).

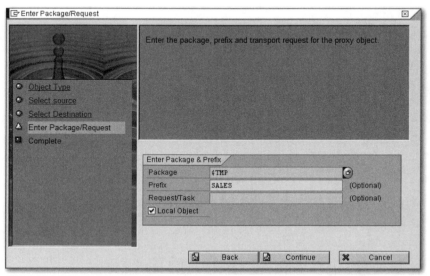

Figure 7.42 Generation Details

When you complete the wizard, similar to the Java EE 5 scenario, the proxy definition, including the proxy classes for service interfaces and data types, is generated.

Now that all the necessary proxy definitions have been generated, we can create the two service groups to manage the customers and sales orders – *SalesClerkApp_Customer_Mngmnt* and *SalesClerkApp_SalesOrder_Mngmnt*. The logical destinations of these service groups are the two process components *SalesOrderProcessing* and *BusinessPartnerDataManagement*.

Creating a service group

As in Java, the destination process component is selected as part of the service group. A service group is created using the ABAP Workbench (Transaction SE80). Choose the option Enterprise service. In the wizard to create a new development object, the object type Service group is selected (see Figure 7.43).

Creating a logical destination

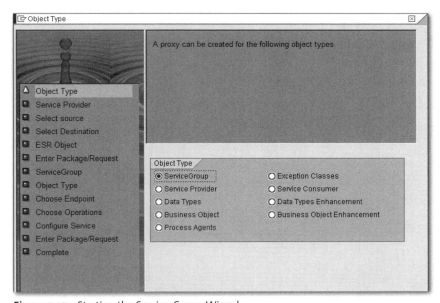

Figure 7.43 Starting the Service Group Wizard

The next step specifies the name and the description of the service group, after which the wizard is closed. This step is first done for the service group *SalesClerkApp_SalesOrder_Mngmnt* (see Figure 7.44).

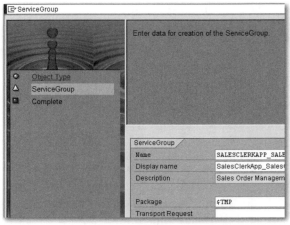

Figure 7.44 Specifying Details for a Service Group

Specifying context When the Wizard is closed, the service group editor is automatically opened. You can use this editor to specify the logical destination for the service group and the business context of the consumer application (for example, industry sector or country), and also to classify the service group. In this case, the logical destination Sales Order Processing is the reference used (see Figure 7.45).

Figure 7.45 Defining the Logical Destination for the Service Group

Now you can add service references to the service group. To do this, select the tab Consumer and then the generated proxy definition. For the service group *SalesClerkApp_SalesOrder_Mngmnt*, this is the proxy definition for the services *ManageSalesOrderIn* and *QuerySalesOrderIn* (see Figure 7.46).

Creating a service
reference

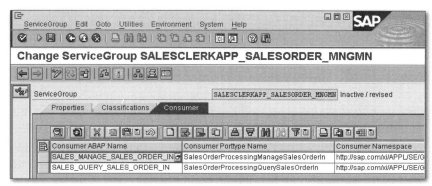

Figure 7.46 Adding the References to the Consumer Proxy Definitions

Classifying the Consumer Application

After all the references to the required proxy definitions have been added, the service group can be classified. In this example, it is classified using the classification *Composite Application* and assigned to the composite application Sales (see Figure 7.47).

Figure 7.47 Classifying the Consumer Application

Implementing the Consumer

When the service group development objects have been created, an application developer can use a dedicated API in the program code to instantiate the consumer proxies, based on the service groups.

Creating a service group object

First, an instance of the generic service group object is created:

```
l_sg_handler type ref to if_srt_public_sv_group_handler.
l_sg_handler =
       cl_srt_public_factory=>get_service_group_handler( ).
```

This can be used to find all of the configured provider applications for a particular service group. This is particularly useful if multiple provider applications potentially provide the same service and the most suitable system has to be selected in the program code of the consumer application. In this example, all the provider systems are found that offer the services needed by the service group *SalesClerkApp_SalesOrder_Mngmnt*:

```
lt_provider_appls type srt_public_provider_appls.
 lt_provider_appls[] = l_sg_handler->get_provider_applications
                      ( 'SALESCLERK_SALESORDER_MNGMNT' ).
```

Creating proxy instances

Now we can go through the list of suitable provider systems and select the system to use and generate proxy instances for the services to be called. In the following example, proxy instances are generated to call the services *ManageSalesOrder* and *QuerySalesOrder*:

```
l_managesalesorder type ref to
          co_sale_order_processing_manage_sales_order_out,
l_querysalesorder  type ref to
          co_sale_order_processing_query_sales_order_out.


loop at lt_provider_appls into l_provider_appl.
  lt_webservices[] = l_provider_appl->get_webservices( ).
  loop at lt_webservices into l_webservice.
    case l_webservice->proxy_class.
      when 'CO_SRT_MANAGESALESORDER_OUT'.
        create object l_managesalesorder
          exporting
          logical_port_name = l_webservice->logical_port_name.
```

```
      when 'CO_SRT_QUERYSALESORDER_OUT'.
        create object l_querysalesorder
          exporting
          logical_port_name = l_webservice->logical_port_name.
      endcase.
    endloop.
  endloop.
```

Listing 7.4 Generating Proxy Instances for the Service Call

Using the instantiated consumer proxies, we can now call the actual service:

Executing a service call

```
* Initialize search criteria

...

* Invoke QuerySalesOrder proxy method

CALL METHOD l_querysalesorder->
    salesOrderBasicDataByBuyerAndBasicDataQueryResponse

EXPORTING

  input = search_criteria

IMPORTING

  output = customers.


* The WS has been invoked and the result has been stored in
customers
```

Listing 7.5 Calling the Service

After the provider side and the consumer side have been implemented, we can configure the overall scenario. This step determines the technical settings that the service runtime uses for communication between the consumer and the provider. These settings include specific security settings, parameters for reliable communication, and the call addresses (i.e., URLs).

8 Configuring an Enterprise Service–Based Scenario

This chapter first describes the goals of configuration and the essential requirements. Then it goes into detail about the integrated configuration of a scenario using the SOA Management Cockpit. The configuration process is also described on a concept level. In particular, it covers the three main phases of the configuration processes: initializing the system landscape, tasks of the technical administrator, and tasks of the application administrator. In addition, it explains how your configuration can react to changes in the system landscape. This configuration process is illustrated with a specific example.

To conclude, we give an outlook on how in the future a scenario can be configured cross-system. The previously described configuration approach is extended through a centralized configuration framework and additional functionalities in the Services Registry.

8.1 Overview of the Fundamental Concepts

The configuration of a scenario can be divided for simplicity into three phases as shown in Figure 8.1:

❶ Configuration of the service on the provider side

❷ Configuration of the service consumer: find the right services or service configuration

Configuration phases

❸ Configuration of the service consumer: create the consumer configuration, based on the service configuration

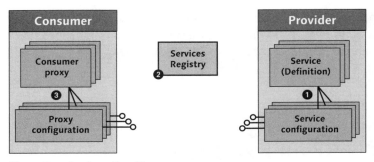

Figure 8.1 Configuration Phases

Procedure so far

In the past, Web service infrastructures provided only limited support for these three phases:

▶ In phase 1 and 3, it was normally only possible to configure individual services or service consumers, but not multiple services or service consumers together.

▶ In phase 2, there used to be no concepts to allow consumers and providers to be configured together or to provide assistance to easily configure a consumer application by automatically finding suitable providers.

Instead, the provider had first to be configured and a WSDL document generated. This WSDL document then had to be explicitly made known to the consumer, in most cases manually, as a basis for configuring the consumer.

> **Note**
>
> Even using a pure UDDI Registry to find the provider only helps in a few cases, because UDDI only defines technical rules to publish WSDL documents. It does not define (business) classifications, by which services can be searched for intelligently. Using only UDDI resources, a service can be found primarily by its name. However, the service name is only rarely known on the consumer side or uniquely identifiable (as there can be many services with the same name but different semantics). Instead, the service consumer typically knows the business context that identifies the service. That is why the business context is normally the search criterion that you must be able to use to search the registry.

With SOA middleware, system and service landscapes can end up with several thousand services and service consumers, which interact with each other through hundreds of scenarios. More advanced configuration concepts are therefore needed to manage these landscapes. These concepts are described in greater detail in the sections that follow.

8.1.1 Goals of Configuration in SOA Middleware

To make large service landscapes manageable, configuration in SOA middleware aims to achieve the following:

Manage large landscapes

▶ **Simplify the creation of configurations (phases 1 and 3)**
To be able to efficiently configure the potentially large number of services and service consumers, *smart configuration* of services must be possible. With smart SOA configuration, individual configurations are automatically derived for many services or service consumers, based on cross-service configuration settings for one system landscape.

▶ **Intelligent, ideally automatic configuration of consumer applications or entire scenarios (phases 2 and 3)**
SOA middleware:

  ▶ Automatically detects which services are needed for the consumer application or for the scenario

  ▶ Automatically determines the suitable providers in the system or service landscape, based on the business context

  ▶ Automatically configures the service consumers, based on the individual configurations of the provider services and the cross-service settings for the system landscape

▶ **Allow role separation of the system administrator and application administrator**
In large system landscapes, a distinction is made between a *system* or *technical administrator* and an *application administrator*:

  ▶ The system administrator knows the technical system settings in the system landscape, for example, how security settings need to be configured for security-critical or non-security-critical scenarios and which systems are in the system landscape and how they are related to each other. The system administrator is tasked with mak-

System administrator

243

ing the technical configuration settings for all the services — settings that will be used for the configuration of applications or scenarios for individual configuration of the services. The system administrator need not, however, know the actual applications or scenarios.

▶ The application administrator knows the scenarios or applications that need to be configured in the system landscape. The application administrator therefore focuses on releasing and changing these business applications or scenarios, without being compelled to understand the details of the technical settings.

SOA middleware's approach to configuration allows the system administrator to do the preparatory work of defining the basic technical requirements and the application administrator to then focus completely on configuring the applications. SOA middleware then automatically ensures that the settings chosen by the technical administrator are used when services are configured, for example, when a particular application is configured.

8.1.2 Requirements for SOA Middleware–Based Configuration

To be able to attain these goals of SOA middleware-based configuration, two requirements must be met:

▶ The service or system landscape must be managed through a Services Registry that knows all the services and service consumers and their relationships.

▶ Services and service consumers must be fully described through metadata.

These two requirements are examined more closely in the following sections.

Services Registry

For a technical infrastructure to intelligently support the configuration process, it must be able to access a central location, through which it can query all the relevant information or initiate actions that affect multiple systems or components. This central component is the Services Registry, which is shown in Figure 8.2.

Chapter 4, Components of SOA Middleware, examined the concepts of the Services Registry. We will therefore offer here a summary of the main requirements with a focus on the configuration process.

The Services Registry must meet the following requirements:

Requirements

- All service providers are registered in it, specifically:

  - Systems offering services.

  - Services that have not been configured but can potentially be used, because the application behind these services is customized. From now on, they will be referred to as *services*.

  - Services that have been configured, that is, can be called directly. From now on, they will be referred to as *service endpoints*.

- All service consumers are registered in the Services Registry, including the information about which provider (or providers) should be referenced.

- The Services Registry must have a notification mechanism that tells the configuration infrastructure or the systems if changes have been made to the registrations (add, change, or delete registrations). Consequently, the coupling between the Services Registry and the service consumers or providers must be close; that is, as soon as a change is made on the consumer or the provider side, the Services Registry must be notified.

- For all Web service–compliant systems to be able to use the Services Registry, the registration and notification must be standards-based. The relevant standard for a Services Registry is UDDI (Version 3).

- Data and information that is relevant for multiple systems (for example, security settings) must be able to be replicated to these systems through the Services Registry.

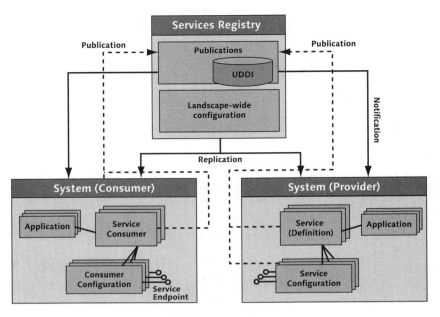

Figure 8.2 Role of the Services Registry in Configuration

Service Description Using Metadata

The metadata that describes the services, that is, the provider side, must meet the following requirements to simplify the three phases:

1. To enable smart SOA configuration, the behavior of the service must be defined in the design time metadata to be able to automatically derive a valid runtime configuration if cross-service configuration options exist. Consequently, the infrastructure must be able to select the options that match the design time behavior of the service from these configuration options.

   This simplifies phase 1, creating the service configuration.

2. You need to give the service a business classification that will enable SOA middleware to automatically find the service in the Services Registry if a service consumer that needs to be configured wants to use the business functionality.

   This simplifies phase 2, finding the matching service for a service consumer.

3. To be able to automatically configure a service consumer, based on the configuration of the service on the provider side, the metadata exchanged between the provider and the consumer must contain all the configuration information relevant for the consumer.

This simplifies phase 3, creating the service consumer configuration.

The following sections examine in greater detail what metadata is needed and how the above requirements are implemented.

The *metadata for a service definition* is the basis for supporting smart SOA configuration, and the business classification of the service allows the service to be found automatically to configure a service consumer. In addition to the interface description (including operations, parameters, and data types), a service definition thus consists of the description of the behavior and the classification (see Figure 8.3).

Metadata for a
service definition

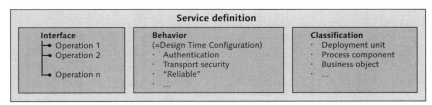

Figure 8.3 Components of a Service Definition

Description of the Behavior and How It Affects Configuration

The behavior (the design time configuration) is defined through a predefined set of abstract properties (i.e. intents) that can be configured differently depending on the service or operation. In this way, the security that the service requires is defined more precisely through properties such as Authentication (with the permitted values None, Basic, or Strong) or Transport security (with the permitted values None, Integrity, Confidentiality, or Integrity and Confidentiality). You can also specify whether the service is reliable or nonreliable or stateless or stateful. It is important that these properties are abstract and not bound to a technical configuration setting.

These abstract properties and the technical configuration settings are only linked when the service configuration is created, and SOA middle-

Rules

ware manages this linking. SOA middleware has rules that assign a permitted set of technical configuration options to particular values in an abstract property. For example, you can define the following:

▸ If the property Authentication has the value Basic, the technical configuration options HTTP Basic Authentication or (X.509) certificates are permitted. For the value Strong, the infrastructure would only allow configuration through certificates.

▸ If the property Reliable is used, the actual protocol to ensure reliable configuration must be specified as a technical configuration option. This can be either WS-Reliable Messaging with specification version 02/2005 or WS-Reliable Messaging with version 1.1.

Using these rules, SOA middleware can automatically derive the configuration for individual services if the technical configuration options to be used in a system landscape have been defined.

Smart SOA configuration

Smart SOA configuration is done in two steps:

1. The administrator determines which technical configuration options will be valid for the system landscape. As in the above examples, the administrator determines:

   ▸ Whether to use only certificates or both HTTP Basic Authentication (for Authentication = Basic) and certificates (for Authentication = Strong)

   ▸ Which standard version to use for reliable communication

   All the settings are made for the system landscape, independently of the actual services.

2. After the administrator has defined which services to configure, SOA middleware does the following:

   ▸ Reads the abstract design-time properties from the service definitions

   ▸ Searches for the matching technical configuration for the abstract properties from the previously defined settings

   The infrastructure generates the appropriate service configuration, based on the applicable technical configuration.

These two steps show that the tasks of a system administrator (step 1) are distinguishable from the tasks of an application administrator (determine the services to configure in step 2). This is covered in greater detail in the following sections.

Classifying a Service and How This Affects Discovering the Service

The second important component of a service definition that simplifies the configuration process is service classification.

The service definition is assigned a business classification to enable a service consumer wanting to use a particular business functionality to find the service. This classification includes a minimum set of predefined classification systems that are used to structure applications based on enterprise services. These are:

Predefined classification systems

▶ Deployment unit or software component

▶ Process component

▶ Business object

The semantics of these entities are described in greater detail in Chapter 3, Model-Driven Business Process Development. In addition to these predefined classification systems, the business context of a service definition can be further restricted using classification attributes such as industry and country.

When a service or a service endpoint is published, the classification of a service definition is also published to the Services Registry. Consequently, the Services Registry contains not only the information that the service exists, but also information about to which deployment unit or software component, process component, and business object it belongs to. Information published to the Services Registry also includes the physical system that offers a service.

The Services Registry contains all the information that a configuration infrastructure needs to automatically discover the appropriate service for a service consumer.

Figure 8.4 uses an example to illustrate what information service definitions can contain. The example shows a CRM service that processes orders and a service from customer invoicing that enables invoices to be created.

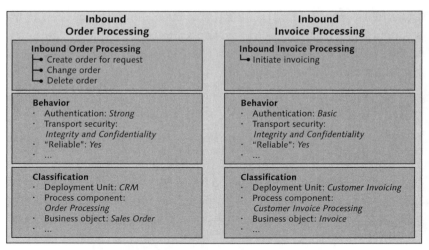

Figure 8.4 Example of the Use of Service Metadata

Description of Service Configuration

A service definition contains metadata that allows services to be configured in a smart way and to classify a service so that it can be automatically matched to a suitable service consumer.

What is missing now is provider-side support for phase 3 of the configuration process, that is, creating the consumer configuration. To enable this, the provider must describe the (standardized) information needed to create the consumer configuration and be able to transmit it to the consumer.

WS-Policy SOA middleware ensures this as it generates a WSDL document including the WS-Policy expressions that contain the information needed for each service or service endpoint. WS-Policy is needed in addition to WSDL, because although WSDL can described the signature of a service and some call information (such as the URL), it cannot describe the behavior (that is, the previously described abstract properties) or technical configuration settings such as security settings. This information is specified using WS-Policy expressions integrated into the WSDL document.

The service provider side is now described fully and is standards-compliant:

- ▸ Services or service endpoints are published to the Services Registry as soon as a consumer can use them. The service can easily be discovered using the additionally published classifications.

- ▸ The service consumer gets the address of the describing WSDL and WS-Policy document from the Services Registry. This document contains all the information needed to configure a service consumer for the service provider.

Describing the Service Consumer with Metadata

The above-described metadata for the service and provider is the basic requirement for an optimized configuration process. The service consumer metadata must also meet a set of conditions if it is to allow the infrastructure to intelligently bring together service consumers and service providers. This consumer-side metadata is described through service groups. These were examined in Section 7.2.2 Service Group, so we will only outline the main facts in Figure 8.5.

Service groups

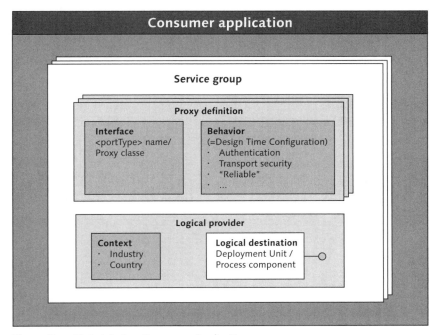

Figure 8.5 Metadata in a Consumer Application

- On a logical level, a service group defines from which provider system to use functionality. The service group stores the logical destination and additional refinements to the business context. The logical destinations recommended for SAP services are process components.

- In addition, the service group points to one or more proxy definitions, which represent references to the services to be called in the logical destination.

Figure 8.6 shows another example to illustrate the metadata in a service group. In this example, an application is defined that first communicates with a CRM system to create an order, and if the order is successful, it also communicates with an accounting system to create the invoice.

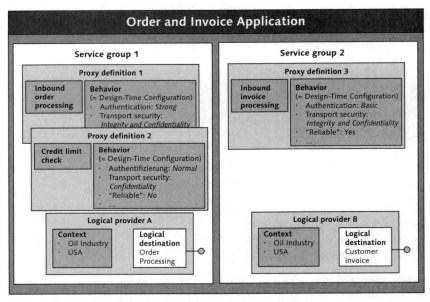

Figure 8.6 Example of Metadata in a Consumer Application

8.2 Integrated Configuration of a Scenario Using the SOA Management Cockpit

The configuration process described here for SOA middleware allows the configuration of a service landscape to be optimized through support for:

- Smart configuration of a set of services
- In ideal situations, automated configuration of the service consumers
- A clear separation of tasks between a technical administrator and an application administrator

In the course of a configuration process, changes will normally be made in multiple systems. It is therefore important for administrators to have an integrated work environment that allows access to all the participating systems. This makes the configuration process significantly easier, because to perform the necessary configuration settings in all the systems, administrators can use the same user interface on ABAP and Java systems, and the work environment guides administrators through the configuration process, ensuring that the necessary actions are performed in the correct order.

SOA Management Cockpit

This work environment is the *SOA Management Cockpit*.

To better illustrate this SOA middleware–based configuration approach, we will first describe the configuration process on a concept level. Then we will examine the process with an example.

8.2.1 The Configuration Process on a Concept Level

Section 8.1, Overview of the Fundamental Concepts, looked at the most important aims and fundamental aspects of configuration. This section looks at the configuration process in greater detail, and the above-described aspects are assigned to a process.

The overall process can be divided into the following phases:

- ▶ **Initialization phase**
  In this phase, all the configuration-relevant components in the configuration framework must be registered. Also, the provider side for all systems is published to the Services Registry. This fulfills the basic requirement for SOA middleware to have all the information available centrally to optimize the configuration process.

- ▶ **System administrator sets up the technical system configuration**
  In this phase, the system administrator fulfills the basic requirements to configure application or scenario communication, by defining the technical settings (such as the security technologies) to be used in a specific system for communication with other dedicated systems. These settings are subsequently used to generate the actual service or service consumer configuration for the applications or scenarios to be configured.

- ▶ **Application administrator configures the communication of the applications and scenarios**
  In this phase, the application administrator decides which applications and scenarios can be executed in a particular system. When the application administrator has defined these applications or scenarios, SOA middleware automatically ensures that the service and service consumer configurations are created.

In the following sections, we examine these three phases more closely. First, here is a brief overview of the main components that are relevant for the configuration process.

Overview of the Main Components

As illustrated in Figure 8.7, the main components are the Services Registry, one or more (physical) systems, the SOA Management Cockpit, and the configuration framework:

- **Services Registry**
  In a system landscape, there is *exactly one* dedicated Services Registry that forms the basis for configuration, particularly on the consumer side. Each of the systems participating in the configuration process knows this Services Registry, and the Services Registry knows each participating system.

- **(Physical) System**
  A physical system is composed of the actual applications or scenarios that will be configured in the configuration process. From the perspective of an ABAP system, a physical system represents a client in this ABAP system.

  The applications, services, and service consumers in a physical system are structured through deployment units and software components or process components. The remaining description of the configuration process is focused on process components, because they are the recommended software structuring units. The process can also be applied unchanged for deployment units or software components.

- **SOA Management Cockpit**
  The SOA Management Cockpit is the work environment of the system and application administrator. It is a browser-based UI that enables an administrator to access all the components in the system landscape from one central location. In this way, an administrator can use the SOA Management Cockpit to browse the Services Registry or to edit content there, make settings in the individual physical systems.

- **Configuration framework**
  SOA middleware's configuration framework ensures that the configuration process is implemented through the APIs provided. In a system landscape, multiple instances of the configuration framework are active, particularly in the individual physical systems and in the SOA Management Cockpit.

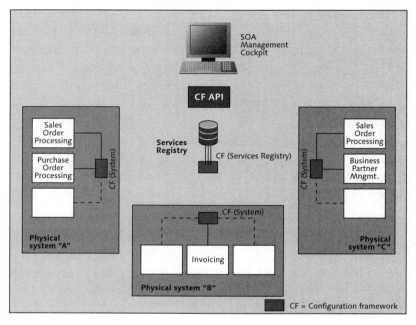

Figure 8.7 Main Components of the Configuration Process

Now that we have described the main components, we will look at how they interact with each other in the different configuration phases.

Initialization Phase

Make the entities known

The aims of the initialization phase are:

▶ To make known all the entities participating in the configuration process, in the configuration framework, and thus in the SOA Management Cockpit. This applies to all of the participating physical systems, services, and service consumers.

▶ To publish the provider sides of all the systems to the Services Registry, that is, all the services that can potentially be called. This is required to find suitable providers automatically when the consumer side is configured.

It is important that the configuration framework is notified and the publication in the Services Registry is updated immediately whenever a system, service, or service consumer is added, changed, or removed. Only in this way is it possible to ensure that SOA middleware can implement the configuration process with up-to-date data.

The initialization phase is not a one-off process that takes place when the system is installed. It must be performed continuously to communicate changes in the system landscape to the Services Registry.

Figure 8.8 provides an overview of the activities in the initialization phase:

❶ Register the systems in the SOA Management Cockpit

❷ Register the services in the configuration frameworks of the individual systems and register the service consumers in the configuration frameworks of the individual systems

❸ Publish the provider side to the Services Registry

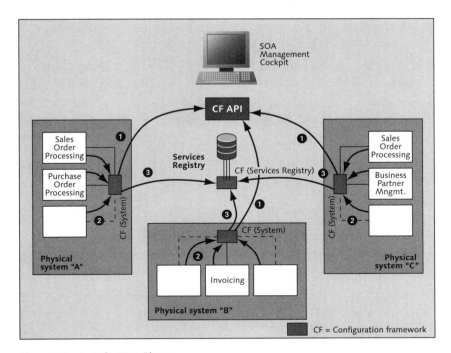

Figure 8.8 Initialization Phase

The main aim of the SOA Management Cockpit is to offer administrators integrated access to the systems to be configured. For this purpose, **Register the physical systems** all the participating systems in the configuration framework of the SOA Management Cockpit must be registered. Each of these registrations contains the metadata needed to later build a connection to a specific system and perform the configuration actions there.

Register services All the services that a service consumer can use are registered in the local configuration framework of each physical system. A registered service is a functionality that can potentially be called, because the application behind the service is configured for production use or has been activated or deployed. Initially, a service normally has no service endpoints that can be called directly.

The purpose of registration is to offer the application administrator an overview of services that can be configured in that system.

When services are registered, the following information is registered:

▶ Service name, description, and reference to the WSDL document that describes the service interface.

▶ Classification values for the service definition are read, and used to categorize the registration. This makes it possible to discover the service, based on its business context, that is, the deployment unit or software component, the process component, or the business object.

Register the service consumers To offer the application administrator an overview of all the service consumers that can be configured in a particular system, the service consumers are also registered in the system's local configuration framework.

These registrations contain the following information that is needed to implement the configuration process on the consumer side:

▶ A list of relevant service groups including information about to which consumer application they belong.

▶ Information about from which logical provider the service consumers will call a service. The logical destination is registered for each service group. The publication of the logical destination contains information about from which deployment unit or software component or process component the services will be used. In addition, the refinement of the business context is published, that is, in which industry or country context the required functionality is provided.

This metadata allows matching provider systems to be found automatically using the Services Registry.

The provider side of all systems is also published to the Services Registry to simplify the configuration of the service consumers by being able to automatically find matching providers. Three types of information can be registered:

Publish to the Services Registry

- ▶ The *physical system* that provides services or service endpoints
- ▶ The *services*, that is, the functionality that can potentially be called and that a service consumer can use
- ▶ The *service endpoints*, that is, the addresses that can be called by a service consumer and that are created for a service when it is configured

Because service endpoints are only created during configuration, they are usually not known during the initialization phase and are therefore only registered in the Services Registry later. Therefore, we will first take a closer look at the registration of physical systems and services. Figure 8.9 summarizes the situation.

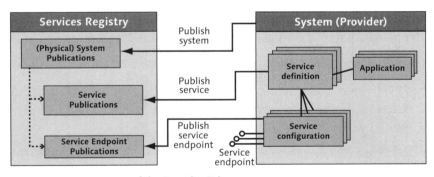

Figure 8.9 Registration of the Provider Side

> **Note**
>
> If a service in the initialization phase does have service endpoints (which were created with different methods), then these service endpoints are registered in the initialization phase. This typically occurs with services created with different Web service infrastructures.

259

> **Note**
>
> When the provider side is registered, it is vital that a service can only be published to the Services Registry if it can potentially be called by a service consumer. This is the case when the application encapsulated by the service has been configured or activated or deployed for production use by the application configuration.

Also, a physical system is only published to the Services Registry as a provider system if it provides at least one service.

Publish the system and the service

The service and the system can be published in two ways:

▶ **Automatic publication by SOA middleware**
If an application is configured, activated, or deployed for production use using application configuration, then, before the process has been completed, SOA middleware ensures that the services for this application are published to the Services Registry.

▶ **Manual publication by an administrator**
In addition to the automatic process, administrators can publish manually through a special publishing interface, which is available in each physical system. This manual publication is described in greater detail in Section 6.3 Classifying and Publishing a Service.

The publication of the provider side is depicted in Figure 8.10.

The following information is published:

Publish the services

▶ When a service is published, the same metadata for the service definitions is published that was previously registered in the local configuration framework. This metadata is:

  ▶ Service name, description, and reference to the WSDL document that describes the service interface.

  ▶ Classification values of the service definition are read to categorize the service publication in the Services Registry.

  ▶ In addition to the service publication, information is added about which physical system provides the service.

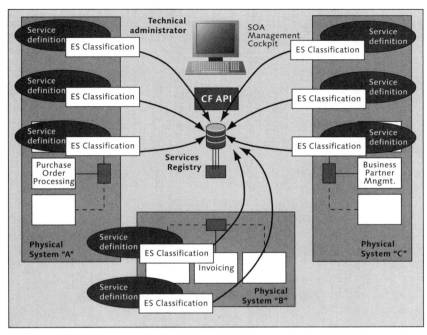

Figure 8.10 Registration on the Provider Side

▶ The physical systems are published when they provide at least one service. The publication is composed of the following data:

> **Publish the physical systems**

  ▶ The general access address for the system, that is, the HTTP host and port.

  ▶ The list of the deployment units or software components and process components that could potentially be used in this system. The Services Registry knows all the services that are provided by a physical system and has information about to which deployment units or software components and process components the services belong. This enables the Services Registry to find out which deployment units or software components and process components the physical system provides. This information is appended to the publication of the physical system.

When the registration of the provider side is completed, the following has been done:

> **Result**

▶ All the provider systems and all the usable services are known.

▶ The services are classified in the Services Registry by the business contexts in which they are provided, that is, by deployment unit or software component and process components. Consequently, a service consumer can now use the Services Registry to find a service by its business context (and no longer just by its name). The configuration framework can also use this information to perform mass operations, such as "Configure all the services in the Deployment Unit/software component ECC."

▶ The publications of the provider systems contain information about which deployment units or software components and process components are active. This enables a service consumer or the configuration framework to use the business context to find out which physical systems provide these functionalities.

Now all the requirements for the provider side to allow a simplified configuration process have been met.

Set Up the Technical System Configurations (System Administrators)

After the initialization phase, the next step is the technical configuration of all the participating systems, that is, determining the technical settings (such as security settings) that are then used when the services or service consumers are configured. In this phase, these settings are initially independent of specific services and apply to the entire system.

Properties to define
This is the task of the system administrator, who is not focused on specific applications or scenarios, but instead determines, for all the systems in the system landscape, which systems can communicate with each other and through which configuration settings.

These settings are made in each participating system:

1. Create the profile

2. Set up the system connections to all the potential provider systems

In the sections that follow, we further examine these two steps.

Create the profile
The configuration profile is the basis for the configuration of multiple services or service consumers. In the configuration *profile*, an administra-

tor defines which settings to use for communication in specific communication scenarios. What an administrator defines in a profile is based on the design time configurations and their various properties. An administrator assigns to each property the technical runtime configurations to be used—known as policies. The profile determines, for example:

▶ The technical security settings to use in the following cases:

  ▶ Authentication = Basic (for example, HTTP Basic Authentication) or Authentication = Strong (for example, X509 certificates through HTTPS)

  ▶ Transport-security = Confidentiality (for example, XML Encryption) or Transport-security = Integrity & Confidentiality (for example, HTTPS)

▶ The protocol to use for reliable scenarios (for example, WS-Reliable Messaging)

▶ How to handle stateful communication (for example, HTTP cookies)

These policies are then used in the system to which the profile has been assigned. This is done using the smart SOA configuration, which is described in the sub-section "Configure application and scenario communication" — by the application administrator. For each service or service consumer to configure, the design-time configuration is read and the appropriate technical policies are extracted from the profile.

Smart SOA configuration

A system administrator can define one or more profiles in a system. For example, it makes sense to define different profiles for A2A scenarios and B2B scenarios, because different systems must or can communicate with each other and because different technical settings are normally used in these scenarios.

An administrator creates the profile using the SOA Management Cockpit:

▶ The administrator uses the SOA Management Cockpit to connect to the system in which to create the profile.

▶ Then the administrator specifies the policies to be used for the service calls that will be assigned later.

These two steps are repeated for all the systems to be configured.

Figure 8.11 summarizes this situation.

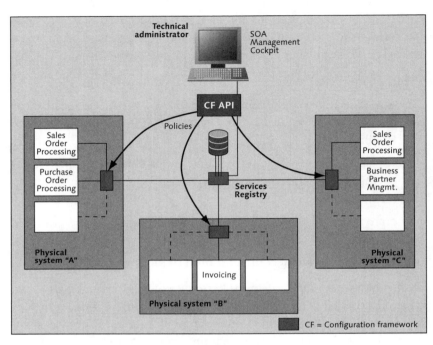

Figure 8.11 Creating and Managing Profiles

Set up system connections

Once an administrator has defined the profile and the configuration options, he can generate the technical communication channels between the systems.

Before we look more closely at the individual steps in this phase, we should explain the most important entity that comes out of this phase.

As we mentioned earlier, this phase sets up the technical communication channels between a consumer system and its potential target systems. These communication channels are known as *system connections*. They have the following properties:

▶ They are independent of specific service calls.

▶ They define the technical configuration settings to be used for an entire consumer system if the consumer system communicates with a particular target system.

► A system connection contains the technical configuration settings from the profile as well as the system-specific settings of the target system, which is accessed through a specific system connection (such as the URL prefix of the system).

In addition, the system connection is used to specify which channel to use to read the metadata (that is, the WSDL and WS-Policy documents) for the individual services from the provider system. This metadata is needed when configuring a particular consumer application, to configure the individual proxy definitions of the consumer application with the service-specific settings of the corresponding services in the provider system. The channels available to read the WSDL and WS-Policy documents are either the Services Registry (recommended option) or Web Services Inspection Language (WSIL) for provider systems that are not registered in the Services Registry.

It is thus clear why the profile alone is not sufficient to configure a service consumer: A profile only contains system-independent settings. However, to establish a communication channel between two systems, system-specific settings must also be defined (such as the destination address of the provider system and the channel to find the service metadata). This combination of system-independent with system-specific settings is made in one system connection.

System-specific settings

Figure 8.12 uses an example to illustrate the significance of system connections.

In this example, the consumer application in system A wants to call the logical destination process component *SalesOrderProcessing*. As this system landscape has two physical systems that provide the process component *SalesOrderProcessing* (system B and system C), two system connections are created in the consumer system. Both system connections contain the configuration settings from the profile, and each has the system-specific data for system B or system C.

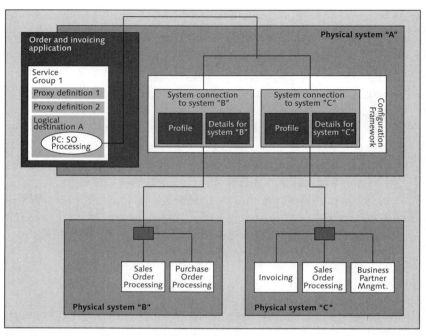

Figure 8.12 Example of the Role of System Connections

Later in the last phase of the configuration process, the system connections form the basis for automatically generating the individual service consumer configuration. At this stage, only the system connections between potential consumer systems and potential target systems are generated. The required steps are summarized in Figure 8.13 and are examined more closely in the following sections.

❶ A technical administrator uses the SOA Management Cockpit to connect to the system for which to maintain the connections to other systems. He gets a list of logical destinations, through which calls can be made from the current system to other systems. This list of potential logical destinations is managed in the configuration frameworks in each system. Each potential service consumer registered there when it was activated or deployed, and the registered metadata specifies the logical destinations that each service consumer wants to call.

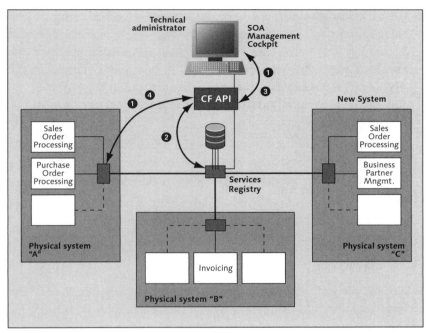

Figure 8.13 Setting up System Connections

❷ Next, the configuration framework finds the provider systems for these logical destinations, for which system connections can be created. For each of these logical destinations, the configuration framework queries the Services Registry to determine the physical systems that provide the entity referenced by the logical destination (for example, the referenced process component). This list of potential provider systems is displayed to the technical administrator.

> **Note**
>
> Automatic finding of provider systems for a logical destination is possible because the provider side was published to the Services Registry when it was activated or deployed. When it was published, its business context (in the form of process components and business objects) was recorded, and it is precisely this business context that is specified in the logical destination of a service consumer to indicate which functionality the service consumer wants to call. In this way, a connection can be established between a service consumer and its provider systems in the Services Registry.

❸ The technical administrator selects all or a subset of the potential provider systems and starts generating the system connections. For each of these system connections, the technical administrator selects the profile to use and defines the ways in which the metadata (that is, the WSDL and WS-Policy documents) for the services in the provider system will be discovered (for example, through the Services Registry or WSIL).

Next, the configuration settings from the profile are passed to the system connections to be created. The system-specific settings (such as a URL prefix) of the respective target system are added.

❹ The system connections created are then saved in the consumer systems.

The technical administrator repeats these for all the other systems in which system connections are going to be set up.

When this phase has been completed, each physical system has all the technical information to create:

▸ Service configuration (the profile data)

▸ Service consumer configuration for all potential target systems, because system connections were created to all target systems that contain the configuration settings for communication with these systems for all the logical destinations used in this system

The configuration framework has all the information necessary to automatically create the service and service consumer configuration for all the services or service consumers selected in the next phase.

Configure Application and Scenario Communication (Application administrators)

When the the technical administrator has prepared the system landscape, the application administrator can configure the individual applications and scenarios. We distinguish here between two cases:

▸ Configure provider groups (independently of specific service consumers).

▶ Configure a particular consumer application, that is, the corresponding service groups.

When the application administrator wants to configure the provider side, the following steps are performed (see also Figure 8.14).

❶ The application administrator connects from the SOA Management Cockpit to the system with services to configure. In this system, the administrator selects the service definitions to configure by searching the classifications. For example, the administrator decides to configure all the service definitions for the process components *SalesOrder-Processing* and *Invoicing*.

❷ The application administrator next selects the profile that contains the configuration settings to be used and assigns it to the selected service definitions. Now the part of configuration visible to the administrator is completed. The configuration framework performs the remaining steps automatically.

❸ The assignment between the profile and the service definitions is saved in the system, and the configuration framework generates the necessary service endpoints for each of the selected service definitions. The configuration of the service endpoints is based on the policies of the assigned profile and is generated using the described mechanism for smart SOA configuration. For each service definition, the design-time configuration (that is, the modeled behavior of the service definition) is read. For the specific properties of this design-time configuration, the configuration options are extracted from the profile and used to generate the service configuration.

❹ Once the service endpoints have been successfully created, they are published together with the relevant metadata to the Services Registry. Now they can be discovered and used for consumer configuration. You can find details of the published metadata in Section 4.3 under, "Publish and search with the Services Registry."

The configuration process for the provider side is now completed.

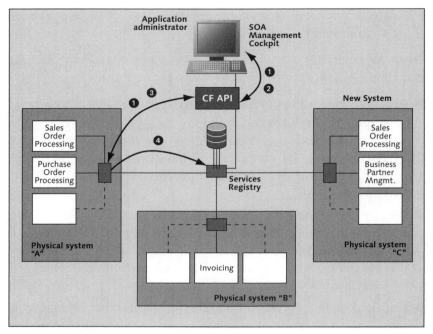

Figure 8.14 Configuring the Service Providers

Configure the service consumer

In an ideal situation, the configuration of service consumers can be completely automated because of the following:

▶ Metadata in the consumer application

▶ Publication of the provider side to the Services Registry

▶ Already-created system connections to the potential provider systems

When the application administrator configures the service consumers, the following steps are performed (see also Figure 8.15):

❶ The application administrator connects from the SOA Management Cockpit to the system in which to configure the service consumers. In this system, the application administrator selects the service groups to be configured for a particular scenario. This is normally done based on the name of the consumer application or scenarios (for example, all the service groups for the composite application *SalesClerkApplication*).

❷ For each of these service groups, the configuration framework checks the Services Registry to find the provider systems that provide all the required services. This involves two steps:

▶ First, it finds in the Services Registry all the provider systems that offer the business context that is referenced through the logical destination.

▶ Next, it checks whether these provider systems offer the appropriate services for all the proxy definitions in the service group.

Only the systems that meet both conditions are used as permitted target systems for the next configuration steps.

❸ The list of the provider systems is displayed to the application administrator, together with the information about whether a system connection to them has already been set up. If a system connection has already been created, the configuration framework can perform the complete configuration. If there is no system connection, the administrator must create one before the configuration process can continue.

❹ The application administrator selects the provider systems to use for each service group. This information is stored in the consumer system, and the creation of the consumer configuration is initiated. The visible part of configuration is now completed for the administrator. The configuration framework performs the remaining steps completely automatically.

❺ Next, the configuration framework creates the individual service consumer configuration for each proxy definition in the service group. It performs the following steps:

Create service consumer configuration

▶ For the service group to be configured, all the system connections that contain the configuration settings for all the relevant target systems have been selected. The system-wide configuration settings for communication are now known. What is still missing for the configuration of the service calls (proxy definitions) are the service-specific settings, such as the endpoint URLs of the services. To find these service-specific settings, the names of the services to be called are read for each proxy definition in the service group.

- ▶ With these names, the configuration framework searches the Services Registry to find the WSDL and WS-Policy documents for the services (**5**a in Figure 8.15) (these were already published when the service endpoints were published).

- ▶ Next, the configuration framework reads these WSDL and WS-Policy descriptions from the potential provider systems (**5**b). The WSDL and WS-Policy descriptions contain all the relevant service-specific settings for the configuration of the service consumers.

- ▶ Finally, the individual configurations for the proxy definitions are generated. The configuration framework merges the general settings from the system connections with the service-specific settings from the WSDL and WS-Policy descriptions.

The configuration process is now completed for the consumer side.

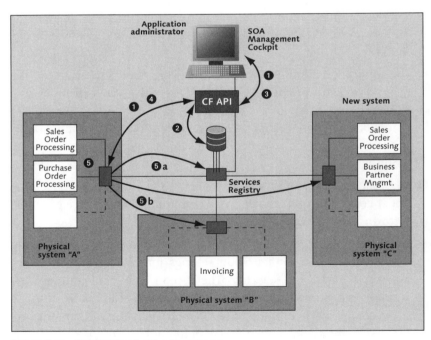

Figure 8.15 Configuring Service Consumers

> **Note**
>
> In the above process, it was assumed that the service endpoints needed to configure the consumer application already existed, that is, that the provider side was already configured.
>
> The configuration framework also supports scenarios in which the endpoints do not already exist. In these cases, the configuration framework *automatically* initiates the configuration of the provider side as soon as it detects that a required service endpoint does not exist. In these cases, we talk of a consumer-driven configuration, because the provider side is only configured if a consumer wants to access it.

Implementing Change Scenarios

Whereas up to now, the description of the configuration process was based on creating the configuration, we will now briefly look at change scenarios.

We focus here on changes to technical settings in the profile, the steps for which can be summarized as follows (see also Figure 8.16):

❶ The technical administrator connects from the SOA Management Cockpit to the system in which the configuration settings will be changed (in this case, system C). There, the technical administrator changes the settings in the profile. For example, the technical administrator decides to increase the security settings; that is, in scenarios, in which Authentication = Basic, instead of HTTP Basic Authentication, from now on only X.509 certificates will be permitted. This change to the profile data causes the configuration framework to generate a new version of this profile.

❷ For each service endpoint in the system that was created based on the old profile version, the configuration framework generates a new service endpoint based on the new profile version (that is, with the new profile values).

❸ These new service endpoints are published to the Services Registry.

❹ The technical administrator then connects from the SOA Management Cockpit to the consumer systems (in this case, system A), which must use the same profile and consequently must be updated to accommodate the configuration change. In this system, the adminis-trator makes the same changes to the profile.

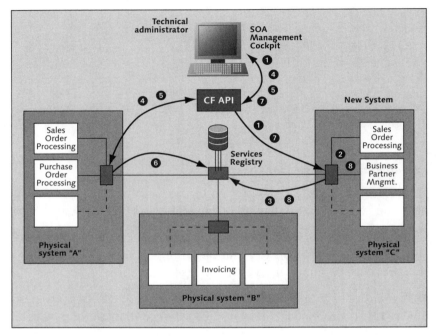

Figure 8.16 Changes to the Technical Profile

❺ Next, the administrator updates the profile version in the system con-nection for the changed provider system. In this case, the administra-tor updates the system connection that was defined in system A to system C.

Update proxy definition ❻ Next, the individual configurations for all the proxy definitions that were configured using this system connection must also be updated based on the new settings. The configuration framework searches the Services Registry to find the service endpoints that were created for this new profile version on the provider side. Then it reads the WSDL and WS-Policy documents for these new service endpoints and updates the individual configurations of the proxy definitions on the consumer side accordingly.

When the new consumer configurations are created, they are used by the consumer application (instead of the old configuration). Then the old consumer configuration is deleted.

❼ When all the consumer systems have been migrated to the new profile version, the administrator connects to system C and deactivates the old profile version.

❽ The configuration framework then removes the publications of the old service endpoints from the Services Registry and deletes the service endpoints.

8.2.2 Configuration Process: Example

To further illustrate the configuration process, we will use a concrete example. We again reference the scenario with sales order management from Chapter 6, Developing an Enterprise Service, and Chapter 7, Developing an Enterprise Service–Based Consumer Application. We will configure a consumer application to manage sales orders and the corresponding provider systems with the process components *SalesOrderProcessing* and *BusinessPartnerDataManagement*. The consumer application is run on SAP NetWeaver Application Server Java, whereas the provider components are run on Application Server ABAP.

Initialization Phase

As already mentioned, the requirements for smart SOA configuration must be met at development time by storing the metadata with the service development objects.

On the provider side, this is the definition of the design-time configuration, that is, the behavior, and the classification of each service definition.   Provider side

Figure 8.17 shows this modeled behavior for the service definition *QuerySalesOrderIn*.

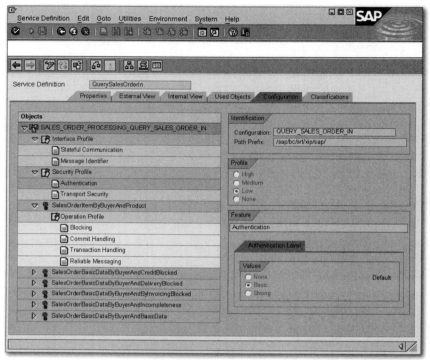

Figure 8.17   Design-Time Configuration of the Service Definition QuerySalesOrderIn

For this service definition, the property Authentication was set to Basic.

In addition, the modeled classification for this service definition is managed in the ES Repository. In this example, this is the assignment to the deployment unit ECC, the process component *SalesOrderProcessing*, and the business object *SalesOrder* (see Figure 8.18).

Publish the relevant service definitions   When the design-time metadata meets these requirements, the potentially usable service definitions, including the relevant metadata, can be registered in the local configuration framework when a provider system is being set up, that is, during the customizing or activation of the deployment of the required application. In addition, these service definitions are published to the Services Registry. Then all the provider metadata required for the configuration process is available. In our example, the process components *SalesOrderProcessing* and *BusinessPartnerDataManagement* are updated and their services are registered and the published to the Services Registry. For the process component *SalesOrderProcessing* and, in particular, for the service *QuerySalesOrderIn*, the result of the Services Registry publication is similar to that shown in Figure 8.19.

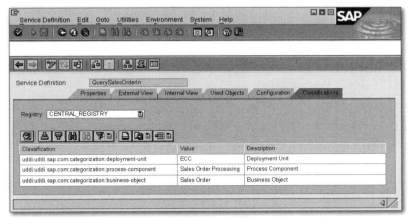

Figure 8.18 Classifications of the Service Definition QuerySalesOrderIn

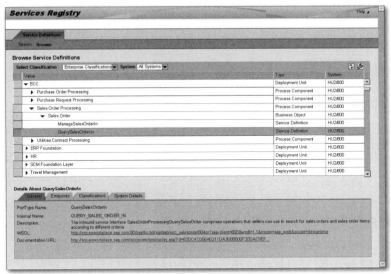

Figure 8.19 Result of the Publication of the Service QuerySalesOrderIn to the Services Registry

Consumer side Similar requirements apply on the consumer side. Here too, the metadata needed for an optimized configuration must be updated at development time. This metadata is composed of the definitions of the service groups, their logical destinations, and the required proxy definitions. Following the example from Chapter 7, Developing an Enterprise Service–Based Consumer Application, this metadata for the *SalesClerk* application is composed of the two service groups *SalesClerkApp_SalesOrder_Mngmnt* and *SalesClerkApp_Customer_Mngmnt*. These service groups reference the logical destinations *SalesOrderProcessing* or *BusinessPartnerDataManagement*.

When the consumer side, that is, the deployment of the consumer application, is being initialized, the corresponding metadata is registered in the local configuration framework of the respective system. The result of the registration of the *SalesClerk* application looks like that shown in Figure 8.20.

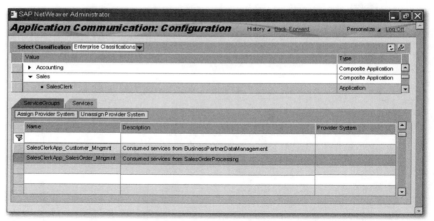

Figure 8.20 Result of the Registration of the Consumer Side in the Local Configuration Framework

The initialization phase is now completed.

Set Up the Technical System Configuration

In the next phase, the technical administrator first defines the technical configuration settings for the entire system landscape. The administrator creates one or more profiles in all relevant systems and specifies the configuration settings to use.

In our example, the relevant systems—both provider systems and consumer systems—are two ABAP systems that provide the required ERP functionality and a Java system, on which the *SalesClerk* application is running. The ABAP systems are named *ERP_1(100)* and *ERP_2(200)* (100 and 200 indicate the clients), and the Java system is named *SalesServerA*.

In all three systems, the administrator creates the profile *Intranet*, as both **Create profiles** consumers and providers will be run in the same company. To do this, the administrator uses the SOA Management Cockpit to connect to all three systems and in each one he creates the profile via the user interface shown in Figure 8.21. In the profile, the administrator then changes, for example, the security setting to be used to Transport Security. This situation is shown in Figure 8.21 for the system *ERP_1(100)*.

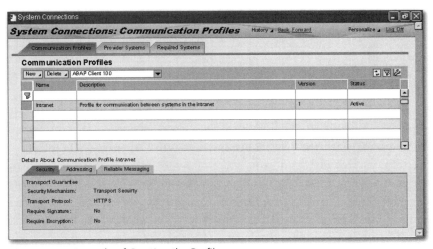

Figure 8.21 Example of Creating the Profile

In the second step, the administrator specifies the outbound channels for **Set up system** each system to all the potential provider systems; that is, the administra- **connections** tor creates the system connections.

To do this, the technical administrator first connects from the SOA Management Cockpit to the system whose system connections need to be changed. In this case, it is the *SalesServerA* system. The SOA Management Cockpit then displays the logical destinations, through which calls will be made from the system to other systems. Following our example, the administrator identifies the two logical destinations *SalesOrderProcessing* and *BusinessPartnerDataManagement*, which must be called by the *Sales-Clerk* application. The *SalesClerk* application registered this metadata when it was deployed in the local configuration framework. Figure 8.22 summarizes this situation.

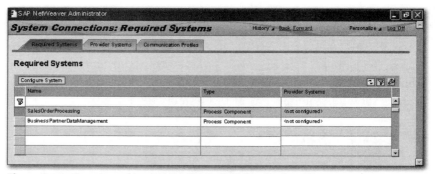

Figure 8.22 Overview of Logical Destinations To Be Configured

Identify provider systems
Next, the administrator initiates the creation of the system connections to each of these logical destinations. To do this, the administrator selects the logical destination to use and then starts the Creation Wizard. In the first wizard step, the configuration framework identifies the provider system for this logical destination, for which system connections can be created. To do this, the configuration framework queries the Services Registry to find the physical systems that provide the entities referenced through the logical destination. Figure 8.23 shows this step for the logical destination *SalesOrderProcessing*. The configuration framework has identified the *ERP_1(100)* and *ERP_2 (200)* systems as appropriate provider systems.

The technical administrator selects all or a subset of the potential provider systems for which to create system connections. In this case, the administrator decides to use both provider systems. The Creation Wizard then guides the administrator through the steps to create the system connection for the provider system *ERP_1(100)*.

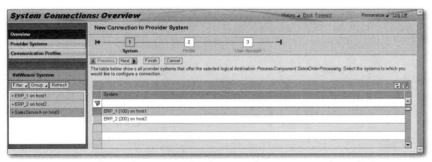

Figure 8.23 List of Provider Systems for the Logical Destination SalesOrderProcessing

For this system connection, the administrator selects the profile to use and defines the path through which the metadata (that is, the WSDL and WS-Policy documents) for the services can be found in the provider system (for example, through the Services Registry or through WSIL). Figure 8.24 shows that the administrator for the system connection to the *ERP_1(100)* system wants to use the Intranet profile.

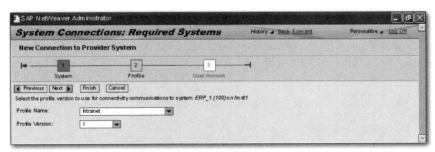

Figure 8.24 Select the Profile To Use in the System Connection

To complete the procedure, the administrator specifies the consumer-specific configuration settings for the system connection. These are primarily the definition and details of the logon procedure. In our example, the administrator decides to use the SAP logon ticket, which is shown in Figure 8.25.

Logon procedure

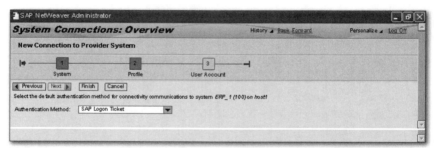

Figure 8.25 Select the Logon Procedure To Use in the System Connection

The Creation Wizard procedure is now complete, and the configuration framework now creates the system connection. To do this, it takes the configuration settings from the profile and adds the defined logon procedure and the system-specific settings (such as the URL prefix) of the target system. It reads these system-specific settings from the Services Registry publication for the provider system. The system connection created is then saved in the consumer system.

Now the system connection is visible in the SOA Management Cockpit and can be used to configure service consumer applications. The system connection to the provider system *ERP_1(100)* is as shown in Figure 8.26.

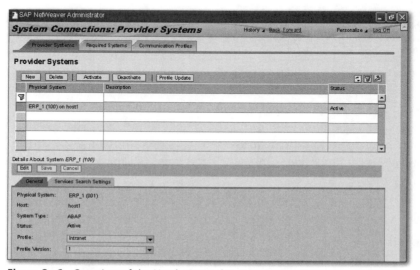

Figure 8.26 Overview of the Newly Created System Connection

The administrator repeats these steps to create the system connection to the second provider system, *ERP_2(200)*. Now the technical configuration is complete.

At this stage, because only the main connections between the systems, but no specific applications, have been configured these connections are still only potential connections. Actual connections (service endpoints and the consumer configuration) are only created when an actual application is configured.

Configure the Applications

In the final phase, the applications must be configured. In our example, these are the process components *SalesOrderProcessing* and *Business-PartnerDataManagement* in the ABAP system *ERP_1(100)* and the *Sales-Clerk* application in the Java system *SalesServerA*.

First, the process components on the provider side are configured. To do this, the application administrator connects from the SOA Management Cockpit to the physical system in which to configure the provider side—*ERP_1(100)*. Then the administrator selects the services to configure, by navigating through the classifications and selecting the configuration-relevant business context. In this case, the administrator selects both process components, *SalesOrderProcessing* and *BusinessPartnerDataManagement*. Figure 8.27 shows this step.

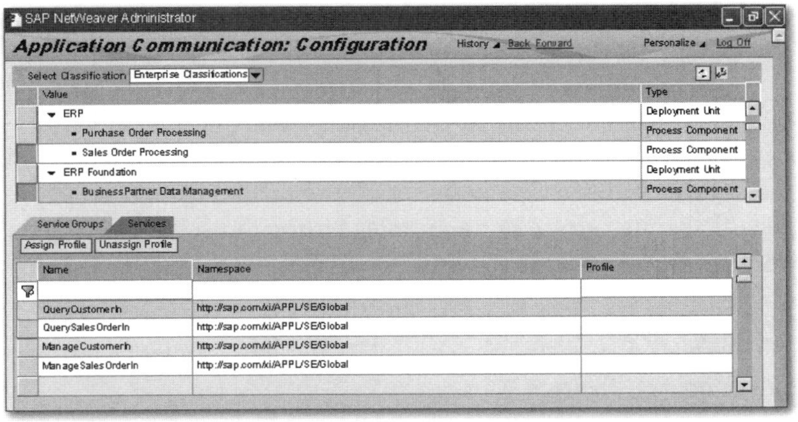

Provider side

Figure 8.27 Selecting the Process Components SalesOrderProcessing and BusinessPartnerDataManagement

When the administrator has performed this step, the SOA Management Cockpit displays an overview of the services to be configured. In our example, these are the four services, shown in Figure 8.27: *QuerySalesOrderIn*, *ManageSalesOrderIn*, *QueryCustomerIn*, and *ManageCustomerIn*. The administrator then selects the profile with whose configuration settings the business functionality will be configured. In our example, this is the Intranet to configure. The result of selecting this profile is illustrated in Figure 8.28. Next, the configuration framework configures all of the services for the selected process components with the settings from the selected profile.

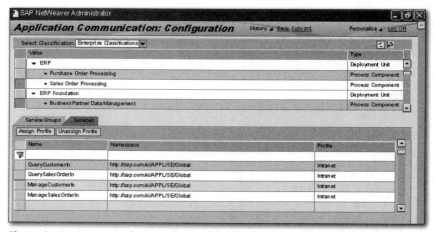

Figure 8.28 Overview of the configured Services, including the Profiles used

The service endpoints created, including the details of the automatically created configuration settings, are available in the SOA Management Cockpit. Here, for example, you can verify that the authentication is actually done through SAP single-sign-on tickets (as defined in the technical system configuration; see Figure 8.25). Figure 8.29 shows the details for the service endpoint created for the service definition *QuerySalesOrderIn*.

Publish service endpoints

The service endpoints are automatically published to the Services Registry, where they are available, for example, for the subsequent consumer configuration (see Figure 8.30).

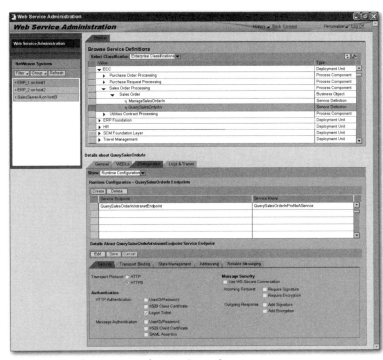

Figure 8.29 The Service Endpoints Created

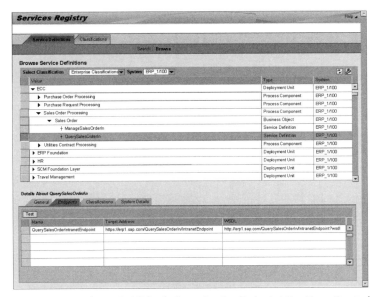

Figure 8.30 What is Published after a Service Endpoint Has Been Created

For each of the service endpoints, the Services Registry can be used to query the WSDL and the WS-Policy document and to configure the consumer application. For the newly configured service *QuerySales-OrderIn*, the WSDL and WS-Policy document (simplified) looks like the following:

```
<Policy xmlns="http://schemas.xmlsoap.org/ws/2004/09/policy"
  xmlns:wsu="http://docs.oasis-open.org/wss/2004/01/oasis-
  200401-wss-wssecurity-utility-1.0.xsd" wsu:Id="P1">
  <ExactlyOne>
    <All>
      <wsp:ExactlyOne xmlns:wsp=
          "http://schemas.xmlsoap.org/ws/2004/09/policy">
  <!-- Binding for AuthenticationMethod sapsp:HTTPBasic -->
      <wsp:All>
        <sp:TransportBinding xmlns:sp="http://docs.oasis-
              open.org/ws-sx/ws-securitypolicy/200702">
          <wsp:Policy>
            <sp:TransportToken>
              <wsp:Policy>
              <!-- AuthenticationMethod sapsp:HTTPBasic -->
                <sp:HttpsToken>
                  <wsp:Policy>
                    <sp:HttpBasicAuthentication />
                  </wsp:Policy>
                </sp:HttpsToken>
              </wsp:Policy>
            </sp:TransportToken>
            <sp:AlgorithmSuite>
              <wsp:Policy>
                <sp:TripleDesRsa15 />
              </wsp:Policy>
            </sp:AlgorithmSuite>
            <sp:Layout>
              <wsp:Policy>
                <sp:Strict />
              </wsp:Policy>
            </sp:Layout>
          </wsp:Policy>
        </sp:TransportBinding>
```

```
      </wsp:All>
    </wsp:ExactlyOne>
  </All>
</ExactlyOne>
</Policy>
...
<binding name="QuerySalesOrderInProfileABinding"
  xmlns:soap="http://schemas.xmlsoap.org/wsdl/soap/"
  type="p1:QuerySalesOrderIn">
<PolicyReference
  xmlns="http://schemas.xmlsoap.org/ws/2004/09/policy"
  URI="#P1" />
<soap:binding style="document"
  transport="http://schemas.xmlsoap.org/soap/http" />
  ...
</binding>
...
<wsdl:service name="QuerySalesOrderInProfileAService">
  <wsdl:port name="QuerySalesOrderInProfileAEndpoint"
    binding="p0: QuerySalesOrderInProfileABinding">
    <soap:address
      xmlns:soap="http://schemas.xmlsoap.org/wsdl/soap/"
      location="https://erp1.sap.com/QuerySalesOrderIn/
      ProfileAEndpoint"/>
  </wsdl:port>
</wsdl:service>
```

To complete the scenario, the consumer side, that is, the *SalesClerk* application, must now be configured. To do this, the application administrator connects again from the SOA Management Cockpit to the physical system in which to configure the consumer side—*SalesServerA*. Then the administrator navigates through the classifications to the configuration-relevant business context—the *SalesClerk* application.

Complete the consumer side

An overview of the service groups in the *SalesClerk* application is then displayed, as shown in Figure 8.31.

Service groups

287

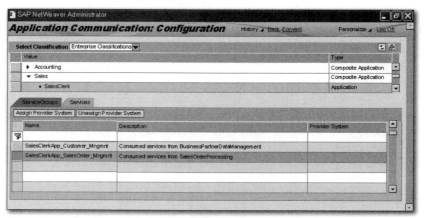

Figure 8.31 Overview of the Consumer Application To Configure

In our example, the two service groups are *SalesClerkApp_SalesOrder_ Mngmnt* and *SalesClerkApp_Customer_Mngmnt*. The administrator now needs to configure both service groups for the provider systems to be used. To assist the administrator, the SOA Management Cockpit lists all the physical systems that provide the appropriate business context, that is, the one referenced by the logical destinations. In this case, it is two systems, *ERP_1(100)* and *ERP_2(200)*, for which the system connections were already set up as part of the technical system configuration. This situation is shown in Figure 8.32.

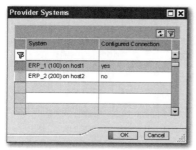

Figure 8.32 Overview of all of the Potential Provider Systems for the SalesClerk Application

Select systems

From this list, the administrator can then select the system(s) for which to configure the consumer application. In our example, the administrator decides to only use system *ERP_1/100*. The result is illustrated in Figure 8.33.

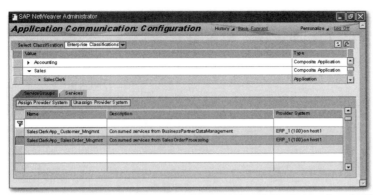

Figure 8.33 After the Consumer Applications Have Been Assigned to the Provider System

The configuration process can be completed when the configuration framework, based on the selection made, creates one individual configuration for each selected provider system for all the proxy definitions in the consumer application. Figure 8.34 shows the individual configuration created for the proxy definition for the *QuerySalesOrderIn* service.

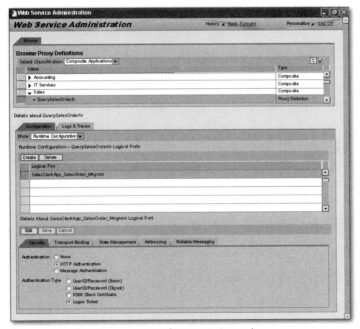

Figure 8.34 The Consumer Configuration Created

8.3 Outlook: The Cross-System Configuration of a Scenario

The above-described integrated configuration process is a part of SOA middleware that is available in SAP products starting in 2008. This section offers an outlook on how support for SOA middleware–based configuration will be enhanced in future versions of SAP products.

Features

The cornerstones of this enhanced support are:

▶ The previously-described configuration process offers administrators an integrated work environment in which to perform required configuration steps. Nevertheless, administrators must explicitly select the systems to be configured, connect to them in the correct sequence, and explicitly make the necessary settings. The enhanced version of the configuration will allow administrators to define the complete configuration scenario cross-system in the central SOA Management Cockpit. Invisible to administrators, SOA middleware will find all the appropriate systems and configure them automatically.

▶ The Services Registry offers enhanced functionality to manage both the provider side and the consumer side, including the relationships set up between the service consumers and the service providers. This enables SOA middleware to centrally manage change scenarios, because if changes are made on the provider side, it is possible to automatically identify which service consumers must be updated as a result. This process will also be fully managed by SOA middleware.

To illustrate this enhanced configuration support, this section first describes the configuration process on a conceptual level and then illustrates this with an example.

8.3.1 Configuration Process on a Conceptual Level

Similar to the integrated configuration, the centralized configuration process is composed of the following three phases:

- ▸ Initialization phase

- ▸ The system administrator sets up the technical system configurations
- ▸ The application administrator configures the applications and scenarios

In the following sections, we will take a closer look at these three phases. The main components are, again, the Services Registry, the physical systems, the SOA Management Cockpit, and the configuration framework. In particular, the Services Registry and the configuration framework in the central SOA Management Cockpit perform the additional tasks, in contrast to the integrated configuration approach.

Initialization Phase

The initialization phase aims to make known all the artifacts that will be involved in the configuration process. Unlike the integrated configuration approach, where only the provider side is published to the Services Registry, it is the basic rule of central configuration that all the relevant artifacts be made known to the Services Registry. This includes all the physical systems, services, and service consumers. Here too, it is vital that the Services Registry is notified as soon as a system, service, or service consumer is added, changed, or removed. Only in this way is it possible to ensure that SOA middleware can perform the configuration process with up-to-date data.

Clearly, the initialization phase is not a one-off process during the system installation. It must be continuous so that changes to the system landscape can be communicated to the Services Registry.

In the initialization phase, two subtasks can be distinguished: publishing the provider side and publishing the consumer side.

The registration of the provider side does not change compared to publishing as part of the integrated configuration approach: The *physical systems*, the *services*, and the *service endpoints* are published to the Services Registry, based on the already described rules.

Result When the provider side has been registered, the following has been done:

- ▶ All of the provider systems and all of the usable services are known.
- ▶ The services are classified in the Services Registry by the business contexts in which they are provided, that is, by deployment unit or software component and process components.
- ▶ The publications for the provider systems contain information about which deployment units or software components and process components are active in them. This makes it possible for a service consumer or the configuration framework to use the business context to find out which physical systems provide these functionalities.

Publish the consumer side A new feature of centralized configuration is that the consumer side is also published to the Services Registry. This makes it possible to also perform the configuration for the consumer side centrally using the Services Registry. To enable this, two important pieces of information are published to the Services Registry:

- ▶ Which service consumers are relevant for the system landscape, that is, which need to be configured. Therefore, all the relevant service groups are published, including the information about which consumer application they belong to and which physical system is providing them.
- ▶ From which logical provider these service consumers want to call a service. Therefore, the logical destination is published for each service group. The publication of the logical destination includes the information about by which deployment unit or software component or process component the services will be used. In addition, the refinement of the business context is published, that is, in which industry sector or country context the required functionality is provided.

Figure 8.35 summarizes this situation.

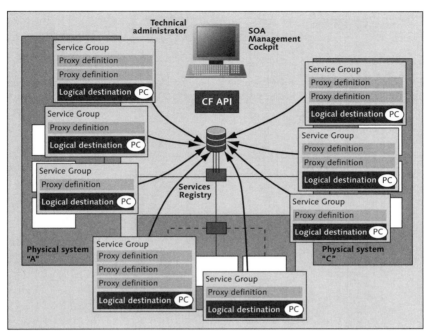

Figure 8.35 Registration on the Consumer Side

The same rules apply as on the provider side, both for the time of pub- **Rules**
lication and the publication mechanisms: The service consumer side is
only registered in the Services Registry if the consumer application was
configured or activated or deployed for production use through the application configuration process. Service groups and logical destinations can
be published either automatically when they are activated or deployed
or manually by an administrator.

After both the provider side and the consumer side have been registered in **Find providers**
the Services Registry, the Services Registry not only contains all the relevant
information about both sides, but it can now be used to find appropriate providers for a service consumer. For each service consumer, the logical destination in the Services Registry is known, and consequently so is
which deployment unit or software component or process component will
be called. The publications for the provider side also contain information
about which deployment unit or software component and process compo-

nent a service belongs to or which deployment units or software components and process components a physical (provider) system provides.

The configuration framework uses this information and the Services Registry to find for each service consumer the physical systems that provide the desired business functionality and to find out whether these systems also provide the actual service, whether service endpoints already exist for this service or need to be created, and so on.

These steps are performed by the configuration framework and only in the following two phases of the configuration process.

Set Up the Technical System Configurations (System Administrator)

As already mentioned, this phase consists of the technical configuration of the system landscape, that is, the definition of the technical settings (such as security settings) that will be applied when the services or service consumers are configured.

The system administrator defines for all systems in the system landscape:

Properties to be defined

- ▶ Which systems can communicate with each other
- ▶ Which configuration settings they use to communicate

This is defined in two steps:

1. Create the domain and the profile
2. Create the physical systems for this domain

We examine these steps more closely in the following sections.

Create the domain and the profile

In contrast to the integrated configuration approach, the central configuration approach also includes domains. A *domain* describes a clearly defined set of physical systems that can communicate with each other and that use the same technical settings to implement communication scenarios.

A domain is essentially composed of a list of physical systems and a *profile*, through which the configuration options for entire communication scenarios are defined, similar to the integrated configuration approach. What is new in the centralized configuration approach is that this profile is applied directly to all the systems in a domain, not just one individual system.

The administrator creates the domain and the profile from the SOA Management Cockpit. Both of these artifacts are managed centrally in the Services Registry by the SOA Management Cockpit. Figure 8.36 illustrates this situation.

After the administrator has defined a domain and has set its configuration options by creating a profile, he can add the physical systems to the domain and create the technical communication channels between the systems. With these steps, the technical administrator creates the system connections necessary to define the communication of a consumer system with its potential provider systems.

Add systems to a domain

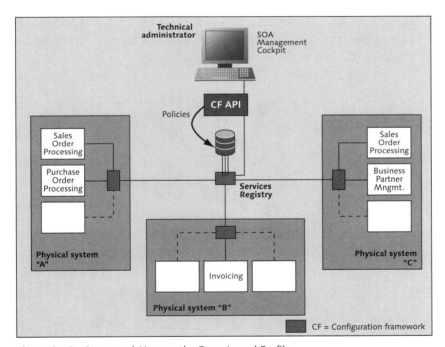

Figure 8.36 Create and Manage the Domain and Profile

In this phase, all of the system connections between all of the potential consumer systems and all of the potential target systems are created cen-

Final phase of configuration

trally. The steps are summarized in Figure 8.37 and will be examined in more detail in the following sections.

❶ From the SOA Management Cockpit, the system administrator first selects the physical system to be added to the domain. The administrator selects this system from the systems published in the Services Registry. In addition to the system-specific configuration data (such as the HTTP host and port) found through the Services Registry, the administrator also specifies the logon procedure to be used.

❷ Next, the configuration framework uses the profile to replicate the metadata for the domain, that is, the permitted configuration options, to the new physical system. Now the physical system has all the information needed to create the service configuration in a later step.

If it was not already done during the initialization phase, the new physical system now publishes all of the services (including classifications), service groups, and logical destinations used to the Services Registry. This ensures that all of the artifacts relevant for the configuration are in the Services Registry.

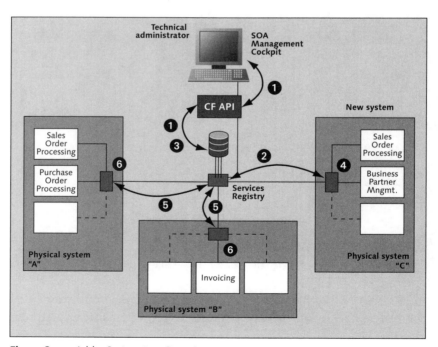

Figure 8.37 Add a System to a Domain

❸ The configuration framework API creates a new system connection for the new system in the Services Registry. This system connection will later be replicated to each physical system, from which the newly added system can be called.

❹ Next, in the newly added system, the configuration framework creates all of the potential communication channels (system connections) from this system to the other physical systems in the domain that can be accessed by this system. This is done in the following steps:

  ▶ The configuration framework reads from the Services Registry all of the logical destinations that are used in this system. The configuration framework has now found all of the potential outbound channels.

  ▶ The name of the deployment unit or software component or of the process component is selected from each logical destination that references it.

  ▶ The Services Registry is queried about which physical systems these deployment units or software components or process components provide. The systems found in this step represent all of the potential destinations for these logical destinations.

  ▶ For each potential target system found, a system connection is created in the consumer system and assigned to the logical destination in this system. Here, the configuration settings from the profile are copied to the system connections, then the system-specific settings (such as the URL prefix) of the target systems are added.

❺ As not only the system that was just added to the domain needs new communication channels for its potential target systems, but itself can also represent a new potential target system for systems that are already in the domain, the configuration framework also needs to check whether system connections for this new system need to be created in the other systems.

Opposite direction

It does this as follows:

  ▶ It searches all of the logical destinations registered in the Services Registry to check whether they reference a deployment unit or software component or process component that is also provided by this new physical system.

- ▶ If this is the case, the configuration framework finds out which physical systems use these logical destinations.
- ▶ Next, a new system connection is created in these physical systems and assigned to the logical destination.

Update applications and scenarios

❻ When the new physical system is added to the domain, applications or scenarios may have already been configured. The new system may be relevant for these applications or scenarios that are already in use, and it may be a potential destination. This will be the case if the new system represents a logical destination used in these applications or scenarios. These applications or scenarios are highlighted in the SOA Management Cockpit for the application administrator, who can decide to update these applications or scenarios.

> **Important**
>
> In this phase, only step 1, the selection of the physical systems to add, is visible to the administrator. All of the other steps are performed automatically by the configuration framework, based on the available metadata.

When this phase is completed, each physical system has all the technical information to create:

- ▶ Service configuration (the profile data)
- ▶ Service consumer configurations for all of the potential physical target systems, because system connections to all the target systems were created for all the logical destinations used in this system, containing the configuration settings for communication with these systems

The configuration framework now has all of the information to automatically create the service and service consumer configuration for all of the services or service consumers selected in the next phase.

Configure the Application and Scenario Communication (Application Administrator)

After the system administrator has prepared the system landscape, the application administrator can configure the individual applications and scenarios. There are two distinct cases here:

▶ Configure provider groups (independently of service consumers)

▶ Configure a specific consumer application, that is, the relevant service groups

When the application administrator wants to configure the provider side, the following steps are performed (see also Figure 8.38).

Configure the
service providers

❶ From the SOA Management Cockpit, the administrator searches the Services Registry using the classifications. The administrator selects the classification values for the business contexts to configure and decides, for example, to configure the process components *SalesOrderProcessing* and *Invoicing*.

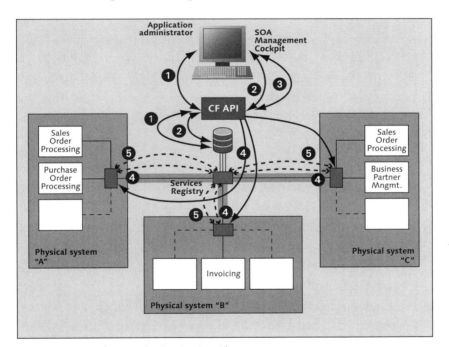

Figure 8.38 Configuring the Service Providers

❷ The configuration framework uses the Services Registry to find which physical systems provide these selected classification values. The SOA Management Cockpit displays a list of the appropriate provider systems. The administrator decides in which of these systems to configure the selected business contexts and initiates the creation of the configuration in these systems.

❸ The administrator selects the domain in which to configure the services and the profile and the policies to use for configuration. The part of configuration visible to the administrator is now completed. The remaining steps are performed automatically by the configuration framework.

❹ The configuration framework starts the configuration of the services in the selected provider systems. In each of the systems, the local configuration framework finds out which services belong to the classification values to configure. The result it gets is the names of the relevant service definitions.

For this list, the local configuration framework initiates individual service configuration, that is, the creation of the service endpoints, based on the above-described mechanism of smart SOA configuration.

❺ When the service endpoints have been successfully created, they are published to the Services Registry. Then they can be found and used for consumer configuration.

The configuration process for the provider side is now complete.

Configure the service consumer

When the application administrator wants to configure the service consumers, the following steps are performed (see also Figure 8.39).

❶ From the SOA Management Cockpit, the application administrator searches the Services Registry for the service groups to configure. This is normally done based on the names of the consumer application or scenarios to be configured.

❷ The configuration framework checks the Services Registry to find out which physical systems provide these service groups. The SOA Management Cockpit displays a list of the appropriate systems for the administrator.

The administrator decides in which of these systems to configure the selected service groups and initiates the creation of the configuration in these systems. For the administrator, the visible part of the configuration process is now complete. The configuration framework automatically performs the remaining steps.

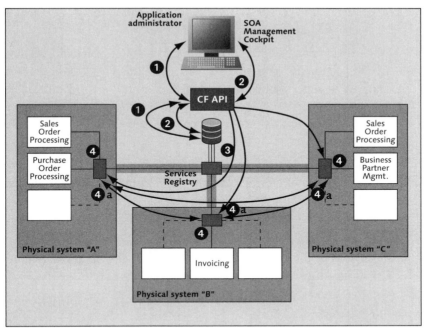

Figure 8.39 Configuration of the Service Consumers

❸ The configuration framework initiates the configuration of the service groups in the selected systems. It calls the local configuration frameworks in the individual systems and passes to them the list of service groups to be configured.

❹ The local configuration frameworks in the systems create the individual service consumer configuration for each proxy definition in the service groups. They perform the following steps:

▶ For each service group, the logical destination to be addressed is known. The system administrator previously created the system connections with the configuration settings for all the potential target systems for the logical destination. The system-wide configuration settings for communication are now known. However, what is still missing for the configuration of the service calls (the proxy definitions) are the service-specific settings, such as the call URLs for the individual services. To find out these service-specific settings, the names of the services to call are read in the service group for each proxy definition.

▶ With these names, the WSDL and WS-Policy descriptions are selected from the potential provider systems. The configuration framework checks the Services Registry to find out the address of the WSDL and WS-Policy descriptions for the service endpoints (they were published there when the service endpoints were configured).

▶ The WSDL and WS-Policy descriptions contain all of the service-specific settings relevant for the configuration of the service consumers.

▶ Last, the individual configurations for the proxy definitions are created when the configuration framework adds the service-specific settings from the WSDL and WS-Policy descriptions to the general settings from the system connections.

The configuration process is now completed for the consumer side.

> **Note**
>
> In this process, it was assumed that the service endpoints needed to configure the consumer application already existed, that is, that the provider side was already configured.
>
> The configuration framework also supports scenarios in which the endpoints do not already exist. In these cases, the configuration framework *automatically* initiates the configuration of the provider side as soon as it detects that a service endpoint needed does not exist. In these cases, we talk of a consumer-driven configuration, because the provider side is only configured if a consumer wants to access it.

Implementing Change Scenarios

We will now briefly look at how change scenarios are managed in the centralized configuration approach.

The changes result from changes to the technical settings in the profile. The steps can be summarizes as follows (see also Figure 8.40):

❶ From the SOA Management Cockpit, the system administrator changes settings in the profile. For example, the system administrator decides to increase the security settings; that is, in scenarios in which Authentication = Basic, instead of HTTP Basic Authentication, from now on only X.509 certificates will be permitted.

❷ Next, the configuration framework saves this change as a new version of the domain to the Services Registry (2a) and replicates this new version of the domain or profile to each physical system in the domain (2b).

❸ In each physical (provider) system in which service configurations, based on the old profile version, existed, the configuration framework creates new configurations, based on the new profile version (with the new profile values) for each of these service configurations.

❹ Next (using the Services Registry), all of the service consumers that are using a service endpoint based on the old profile version are notified that there is a new service endpoint.

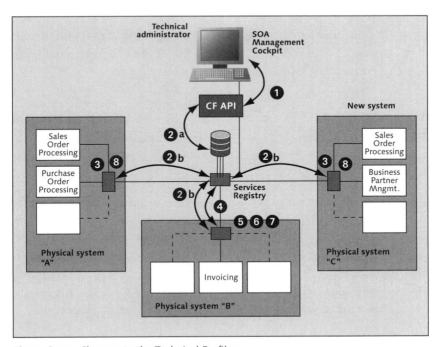

Figure 8.40 Changes to the Technical Profiles

❺ In the physical systems, where these service consumers are, new consumer configurations are created, based on the new service endpoints and the new version of the profile (the new profile data).

❻ As soon as the new consumer configurations are created, they are used by the consumer application (in place of the old configuration).

❼ The old consumer configuration is deleted. When all the old consumer configurations in a system have been deleted, the system notifies the Services Registry that the old profile version and the configuration based on it are no longer being used.

❽ When the old profile version and the configuration based on it are no longer used in any consumer system in the domain, the Services Registry initiates the deletion of the old service configuration in the provider systems.

8.3.2 Configuration Process: Example

To better illustrate the configuration process, we will explain it here using the same example as in Section 8.2.2, Configuration Process: Example. Again, the consumer application used to manage sales orders and the relevant provider systems will be configured with the process components *SalesOrderProcessing* and *BusinessPartnerDataManagement*.

Initialization Phase

The initialization phase on the provider side is equivalent to the integrated configuration described in Section 8.2.2 and is therefore not explained further here.

Consumer side   On the consumer side, the service consumers are published to the Services Registry, as well as being registered in the local configuration framework. After that, the configuration of the consumer side can also be initiated through the Services Registry. In our example, this is the *SalesClerk* application with the two service groups *SalesClerkApp_SalesOrder_Mngmnt* and *SalesClerkApp_Customer_Mngmnt*. They reference the logical destinations *SalesOrderProcessing* or *BusinessPartnerDataManagement*.

The result of the publication of the *SalesClerk* application to the Services Registry looks as shown in Figure 8.41.

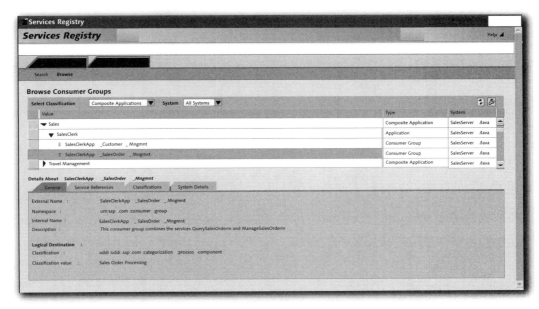

Figure 8.41 Result of the Publication of the Consumer Side to the Services Registry

The initialization phase is now completed.

Set Up Technical System Configuration

In the next phase, the technical administrator defines the technical configuration settings that will apply to the whole system landscape. The technical administrator creates a domain and specifies these configuration settings in the profile.

In our example, the technical administrator creates the domain Intranet, as both the consumer and the provider are running in the same company. In the profile, the administrator then sets, for example, the security setting Transport Security. This situation is shown in Figure 8.42.

Domain and profile

305

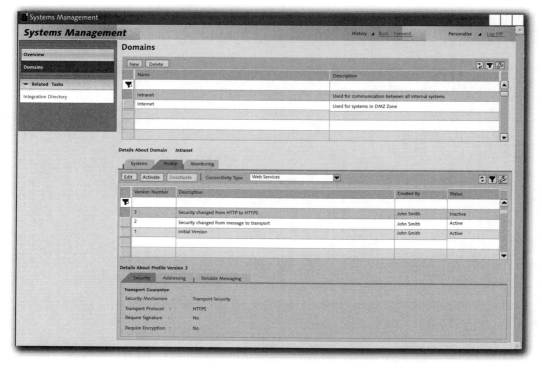

Figure 8.42 Example of Creating a Domain, Including the Profile

Add systems to the domain

Then the technical administrator includes all of the relevant systems in the domain—both the provider systems and the consumer systems. Here, it is two ABAP systems that provide the required ERP functionality and a Java system, on which the *SalesClerk* application is running. The ABAP systems are called *ERP_1/100* and *ERP_2/200* (100 or 200 indicate the clients), and the Java system is called *SalesServerA*. For each system, the administrator also defines the system-specific settings for how the system can be accessed. These settings include the HTTP host and port and the authentication type. Figure 8.43 shows how the *SalesServerA* system is represented in the domain.

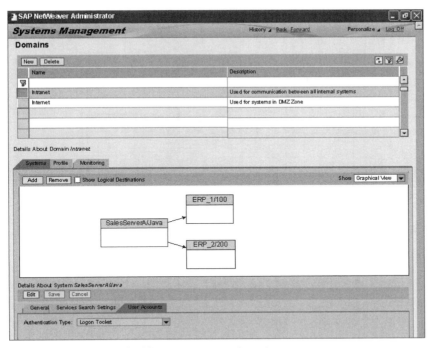

Figure 8.43 Example of Adding a System To a Domain

In this case, it was decided that the authentication in this system would be done through SAP single-sign-on tickets.

If a system was added to the domain, the SOA middleware's configuration framework would find out which of these systems must potentially communicate with each other. As previously described, this is done by comparing the logical destinations in a system with the functionalities provided in the other systems in the domain (described through classifications). For each match, a system connection to the corresponding provider system is created in the consumer system, and the relationship between the systems is displayed to the administrator. In our example, four system connections are created in the Java systems *SalesServerA* for the logical destinations *SalesOrderProcessing* and *BusinessPartnerDataManagement* for the ABAP systems *ERP_1/100* and *ERP_2/200*. Figure 8.44 shows the result of this.

Create system connections

307

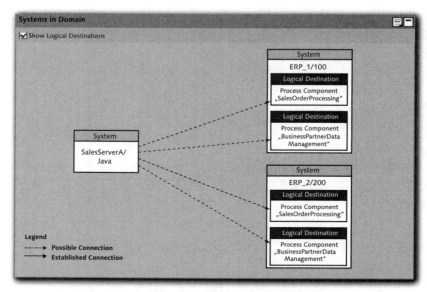

Figure 8.44 Example of the Creation of the Connections between the Systems

Because only the main connections between the systems, and no actual applications, have been configured, these connections are still only potential connections. Only when an actual application is configured will actual connections (service endpoints and consumer configurations) be created. Figure 8.44 illustrates this situation. Now the technical configuration is complete.

Configure the Applications

In the last phase, the required applications need to be configured. In our example, these are the process components *SalesOrderProcessing* and *BusinessPartnerDataManagement* in the ABAP system *ERP_1/100* and the *SalesClerk* application in the Java systems *SalesServerA*.

Provider side First, the process components on the provider side are configured. Figure 8.45 shows this situation for the process component *SalesOrderProcessing*.

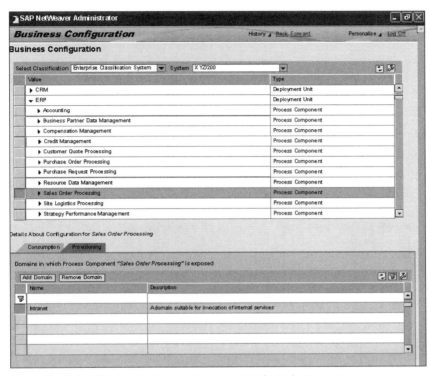

Figure 8.45 Configuring the Process Component SalesOrderProcessing

The application administrator first selects the physical system in which to configure the provider side (*ERP_1/100*) and then navigates through the classifications to the configuration-relevant business context to the *SalesOrderProcessing* process component. Then he selects the domain for which to configure the business functionality. In our example, this is the domain Intranet. The configuration framework configures all of the services for the selected process components with the settings from the selected domain.

The created service endpoints, including the details of the automatically created configuration settings, are now available from the SOA Management Cockpit. Here, for example, an administrator can verify that the authentication really is through SAP single-sign-on tickets (as defined in the technical system configuration). Figure 8.30 in Section 8.2.2, Configuration Process: Example, shows the details of the created service endpoints for the service *QuerySalesOrderIn*.

The created service endpoints are also automatically published to the Services Registry, where they can be used, for example, for subsequent consumer configuration. For each of the service endpoints, the WSDL and WS-Policy document can be queried and the consumer application can be configured through the Services Registry.

Complete the consumer side To complete the scenario, the consumer side, that is, the SalesClerk application, must be configured. This situation is shown in Figure 8.46.

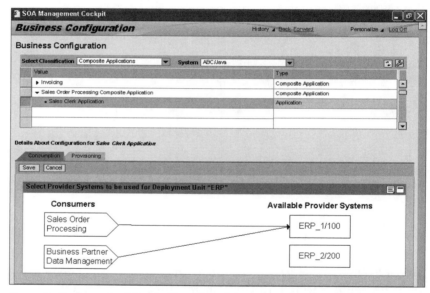

Figure 8.46 Example of the Configuration of the Consumer Side

Here again, the application administrator selects the physical system in which to configure the consumer side (*SalesServerA*) and then navigates through the classifications to the configuration-relevant business context to the *SalesClerk* application.

Service groups The system displays an overview of the service groups in the consumer application, including their logical destinations. In our example, there are two service groups, with the logical destinations *SalesOrderProcessing* and *BusinessPartnerDataManagement*. Also, the system lists the physical systems that provide the matching business context, that is, the business context referenced by the logical destinations. In this case, these are the systems *ERP_1/100* and *ERP_2/200*. From this list, the administrator can then select the system(s) for which to configure the consumer application. In our example, the administrator decides to only use the system *ERP_1/100*. Now the configuration process can be completed, as the configuration framework creates an individual configuration for each selected provider system, based on the selection made, for all the proxy definitions in the consumer application.

Figure 8.34 in Section 8.2.2 shows the individual configuration created for the proxy definition for the service *QuerySalesOrderIn*.

Appendices

A   Standards for Service-Oriented Architectures

SOA middleware can only be usefully implemented using open standards. With this appendix, we therefore offer a short excursion through the main standards used in the infrastructure. It would go beyond the scope of this book to present all the standards used.

A.1   Standards for Design Time

A.1.1   WS-MetadataExchange

WS-MetadataExchange defines how metadata is appended to the description of a Web service endpoint and how that metadata can be read from there. This standard enables Web services to be described with greater precision, and above all, not only technically, but also semantically.

A.1.2   Service Component Architecture

Service Component Architecture (SCA) defines a set of specifications that describe how to build service-oriented applications and systems. SCA is based on Web service standards and unifies other approaches to describe SOA applications.

A.2   Configuration and Management

A.2.1   Web Service Reliable Messaging

Web Service Reliable Messaging (WS-RM) is used to secure the transfer of data. WS-RM supports the following scenarios:

Secure transfer

▶ Guaranteed delivery of a message (*Guaranteed Delivery*). The infrastructure ensures that a message will be delivered to its recipient. If this proves to be impossible, the sender is notified of the error.

▶ The second scenario ensures that messages are only processed once (*Deliver Once*) on the recipient side. This functionality combined with the above-described scenario ensures that the message can arrive and be processed only once.

▶ In the third scenario, WS-RM helps ensure the sequence of messages (*Deliver in Order*). This is important in many business scenarios, as the processing of steps is typically critical for process execution.

A.2.2 WS Addressing

WS Addressing defines a mechanism that allows Web services to exchange address information for message transport. It defines how the message headers determine the transport path, how direct responses or errors are diverted to particular locations, and what the reference to the service endpoint looks like.

A.3 Generic XML and Communications Standards

A.3.1 Extensible Markup Language

Data exchange
The common denominator for all other standards is the *Extensible Markup Language* (XML). XML is a standard for creating hierarchical, machine- and human-readable text documents in a tree structure. XML defines the rules for building the documents. The Enterprise Services Infrastructure uses XML to exchange data. At runtime, the data in an interface call is represented by XML documents. For an actual application case, the details of the data structures need to be specified. This is particularly important for the definition of the structure elements and for their sequence in the hierarchical XML data structure. Any names can be used for the structure elements (XML elements) and attributes (XML attributes). An XML element can contain and describe very diverse data, prominent examples being free text, as well as graphics or abstract knowledge.

A.3.2 XML Schema

Description of
XML documents
XML Schema (XSD) is the modern method of describing the structure of XML documents. XML Schema also allows you to restrict the con-

tent of elements and attributes, for example, to numbers, dates, or text, using regular expressions. A schema itself is an XML document that allows more complex concepts to be described. In SAP NetWeaver, XML Schema is used as a special type of system to describe the data structures of service interfaces.

A.3.3 SOAP

SOAP is a protocol that is used to exchange data between systems and to execute service calls. SOAP is based on the services of other standards: XML to represent the data and Internet protocols of the underlying transport layer and HTTP to transmit messages. Originally, SOAP stood for Simple Object Access Protocol, but since version 1.2, SOAP is officially no longer an abbreviation, as it is no longer solely used to access objects.

A SOAP message is an XML document that is based on the Header-Body model. It essentially consists of a (optional) header element and a body element. The header region is used to store meta information about the message. This information can be about the recipient, the message routing, encryption, or an assignment to a transaction. The message body contains, as with HTML, the payload data. This data must be interpreted by the message recipient; any locations that the message passes through on its route can ignore the payload data. The data can be used for remote method calls, (error) messages, or pure data. Any attachments are appended to the message in accordance with the transport protocol. Binary files (sound, video, graphics) can be appended using MIME mechanisms (see below).

SOAP message

A.3.4 MIME

MIME (Multipurpose Internet Mail Extensions) is used to describe the design and the structure of Internet messages. MIME makes it possible to describe the message type and to send the payload data coded as text. This means non–text-based payload data, such as videos or images can be sent in text-based systems, such as email.

A.3.5 HTTP

HTTP stands for *Hypertext Transfer Protocol*. HTTP is a stateless protocol for transmitting data. In spite of its name, it is not restricted to the exchange of hypertext; it can now be used to exchange any data.

A.3.6 WSDL

Description of
Web services

Web Services Description Language (WSDL) defines an XML standard used to describe Web services that is independent of platforms, programming languages, and protocols. WSDL (pronounced "whistle") is a meta-language that can be used to describe the functionality of a Web service. WSDL essentially defines the individual operations with their parameters and return values. A WSDL document contains functional information in machine-readable format:

- Interface (XML Schema is used to describe the data structures)
- Access protocol (for example, SOAP)
- All information needed to access the service

A.3.7 Web Services

Web service is used to mean a service whose XML description and call are based on universal Internet standards. A Web service is used for direct platform- and programming language–independent interaction between applications through Internet-based protocols. Currently, mainly SOAP (see the definition of SOAP) is used through HTTP. Web services are described by WSDL.

A.3.8 Enterprise Services

Enterprise services use open standards to describe business processes. This allows applications, processes, or data to be brought together independently of the operating system. From a technical perspective, enterprise services are Web services. Flexible, fast, and simple, they can be used by partners, vendors, and customers alike. Company strategy and IT strategy go hand in hand. A collaborative partnership between IT and business experts produces process-oriented solutions that open up new competitive advantages.

A.4   Security

A.4.1   WS-Security

WS-Security is a security concept in the form of a framework. It brings together diverse standards that are needed for secure Web services. It includes support for standards such as SAML, PKI, and SSL, but also allows SOAP to be enhanced with security-relevant encryption and message signatures. Here again, universally accepted standards such as XML encryption or XML signatures are used. WS-Security is more like a construction kit that allows you to implement complex models and security requirements.

A.4.2   SAML

SAML stands for *Security Assertion Markup Language*. This standard was codeveloped by SAP in the OASIS consortium. SAML defines a set of application cases to simplify secure communication. The first case is used to enable so-called *single sign-on*. After a user logs on to the first application, that user is authorized to work with subsequent applications. SAML also allows security information to be shared in distributed applications by multiple users. In the third application case, an authorization service—at a separate intermediate location—checks the user authorizations independently of the actual application, and releases or locks the application.

B   The Authors

Timm Falter studied business informatics at the Wilhelms University at Münster, Westphalia. He joined SAP AG in 1999, where he initially focused on business framework architecture.

In 2001, he took on the role of development lead for the implementation of SAP Web service infrastructure for SAP NetWeaver 7.0. His work as a development manager for SOA Management began with the evolution of the Web services infrastructure in the direction of SOA middleware. During this time, Timm was responsible for development of SOA configuration, SOA monitoring, and the Services Registry.

Since 2008, he has been in charge of the central SOA middleware architecture group, which is tasked with elaborating the overarching SAP middleware architecture and supporting its implementation.

Timm has been a regular speaker at conferences, such as SAP TechEd, on subjects including Web services and Enterprise Services Infrastructure.

Thomas Fiedler studied physics at the Technical University of Karlsruhe. In 1999, he joined SAP AG as a developer for the ABAP Workbench. In this role, he was responsible for developing tools for object-oriented language ABAP objects, such as the Class Builder and the Refactoring Assistant. During this time, Thomas was a regular speaker at SAP TechEd, and led Workshops on ABAP Workbench.

After Thomas switched to Java development, he built the development environment for SQLJ on the Eclipse platform. Thomas later joined the project team that developed the foundations for SAP's service-oriented architecture. As an architect, he developed central components for the programming model for SOA middleware. Since 2005, Thomas has been a member of the central architecture group for SOA middleware, where he is responsible for the architecture of the Business Object Infrastructure, which forms the basis of the application platform and the mid-sized business solution SAP Business ByDesign.

After completing his degree in business informatics, **Martin Huvar** first worked on developing business applications in a mid-sized company. In 1993, he joined an SAP subsidiary, where he worked on a variety of technology development and consulting projects.

In 1997, he moved to SAP headquarters at Walldorf, where he took on responsibility for technology knowledge transfer for the SAP subsidiaries in Europe. This work saw him in charge of the then-new SAP Internet Transaction Server (ITS). Later, Martin worked in SAP Basis Product Management, which grew into SAP NetWeaver. Here, Martin's responsibilities included the SAP Business Connector and areas of XML.

In 2001, he assumed the role of product manager in charge of the Web service infrastructure, and led the PM team for that area. Martin supported development of the Web service infrastructure in the direction of SOA middleware. In 2005, he led Product Management for User Interface Technologies at SAP, where he us currently still active.

Alexander Zubev studied computer science and technology at the Technical University of Sofia, Bulgaria. While still a student, he started work at InQMy, a subsidiary of SAP AG, which subsequently became SAP Labs Bulgaria. Here, he worked on the development of the XML Toolkit. Later, he developed parts of the Web Service Framework in SAP NetWeaver. One of his projects was the Web Service Navigator—a tool to test a Web service without coding, based on its WSDL description. His other projects included Web service configuration and UDDI integration into SAP NetWeaver SOA middleware.

In 2007, Alexander took on the role of development manager for the SOA configuration team at SAP Labs Bulgaria. He is also the project manager in charge of the Connectivity Configuration project in the SOA Middleware Management program.

Index

T

A developer's guide to new technologies and techniques in SAP NetWeaver 7.0 (2004s)

Discusses the new ABAP Editor, ABAP Unit testing, regular expressions, shared memory objects, and more

485 pp., 2007, with CD, 69,95 Euro / US$ 69,95
ISBN 978-1-59229-139-7

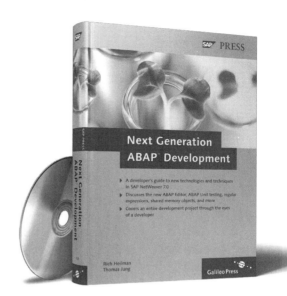

Next Generation ABAP Development

www.sap-press.com

Rich Heilman, Thomas Jung

Next Generation ABAP Development

This book takes advanced ABAP programmers on a guided tour of all the new concepts, technologies, techniques, and functions introduced in the new ABAP release 7.0. The unique approach of the book gives you a front row seat to view the entire process of design, development, and testing — right through the eyes of a developer. You'll quickly learn about all of the new ABAP programming options at your disposal, while virtually experiencing a detailed series of actual scenarios that could easily be encountered in your own upcoming projects.

Learn about security standards and solution concepts

Discover Web Services Security, Single Sign-On, SAML, SPML, and much more

Explore comprehensive exercises and examples in an Enterprise SOA scenario

approx. 548 pp., with CD, 69,95 Euro / US$ 69.95
ISBN 978-1-59229-180-9, June 2008

The Developer's Guide to SAP NetWeaver Security

www.sap-press.com

Martin Raepple

The Developer's Guide to SAP NetWeaver Security

This practical guide for developers, system integrators, and software architects, describes security technologies in conjunction with SAP NetWeaver Application Server up to and including Release 7.0. The book covers the basic principles of Web Service Security but focuses on practical exercises and examples to help you establish a deep understanding of the standards used. It presents a cross-enterprise scenario — complete with screenshots and sample code — focuses on key application layer areas such as communication, data security, and identity management, where system components are integrated using different standards (Open Source, Microsoft .NET, J2EE, Legacy).

This comprehensive reference enables you to use — and benefit from – open security standards, based on service-oriented architectures (Enterprise SOA).

Master the complete development cycle for mobile applications

Learn how to use SAP's new development tools

Gain insights on performance and security measures

348 pp., 2007, 69,95 Euro / US$ 69.95
ISBN 978-1-59229-141-0

Developing Mobile Applications Using SAP NetWeaver Mobile

www.sap-press.com

Thomas Pohl, Ramprasadh Kothandaraman,
Venkat Srinivas Seshasai

Developing Mobile Applications Using SAP NetWeaver Mobile

This book provides readers with an in-depth, technical introduction to SAP NetWeaver Mobile (SAP NetWeaver MI). Developers, administrators, consultants, and IT managers learn everything there is to know about the development, deployment, and operation of mobile applications. Beginning with the basics of mobile technology, architecture of mobile apps, and device management, the authors efficiently guide you through the complete application development and management life cycle. Critical topics such as programming tools, performance, backend integration, and cross-application functionality, are covered in detail.